I AM SERENA

A MULTIPLE'S JOURNEY
OF PERSONALITY INTEGRATION

A memoir by
Serena-Faith Masterson

Copyright © 2020

by Serena-Faith Masterson

I Am Serena

Written by Serena-Faith Masterson

Book & Cover Design by Rachel Farabaugh

Production & Formatting by Bogdan Onecic

Published by Dream Magic Publications www.dreammagicpublications.com

PUBLICATIONS

Second Edition 2026

Original Publication Date: April 2020

Printed and Manufactured in the United States of America ISBN: 978-1-7330970-6-2

*Some names in this book have been changed to protect their privacy.

The contents of this book are protected and copyrighted under the Library of Congress.

No part of this publication may be reproduced, stored in a retrieval system, or transmitted in any form or by any means, electronic, mechanical, recording, or otherwise, without the prior written permission of the author, except by a reviewer who wishes to quote brief passages in connection with a review written for inclusion in a print or online medium, magazine, newspaper, periodical, or broadcast.

Dedicated to Norma Delaney

ACKNOWLEDGEMENTS

*****

Norma, the gratitude I feel for you is immense. I know that you gave of your own life to set me free. If I had known the price you would pay to support me throughout our integration work, I probably would have stopped working with you. It took every bit of courage I had to accept your gift without turning away in judgment or guilt.

Your commitment to me expressed itself in a love so pure it transformed both of us. I marvel at the journey we took. It was arduous, painful, extraordinary, and always illuminating. I will always be eternally grateful to you for being the guiding light in my life.

To my three blessed sons, taking care of you was my only reason for living. Your presence in my life was a beacon guiding me forward. Those first few years working with Norma were devastating; I wanted to die, but Norma would remind me that if I stayed alive, I could see you grow into men and be a part of your futures someday.

Having a mother who was extremely dissociative meant I wasn't emotionally available to you. But no matter how hard your childhoods were, you kept your hearts open to me, which helped me stay focused on my integration work. Each of you contributed to my memoir in your own unique way.

Aaron, when you left home in the late '90s, your phone calls were a lifeline for me. Despite how difficult it was to hear your mother speak in different children's voices, you didn't reject me. Instead, you were kind to my internal children, which soothed the ache within me. I was desperate to be heard, and you listened. Do you know what that kindness meant to them and me?

You honored my request for solitude by not contacting me. When you drove from Texas to Colorado years later to introduce me to your newborn son, you never mentioned how hurt you were by my actions. Instead, you kept accepting me where I was. You demonstrated more loudly than words could ever express how you felt about me. Your love and acceptance supported me in my healing process, and for that, I will always be grateful.

Stephen, your letters meant the world to me when I had no contact with you or your brothers. They were a lifeline that allowed me to pretend, in some small way, that I was still a part of your lives. I was overwhelmed by my commitment to putting myself first and believed that in staying silent, I would lose the three of you forever. Every time one of your letters arrived, I eagerly read it, which allowed me to re-focus on my integration work with renewed purpose. Plus, the silly faces you drew in the margins made me laugh with delight every time.

When you taught me how to edit my book's manuscript, your guidance and patience were invaluable. It let me focus on the revisions I needed to make without the stress. Your perspective added clarity to what I had written, since you were part of my journey. Your willingness to read it, minus the memories, made it easier for me to relay my message to my readers so they could better understand what I had experienced.

I am thankful for the precious time we had together once you moved to Colorado. The laughter we shared healed some of the guilt I felt about being your mother. I am blessed to have you in my life because your love and acceptance have made a huge difference in my life.

Timothy, our relationship has evolved over the years because of your willingness to always be honest with me. Your candor helped me delve into parts of my journey I had not yet faced, and it opened the door to the new, sweet relationship we have today.

When I visited you in Pittsburgh and watched you dance and teach ballet, those memories will always be cherished. I marveled at the fact that despite your childhood, your creative light still shone brightly.

The photo you took of me for the back cover of my book is the best picture anyone has ever taken of me. I remember laughing as you diligently tried to guide me to hold my head in a certain position while instructing me to look into the camera lens. The laughter we shared was contagious, and we needed several takes before you were satisfied. When I see that photograph on the back cover of my book, it fills me with pride and joy. You are a priceless gift in my life.

Rachel Farabaugh, I appreciate the skill you brought to the publication of my book. I wrote my memoir to introduce people to the truth: that with Spirit, anything is possible! No matter what your past was, you can choose to heal.

The commitment it took to get my manuscript ready for publication was huge. The Universe brought you into my life to share in this final step. You made the cover of my book beautiful, and your attention to detail ensured nothing was overlooked in its presentation.

*****

CONTENTS

INTRODUCTION	11
Chapter 1: A CRACK IN THE WALL	14
Chapter 2: MEETING NORMA	21
Chapter 3: LEARNING TO BREATHE	28
Chapter 4: WEEKEND WITH THE BOYS	44
Chapter 5: THE MOTHERS	62
Chapter 6: SEBRINA INTEGRATES	76
Chapter 7: COMPASSION	84
Chapter 8: ROBBIE INTEGRATES	98
Chapter 9: LIVING FOR ME	105
Chapter 10: HAMBURGERS AND JOY	117
Chapter 11: CHANGES	135
Chapter 12: KEEPING ME SAFE	151
Chapter 13: SUCCESS	182
Chapter 14: I'M YOUR MOTHER	215

Chapter 15: MOVING TO COLORADO	222
Chapter 16: MY NEW HOME	231
Chapter 17: CONNECTIONS	239
Chapter 18: BECOMING AUTHENTIC	247
Chapter 19: MOMENTS OF REAL HAPPINESS	261
Chapter 20: I AM THE DOORWAY	276
Chapter 21: THE DREAM	283
Chapter 22: NEW FREEDOMS	292
Chapter 23: RETURNING TO WORK	295
Chapter 24: FIGHTING NEVER WORKS	305
Chapter 25: WHAT IS SOUL?	313
Chapter 26: ASPECTS	321
Chapter 27: A NEW BEGINNING	331
Chapter 28: I'M DONE WITH DARK ENERGY	349
EPILOGUE	367

INTRODUCTION

*****

In 1953, the Central Intelligence Agency was authorized to begin the top-secret project known as MKUltra. It used people of all ages in a program that was largely focused on brainwashing and mind control. Through the use of LSD and other chemicals, hypnosis, electroshock, sensory deprivation, isolation, verbal and sexual abuse, and other forms of torture, they sought to find a portal into the mind through which they could completely control another human being. After decades of denial, the CIA finally admitted the existence of MKUltra, stating that the project was no longer operational. The program affected over two million Americans and Canadians, and I was one of them.

Satanic cults use mind control on their cult members. The CIA enlisted the participation of satanic cult members who would willingly contract their children to this new project of experimentation. Combining the techniques of both organizations meant the CIA would have a greater chance of success with what they hoped to achieve.

In 1955, when I was born, my parents named me Jennifer. In 1995, I legally changed my name to Serena. Before my birth, my father made arrangements to sign me over to the MKUltra project. He was the head of a satanic cult, so this type of behavior was standard for him. My parents' intent, combined with the CIA's plan, was to create a person with multiple personalities that they could control from the very beginning. The training started when I was three days old, and it affected every area of my life.

When I was thirty-seven years old, I was diagnosed with multiple personality disorder, later termed dissociative identity disorder. I didn't accept that diagnosis, but I knew something was wrong with me since I was in pain on a daily basis. I had lost my three sons to foster care due to my instability, and believed that if I were integrated, I could get them back. I was looking for a quick fix. I had it all planned out, I thought.

Then I met the woman who would change my life. Unlike the doctors and therapists I had previously worked with, she was willing to step beyond the confines of accepted psychological methodology, in favor of something that would secure an authentic integration born of my Soul. I latched onto the idea of integration in shortsightedness. I could only dream of surviving, but my Soul knew a greater truth. With guidance from my Soul and a total commitment from this woman, I began my integration.

*****

This book is my story.

Chapter 1: A CRACK IN THE WALL

I was diagnosed with multiple personality disorder when I was thirty-seven years old. I didn't agree with the diagnosis, but I knew something was wrong with me. I was in constant emotional and physical pain, and struggled to make the simplest decisions. Every area of my life was in chaos.

Six years before my diagnosis, I began working with my first therapist. During one of our sessions, he asked me if I had been sexually abused. I told him I didn't think so, but as I drove home that evening, I asked God to show me the truth.

Pieces of memory began to filter through the veil of my forgetfulness; flashes so unimaginable, I could barely cope. How could this be real? I would have remembered it, I thought. As the flashes became full-fledged memories, I was crippled with such overwhelming emotional pain that I cried every day. I had found being a single parent of three young boys very difficult, but now with these memories becoming more frequent, I could barely function.

After a couple of years dealing with the memories of my father's abuse, I began having memories of men being dressed in hooded, black robes. Pieces of memory flashed before my eyes—images so horrific I wondered if I were insane. With these images came the awareness that these men were part of a satanic cult. How could these things have happened to me without me remembering them?

Julie, my younger sister, began having satanic memories as well. She would call me on the phone and ask me to listen to a memory she just had. She was concerned I would contaminate her memories with my own, so she asked me only to listen.

In October of 1992, she called to share another memory with me. As I listened to Julie recount what had happened to our mother, it seemed as though an invisible wall crumbled, allowing me to see everything in shocking detail. Stopping Julie in mid-sentence, I pressed her for specifics. As she described what she was seeing, I could no longer push the truth away. Our memories matched exactly! Seeing my mother savagely raped by my father and his male cult followers caused chills to run down my spine. I felt like I was plunging headfirst down a dark hole, and I couldn't do anything about it. Every satanic cult memory I had remembered up to this point had seemed too outlandish for them to be true. They were so outside the realm of normalcy that they were easy to repress. But now, I was seeing the memory in real time, and it hit me hard! My denial shattered. I knew I was in trouble.

I scheduled appointments with different therapists in hopes of finding someone I could work with. But when I met with them individually, they all asked me the same question: did I know what multiple personality disorder was? I was offended and angry at their question. I left each appointment totally discouraged. But I had to find someone to help me. Walking into my seventh appointment, I tried to describe the memories I was having. Sobbing, I was incoherent. Once again, I was asked if I knew what multiple personality disorder was. I rebuked the therapist, telling him I knew what it was, and that I didn't have it! Unlike the other therapists who had let the matter go, he disagreed with me and said that he had seen me switch personalities at least six times during the session. I left his office completely discouraged.

Lying my head against the steering wheel of my car, I begged God for help. I told God if this were true, I would be willing to face it. Instantly, I saw a young girl appear on the seat right next to me. She seemed as real as I was, but since she materialized out of nowhere, I knew she must be a personality.

She told me her name was Candee. She couldn't have been more than fourteen years old. She was thin, with blond, curly hair. Her eyes were blue, and she had the sweetest smile. I was so shocked that I didn't remember driving home.

I began working with the therapist who had insisted I was a multiple personality. I would go to his office for a session and be told only minutes later that it was over. He informed me I had been there for the full hour, but I didn't remember a thing! I began recording the sessions so I could hear what was going on with me. When I listened to the cassette tape, I was surprised. I heard different voices, sharing things I had no memory of. Even though the therapist handed me the cassette tape after every session, I still didn't believe what was on it. The stories told by the various voices were too far-fetched to be true; it was easier for me to believe I was crazy.

I began taking notes from the recorded cassette tapes, and when each new personality presented itself, I wrote down its name in my journals. I did this for years. It felt like I was working with a jigsaw puzzle, with the pieces of me scattered everywhere. I believed that if I kept track of all the different names and stories, I would eventually find myself. I went back through my journals many years later and counted the names I had jotted down, and to my amazement, it exceeded three hundred different personalities.

One day, while shopping with my sons, I heard a high-pitched child's voice calling to them. I watched a four-year-old boy with freckles and brown hair repeatedly shout to my boys that they had to come and see the toys. He gestured wildly, racing back and forth through the toy aisle. As I stood there, blocked behind some kind of internal glass wall, I saw my sons' confusion and was powerless to do anything about it. Intuitively, I knew this child was connected to me and my supposed multiplicity. In the next instant, I was back on the other side of the wall, trying to deal with my sons' embarrassment. At the time, I believed what I saw was what everyone else saw. It was years before I understood that the little boy who was running up and down the toy aisle was me! My sons and others saw an adult woman frantically gesturing and shouting loudly, while acting like a small child.

I was getting worse. Suicide promised a way out, but I couldn't do that to my sons. I found a hospital that was willing to help me. It was described as one of the leading institutions in the country dealing with dissociative disorders.

I went into the hospital on August 12, 1993, and what was supposed to be a twenty-eight-day program turned into eight straight months of hospitalization. I deteriorated so completely that foster care was called in to help. They told me that if I didn't willingly sign my sons over to the state, they would take me to court and prove I was unfit, and then I would never get them back. This terrified me, so I willingly signed the papers.

I also began having memories of the government experimenting on me. My doctor told me I wasn't the first patient to share this kind of information with him. He told me that the government had admitted to experimenting on Americans years earlier, but at that point, I was overwhelmed and could not accept any more details about my past, so my Soul put them away until later.

After being released from the hospital, I was re-admitted periodically for the next two-and-a-half years due to my instability. While living on my own between hospital stays, I attended the hospital's outpatient program every day and met with my doctor three times a week, but nothing seemed to help. I was still behaving erratically, and the memories never stopped. I felt hopeless.

In my therapy sessions, I began to hear the words *there is something more*. It began as a quiet whisper, and the more I felt stuck, the louder it got. Finally, in complete despair, I surrendered. Within weeks, I was meeting the woman who would help me integrate. Through compassion, Norma Delaney bridged my self-hatred with a love so pure that she opened the way for me to begin feeling and experiencing things I had never known before. I learned from her; she was my teacher in becoming real.

Unlike the doctors and therapists I had previously worked with, she was willing to step beyond the confines of accepted psychological methodology, in favor of something that would secure an authentic integration born of my Soul.

*****

Using the word "I" in the previous text was only for semantics.

In truth, there was no I. There was no awareness of myself as an individual. Instead, there was a physical body, containing fragmented consciousnesses, held together by my Soul to move the life forward. Imagine a revolving door, quickly ushering people in and out. Each personality that comes forward will pick up the conversation where the last one left off. There can be no indication of the switch, because that will attract your attention. There is a cohesiveness of awareness, which allows all the personalities to flow as one.

When a baby is born, the parents (if they are loving), hold and nurture their newborn. This simple act invites the Soul, through breath, to come into the body. While I was in the hospital, I got that kind of nurturing from the hospital staff. But once I was brought home, the training regimen began.

When I was three days old, my father took me outside and laid me in the grass. Standing back, he watched to see how I would react. As I became hungry and cold, my cries turned into fitful bursts of rage. Weakened from lack of nourishment, I would fall into unconsciousness, but he would have none of that. Kicking me awake would start the process all over again. This went on into the early morning hours.

How many times did my father have to kick me to rouse me out of death? How long would I cry before I gave up? Whatever the criteria, I passed with flying colors. I was the fighter he was looking for.

How do I remember this? My Soul showed me this memory many years ago. She began to share with me the intent of this lifetime. Before my birth, my Soul knew of the thousands of years she had lived in human form, experiencing life through a veil of self-hatred and forgetfulness. She chose that this lifetime would be different. By being born to parents who were masters in the game of fear, I would either get lost in it or discover the truth of who I really am. It was a huge gamble, but my Soul was willing to take it.

Norma held a space of loving compassion that allowed me to feel safe enough to face the truth of my life's experiences, a memory at a time. Only after we had worked for over twenty years and I knew without a doubt that the memories were true, was I able to research online what the government had admitted. It shocked me to my core and validated everything I had remembered. I realized that my parents' intent, combined with the government's mind control program, had one purpose: to create a multiple personality that they could control from the very beginning, and that training affected every area of my life.

This book is about my miraculous journey into integration and the light. It is about my transformation from living in darkness to being a person of higher consciousness. It's about working outside the box to realize a choice that was made before my birth. The multiplicity that had worked so miraculously for thirty-seven years began to unravel because I allowed the first piece of truth to break through the barrier of my denial. That first truth created a small crack in the walls of my dissociation. What looked to the outer world like chaos was, in truth, the beginning of my new life.

How is it possible that integration was finally achieved? Soul wisdom is so much more than what we humans realize. I, the human, needed another human to guide me, to help me see that there was another way. My Soul brought me to

Norma to begin my journey of integration. In being able to touch her and speak to her, in feeling her love and compassion encompass me, I began to trust something other than fear. She was the rock to my instability. I knew nothing about my Soul, but through her, I was introduced to the light within me. I could only dream of surviving, but my Soul knew that life could be so much more. With guidance from my Soul and a total commitment from this woman, I began my integration.

There were many naysayers who told Norma to give up. They said I would never integrate, but she knew that with Spirit, anything is possible.

This book was written to show others that there is another way.

No matter what has happened in your past, if you truly want to heal, you can through the wisdom of your own higher consciousness. You don't have to have a plan. Just say yes to your Soul, and that will be a beginning.

Chapter 2: MEETING NORMA

I'm meeting with Norma today to see if she can help me. Opening the door, she smiles and invites me in. Scanning her appearance, I examine everything, from the color of her pants and blouse to the jewelry that adorns her neck, wrists, ears, and fingers. I am a human computer, memorizing everything for future reference. But there is something beyond the physical that intrigues me. Her eyes emanate a life of their own. They invite me to trust, just by looking into them. Her whole being radiates an energy that I find comforting.

Following her into the living room, I stop and turn around in amazement. Tall Ficus trees stand on either side of the room, with twinkling white lights interwoven between their branches. Various types of potted plants grow everywhere. The sound of a bubbling water fountain and the tinkling of a wind chime add the final touches to a room that is purely magical.

Smiling warmly at me, Norma pats the couch, inviting me to take a seat next to her. Shaking my head no, I sit down on the floor with my back against the wall. Unfortunately, that doesn't help to control my anxiety.

Internally, many voices are speaking.

Will she like me?

Is she safe?

She's so beautiful!

Don't say anything. See what she does first.

My hands fidget nervously; my breathing is fast and shallow. Norma speaks quietly; she asks me what I would like to accomplish.

With a switch and a rush of words, someone cries, "I need to get my sons back! I have been in and out of the hospital since 1993. It was supposed to be a twenty-eight-day program …"

Abruptly, the body transforms, as Roberta defiantly states, "I know they think I'm a multiple personality, but they're wrong! I need to get stable, so I can get my boys back …"

Without as much as a hiccup, the head straightens, and an angry, high-pitched voice demands, "What are your credentials? Have you ever worked with a multiple before? My name is Charlotte. I don't want to work with anyone, unless they know what they're doing."

Before Norma can reply, Roberta is back, and without a pause, she implores, "I have to get my sons back. Can you help me?"

Before Norma utters a word, Roberta is gone again.

There are many who come. Most are unaware of the one that precedes them. Each one leaves before any cohesive conversation is established. Finally, Daniel appears and speaks in a deep voice. "I am a protector. I am thirty-three years old, and I stand at 6'2" tall with blond hair and blue eyes.

I know that I'm part of a system that lives in a female body, but it's important that you see me for who I am. I'm here to help you with the children. They don't trust anyone, not even Dr. Barnes. I will do what I can to help. All you need to do is call my name, and I will come." Without further ado, he leaves.

The body sits motionless. Moments pass in silence before I come forward. "I am Sebrina, the one who made the appointment with you. I'm sorry if the switching scared you, but I knew they were anxious to meet you, so I let them be first."

"I wasn't afraid," Norma acknowledges. "I was just listening."

"Do you think you can help us?"

"I have seen movies about multiples," Norma says, "but I've not studied or read any books on the subject."

"I understand that," I interject. "That's not what I want. I have worked with professionals for years, and we are no closer to being integrated. I need someone who works with the psychic and spiritual realm. We have so many parts of our memory dealing with unusual things that I don't know what to believe anymore. Do you think you can help us?"

Norma's face is aglow with love as she responds. "I work with compassionate energy that seems to know how to do things beyond what the human part of me knows. I call it Spirit, or the psychic realm. I have been working in that medium for many years. I truly believe there is no illness that Spirit can't assist a person in healing."

Before I have a chance to respond, an attractive man walks through the front door. He is in his late forties, with long, white hair drawn back into a ponytail. The aroma of leather and pipe tobacco clings to him as he enters the room.

"It's alright," Norma assures me. "That's my husband, Garret."

Up bounds the body, as a young boy shouts, "Hey, I'm a boy, too!" Racing toward Garret, he exclaims, "I am four years old, and my name is Robbie!"

Imagine if you will, the body of a forty-year-old woman, racing toward this man with the gait of a youngster. Stretching out his arms and smiling widely, Robbie stops within inches of Garret, waiting for his response.

Taking it in stride, Garret graciously nods and responds, "It's nice to meet you, Robbie." Looking over at Norma, he smiles and politely excuses himself.

Completely unperturbed, Robbie plops himself down on the couch beside Norma. Animated and bright, he waves his arms above his head. "Who is you? Do you know Barnie? I love Barnie! Oh ... Sebina is telling me to come back inside, because she wasn't done yet. I was glad to meet you," he happily declares. With that pronouncement, he throws his arms around Norma and gives her a hug before disappearing inside.

Coming back to the front, I laugh while saying, "Robbie is an important part of the system. He's a protector who brings laughter and joy to us all. He adores Dr. Barnes and calls him Barnie. So many of the other children are terrified of men, so they refuse to speak to Dr. Barnes, so large parts of our story are being left out. Don't get me wrong—Dr. Barnes is the best doctor we've ever had. He's able to see and hear things that the other doctors miss. He never judges, no matter what we share, but it seems that no matter how hard we work, there are always more memories waiting to be dealt with. That's why I feel there has to be something more!"

Taking a deep breath, I add, "I feel that the spiritual realm is where our answer is, but don't say anything yet! I need to tell you a bit about our history. Then you can decide if you want to work with us. We were born into a satanic cult, plus my father involved us with the government, where they supposedly did experiments on us, but to be honest, I don't believe that. I don't know what happened, but I know that it was bad! Do you think you can help us?" Holding my breath, I anxiously wait for her to answer.

Smiling warmly, Norma responds, "Yes, Sebrina, I will help you. It will be an adventure for both of us as we discover how Spirit will lead us."

NORMA'S OBSERVATION

Each new client I agree to work with is an opportunity for me to open to further discovery. I'm an energy facilitator in partnership with Spirit, which I recognize as my own intuitive self. Over the years, I have worked with many individuals, each with different issues. I teach them to connect with their own Spirit self for their own healing. Spirit leads me in my work, continually assuring me that all I have to do is show up and I will be led.

I had no idea what meeting with Sebrina would be like. We had met at a Kryon event in Seattle, Washington. These events are opportunities to align ourselves with others who choose to work with Spirit. Many are healers, channelers, and teachers of metaphysical subjects.

Sebrina stood at the microphone and asked for help. I was referred to her as the person best suited to assist her in her healing. She stated that she was diagnosed with multiple personality disorder. My only experience with understanding multiplicity came from the movies The Three Faces of Eve *and* Sybil. *Trust me, the movies are bland compared to the real-life encounter. Sebrina arrived, and my life-changing adventure began.*

It was one of the most unusual experiences I have ever had. I knew from Spirit that I had to be very still in her presence. I watched this woman come into my living room. Her attempt to appear normal was contradicted by the evident tension in her body. Her eyes darted everywhere. I had the impression that she was memorizing her surroundings, possibly looking for an escape route. Despite the time she had taken to apply her makeup, I could see the deep sadness in her eyes. Her whole body exuded a profound weariness.

I invited her to sit on the couch next to me, but she preferred to sit on the floor with her back against the wall. As rapidly as I could talk to one person, another would appear. Some were adults, like Daniel. He displayed a depth of wisdom and kindness as he told me he was ready to assist me in any way he could. He good-naturedly informed me that he understood he lived in a female body, but it was important that I see him for who he truly was. The amazing thing is that, over time, as I got to know Daniel, I saw him for who he was. Despite the fact that he lived in a female body, his large male presence dwarfed the 5'5" frame.

Children appeared, both male and female alike. I had the impression they were the brave ones who were coming out to gauge my reaction. Behind the children's eyes, I could see many other pairs of eyes, watching, too afraid to come out and speak for themselves. I sat there witnessing a miracle of life. Within each human being is the capability to split into multiple fragments, just as anything else that is broken can be shattered. I felt humbled and ready to assist this person with whatever Spirit would lead us to do. It never occurred to me what a giant journey I was undertaking, and I never thought to ask how long it would take, or all the other questions people have asked me since.

We were drawn together by a mysterious force; my mind was never present enough to question it. The only thing I know these many years later is that I still feel the same way. It's like I've been in training in a university program, unlike anything I could have ever imagined. I feel and know I've been blessed to be part of this miracle.

I think back to our beginning and realize how unaware we both were. Innocence has been our strongest suit. It has allowed both of us to be led by Spirit. I truly believe this is a story of a shattered human being, commonly known as a multiple personality, being led to fully integrate.

The reason this integration is so unusual is that it was led by Kuan Yin, who is the goddess of Divine Compassionate Love. When I met Sebrina, I knew I had to channel more than just Kuan Yin's words. I opened myself fully to Kuan Yin's energy, which awakened the compassion already living within me. This solid connection enabled me to easily communicate with Serena's Soul, opening the door to a new, healed human being.

Chapter 3: LEARNING TO BREATHE

Knocking on the door, I listen for the sound of footsteps. Hearing nothing, I knock louder. Still, no response. Standing there aimlessly, I wonder what to do. Finally, after what seems like an eternity, Norma opens the door.

Smiling, she takes my hand, saying, "Just come on in. You don't need to knock, sweetie."

"Are you serious?" *How can she trust us?*

"Of course, Sebrina. I have nothing to fear. If you don't see me, I'm upstairs working with another client. Make yourself comfortable, and I'll be down shortly."

Bewildered by her remark, I remain silent. Following her into the living room, I sit down in the upholstered chair across from her.

"Come sit beside me," Norma suggests.

Taking a seat next to her, I wonder where I should begin.

No need for deliberation: out pops Robbie. "Hi! It's me, Robbie! I missed you. I is glad we is here. I telled Dr. Barnie about you."

Stopping to inhale, he rushes on. "There is lots of kids waitin' to see you.

How come we had to wait so long before we could come to your house again?" Smiling broadly, he waits for Norma to respond.

Before she has a chance to answer, the face transforms, and the eyes grow round with innocence as a switch occurs. "I have to go pee pee," a child's voice whispers. Grabbing her crotch, the child wiggles in discomfort.

Smiling and without comment, Norma gently takes her hand, leading her to the bathroom. The child's gait is stiff and unbalanced, just like a toddler learning to walk. The closer she gets to the bathroom, the more rigid she becomes. Pulling her hand out of Norma's, she curls up on the floor, whimpering.

"I will pee for her!" Robbie exclaims, stepping forward. "I is not afraid." Striding out of the bathroom minutes later, he triumphantly exclaims, "Jennifer is scared of lots of things. She don't talk much, but I always try to help her." With a skip and a hop, he lands back on the couch.

"Barnie don't care if we sees you. I is glad. I want to have time with you today, okay?" Scooting closer, Robbie leans in for a hug. "After all the others talk with you, can we be together?"

"Of course we can, sweetie. I want to be with you, too." Holding him close, Norma gives him a bear hug before letting go.

Looking up at her, he laughs. "I think you had better talk to them, because they is having a hard time." Happily, he steps back, making room for Sebrina.

"I don't know where to start," I remark, rubbing my forehead for clarity.

"Let's start by breathing, so your body can feel more at peace. Sit back and close your eyes. Listen to my voice as you breathe deeply through your nose." Speaking slowly, in a gentle cadence, Norma continues. "Let your shoulders relax as you drop deeper into your body. Keep your mouth closed as you inhale and exhale slowly." Stopping, she allows me to breathe a bit before continuing. "Notice if your breath is coming all the way down into your belly. Feel your belly rise and fall with every breath you take. This type of breathing tells your body that it is safe. Give yourself the time you need to really settle into the sweet rhythm your breath has for you." After a few minutes of leading me to breathe, she asks if I am ready to begin.

"Yes, listening to your voice really helped me feel better. Thanks, Norma."

"Good, now what do you want to talk about today?"

"I've always believed that I chose my parents for a reason. I don't know what that reason is, but I feel it. I've yearned for a spiritual connection for as long as I can remember. It's what led me to try different things in my life. A few years ago, I began meditating. One morning in meditation, I saw a candle flickering underneath a bushel basket. My eyes were closed, but I swear I saw it, Norma! Then I heard a voice say, 'Don't hide your light under a bushel basket.' Even though I knew the words came from the Bible, that didn't change how real that moment was for me. I've had many experiences like that, most of them before I was diagnosed."

"Tell me about another such experience," Norma suggests.

"Well, a few months ago, I began feeling that to truly integrate, I needed to change my legal name. At the time, I had no idea what that would be. When I shared the idea with Dr. Barnes, he thought it was silly. But Norma, the feeling didn't go away—it grew stronger! One morning, when I was still half-asleep, I heard that voice that whispered to me about the light under the bushel basket, say, 'Your new name is to be Serena-Faith Masterson, which means serene faith master of the Christ within. You will need to legally change it for the work that is to come.' And so I did. I legally changed it, but no one calls me that.

"Isn't that strange? Hearing voices? Sometimes I wonder if I'm just plain crazy. I leave out parts of my history on purpose. I never share them with the therapists, because it's too uncomfortable." Grabbing a pillow off the couch, I push it into my stomach, hoping it will stop the anxiety I'm feeling.

"Let's slow this down, so we can look at your concerns one at a time, Sebrina." (Norma frequently speaks my name, saying it loudly to help bring me back to the present moment. She knows I live in a constant state of mental confusion caused by internal voices clamoring to be heard. She uses this method to help me focus so we can continue talking with minimal interruptions.) The first thing I heard you tell me is that you're aware of an intuitive sense that guides and directs you from within yourself. I understand that. Through the years, I have learned that even though my mind has no idea about any given situation, Spirit fully knows what a person needs for their own healing. Discussing Spirit or psychic phenomena does not intimidate me. I believe and know it to be true. It's how I do my work. As we work together, we will discover the truth about what happened to you.

"Now this is important, and I need you to listen to me," Norma emphatically states, while raising her voice. "You are not crazy! In fact, you're a remarkable human being who used your psychic ability to keep yourself alive. Most people would have succumbed to the life you had. Do you realize how brilliant your Soul is?"

Since I don't like compliments, I pretend I didn't hear her question. "I don't know the difference between real and pretend most of the time, and that really bothers me. I know Robbie is real, because I can see him. We are two very different people. I remember when he raced up and down the aisles of Target, yelling for my sons to hurry and come see the toys. People stared, and my sons were mortified, but I couldn't stop him! He does what he wants. I see his freckles, and his upturned nose ... and his smile makes me feel happy. But other people don't see him at all!"

Stopping for breath, I wrap my arms around my middle to repress my mounting anxiety. "When the others come into the body, I usually don't remember it. I know I've lost time, because others tell me about it later. I constantly question myself. I wonder if I want attention so badly, I'd do anything for it."

Brushing the tears off my face, I push on. "I'm always angry with myself, and feel frustrated that I have difficulty with the simplest things! Telling you this much makes my body scream in pain!"

"I'm proud of you for sharing this with me," Norma says encouragingly.

"Do you think it might all be a lie?" I hopefully ask. "I've told you, I don't know what to believe, and it's hard telling the difference between what is pretend and what is real, so maybe what I remember is all a lie ..."

"Why do you think it might be a lie, Sebrina?"

"That thought always pushes at me. How do I go from believing my life was one way, then poof — I discover a totally different story that's so outlandish, anyone would question it?"

"I know you want answers, Sebrina, but this will take time. Can you allow yourself to discover the truth gently?"

"When I'm with you, I believe anything is possible." Squeezing Norma's hand, I add, "Yes, if you will do it with me."

"Of course I will. Now let's go upstairs to do more of the breathing I showed you earlier."

*****

Norma smiles at me, inviting me to lie down on the massage table.

No one's going to touch me!

Can't lie on my back— no, no, no!

"I want to go back to the couch," a young child pleads.

"I know you're afraid," Norma gently responds. "I won't hurt you. If you lie down on your back, I can help you breathe easier."

"I will!" exclaims Robbie. Climbing up onto the table, he scoots to the far end and hangs his head off the side. "Like this?" he playfully asks, giggling.

Laughing, Norma centers him on the table.

"See, I breathe real good." Pointing to his stomach, he pushes it up and down, exaggerating its movement with his breath for effect.

"Yes, Robbie, you do breathe good," Norma gently croons. "But did you know that you breathe backwards?"

Pulling back, he frowns at her questioningly.

Placing her hand on his stomach, she smiles and guides him to slow his breathing down. "When you inhale, your stomach goes in, and when you exhale, your stomach goes out. Did you know that?"

"Yes, that's the right way. I know it!" Robbie insists.

"Actually, it's backwards, sweetie."

"No, that not right, Norma!"

"If you have breathed one way your entire life, it would feel wrong to breathe differently," Norma calmly replies. "But I can assure you, it is backwards. Would you like to learn to breathe in a way that will help all of you?" Speaking in a quiet, melodic voice, she leads Robbie to breathe in a new way. "Play with me and inhale, while pushing your stomach out. Notice where your breath stops. Is it in your chest, or are you bringing it down, deep into your stomach? Allow your stomach muscles to relax. That's it. Now, as you exhale, bring your stomach in."

With the next inhale, I switch in, exclaiming fearfully, "This is too hard!"

"It's alright, Sebrina. We'll do it slowly." Speaking gently, Norma asks, "Have you ever tried something new, and at first it feels so different that you know it must be wrong, but the more you do it, the more comfortable it becomes?"

"Yes, but how could I have been wrong all this time?" I anxiously shout.

"Sweetie, you're not wrong. People who have been traumatized at an early age tend to breathe up in their chests. They're afraid to come deep into their bodies. They blame their body for their pain and want nothing to do with it.

Let's make a game out of it. Pretend you're on a surfboard, on top of a wave, and feel yourself move deeper into your body with each breath. Feel how easily the breath can move."

I try to imagine myself on a surfboard, riding a large wave, but no matter how vividly I see it, I'm unable to go any deeper into my body; my breath catches in my throat, and my body feels like granite rock. There's no way I or anyone else will come into the body like this. "I can't do it, Norma. I'm sorry!"

"Don't apologize, you've done nothing wrong. Practice it as gently as you can without forcing yourself to do it, Sebrina. Lay your hand on your stomach and practice inhaling and exhaling, while letting your stomach move as I showed you. Make it a game, where you discover how it feels to breathe in this new way. You don't have to rush it, seriously sweetie, let it be, and it will become yours naturally."

"Okay, I'll try, but can we go back downstairs to talk?"

"Yes, but it would be helpful to get something to eat before we do anything else today."

Uh-oh, another glitch. There will be more switching, since food is an issue for all of us.

Leading the way into the kitchen, Norma responds to my unspoken dread. "I know you would prefer to keep going and ignore the fact that you need to eat, but we have been working for quite a while, and your body would appreciate a snack before we delve into any other subjects. Can you allow someone who wants to eat to come forward, please?"

"That's me!" Robbie happily declares.

"What would you like?"

"I want dessert, like cake or cookies!"

Rummaging in the refrigerator, Norma answers, "I know sweets sound good, but let's start with something more substantial. Would you like a chicken sandwich or a peanut butter-and-jelly sandwich?"

Running over to where Norma is standing, Robbie shouts, "I want peanut butter and jelly!"

Taking Robbie's hand, Norma leads him back to the table. "I want you to sit and talk with me while I prepare our snack. Can you do that?"

Immediately, Robbie withdraws.

"Hey, you did nothing wrong, sweetie, you're okay. I just need room to make our snack. Tell me why you like sweets so much, and I will listen."

"Well … I likes to eat sweets because it tastes so good! At the hospital, I sneak dessert all the time." Covering his mouth with his hand, Robbie laughs mischievously.

"Why do you have to sneak it?"

"Because the big people say it makes me hyper."

"Is your favorite food anything that is sweet?"

"Yes! I love all sweet things!" he wildly exclaims.

Norma sets the plate with the peanut butter-and-jelly sandwich down in front of him. Robbie grabs it and bites it in half. Leaning directly over his plate, he finishes it almost without chewing.

"Would you like a cookie?"

"Can I have more than one?"

"Let's start with one and see how you feel." Deciding he will have more, Robbie nods obligingly.

Before he finishes, a timid voice asks, "Can I have something to eat, too? I'm so ... hungry."

Smiling, Norma replies, "Of course, you can have something to eat. What would you like?"

"I want peanut butter-and-jelly, just like Robbie."

"Alright, I can do that. Were you watching him eat?"

"Quietly nodding, the child answers, "I wanted something to eat just like him."

Going back into the kitchen, Norma continues talking, knowing that the sound of her voice is comforting. She knows it took courage to come forward and ask for food. Walking back into the room with half a sandwich, Norma sets the plate down in front of her.

"What is your name?" Norma asks, sitting down in the chair next to the little girl.

The child looks around the room fearfully before answering. "I'm Priscilla. I was wanting to come, because I like how you talk."

Leaning back, Norma smiles at her. "I'm glad you came."

Picking up the sandwich, Priscilla takes a bite and swallows quickly. She barely breathes. Keeping her head down, she furtively looks around the room while shoving the rest of the sandwich into her mouth. No sooner does Priscilla finish than another child comes forward to take her place.

Picking up the plate and returning to the kitchen for a third time, Norma makes another half sandwich. Returning to the child, Norma guides her to feel the food as it goes into her tummy. Norma knows that it's important to balance the body's needs while attending to each child who comes forward.

Calling Sebrina to the front, Norma suggests they move back to the living room to talk.

Sitting down on the couch together, I gather my thoughts before speaking. "I feel the medications we're taking aren't good for us. I've felt this for a while. When I take them, it feels like I'm putting a lid on the top of my head, bottling everything up inside."

"The medications you're taking were prescribed to support you through this difficult time in your life," answers Norma. "Their purpose is to keep your emotions in check so that you can cope. That's why you're feeling bottled up, Sebrina."

"I know it helps with our anxiety, but sometimes, it feels wrong to use them."

"It's not wrong, Sebrina. It has helped you when you needed it most, but now that you're sensing it's time for a change, trust that." Patting my hand reassuringly, she asks, "What medications are you currently taking?"

"We take Prozac for depression, Klonopin for anxiety, and Ambien for sleep. But none of it really works; we still wake up several times a night, and the anxiety is out of control. I wonder if any of them really help. I like the Prozac, though, because it helps keep the hunger at bay."

"You said you believed I could help you," Norma replies. "In order for this healing to occur, can you trust that you could be all right without medication? The medication is a temporary fix that covers up the real problem. I know it's been useful in the past, but if you're sensing it's time to come off it, you need to trust that. I'll be here to help you. It's important that you tell Dr. Barnes what you want to do, and ask him what he suggests."

Nodding in agreement, I decide I will bring this up the next time I see him. "I need to talk to you about the boys. Is there time?" I anxiously ask.

"Yes, sweetie. I told you we have as much time as you need." Taking my hand, she looks into my eyes. "It will help everyone if you can hear me when I say, we have as much time as you need. Rushing creates fear, so take your time, I'm not going anywhere."

"Okay, Norma. I'll trust what you're telling me." Smiling, I inhale slowly before beginning. "Like everything else in our life, the situation with the boys is out of control. They fight with each other most of the time, so when I have them on the weekend, it's absolute chaos. I have no downtime.

"Aaron is depressed and stays by himself most of the time. Stephen is angry and ends up yelling at everyone, and Tim …well, I don't know what happens, but all of a sudden, the other two have ganged up on him, and he's screaming … it's utter chaos! They blame each other, so I don't know who to believe. I can't cope with it all!" I hysterically wail. "I end up feeling overwhelmed and guilty. I want to make it right for them, but I don't know what that is!"

"Stop a moment and breathe with me," Norma suggests. "Just focus on your breath, and feel yourself relax."

As I relax, I'm able to speak more easily. "I love them, but I dread the weekends, because I know I hurt them by switching. When I was driving the four of us to the store the other day, something on the side of the road caught the attention of one of the children in the system. She moved to the front of the body, while pointing and telling everyone to look. The boys were upset that I had switched, but for me it was both upsetting and dangerous because no one was driving the car, Norma!"

Without as much as a hiccup, Roberta appears and picks up the conversation from where she left off during the last session. "Do you think you can help me? Dr. Barnes is sure I'm a multiple personality, but I think he's wrong. The boys have been in foster care for a long time! I'm frustrated because I end up getting hospitalized again and again. I have problems, but being a multiple is not one of them!"

Norma has witnessed how quickly Roberta retreats, so she holds very still, while asking, "Why are you so sure you're not a multiple, Roberta?"

"Because … I just know it!" Jumping up off the couch, she furiously shouts, "I don't want to be a multiple!"

"I understand that you don't want to be a multiple, but what is making you so afraid, Roberta?"

"If I'm a multiple, then that means what the others have shared could be true!" Screeching the last few words, she then whines, "Can't you understand, I don't want that?" Struggling to stay, Roberta ponders Norma's question more fully and realizes that the stories she has heard over the past few years were so awful that it was easier to reject them rather than to believe them.

Patting the couch beside her, Norma invites Roberta to sit down. "I know that what you have heard from the others seems unbelievable, but you don't have to do anything with that today. Can we begin with the truth that you're not alone? I can tell you honestly, you are a multiple." Raising her voice, Norma commands, "Don't leave, Roberta!"

Rubbing her forehead, Roberta looks at Norma through a cloud of haze.

"Stay here for one more moment. Can you be honest with yourself first? You don't want to be a multiple, so you can continue to deny the stories. But if we leave the stories out of it, can you tell me honestly that you don't believe you're a multiple?"

Crying softly, Roberta shakes her head no. "At the hospital, there are times when hours have gone by without me knowing it, or all of a sudden, I'm meeting with Dr. Barnes, and I don't even know how I got there, and that scares me!"

"I can understand why, Roberta. If you accepted that you were a multiple, you wouldn't need to be scared anymore, because you would know you had switched."

"Oh, Norma, do you really think I'm a multiple?"

Leaning in and taking Roberta's hand, Norma looks directly into her eyes. "I know you are a multiple, sweetie. I have seen it first-hand. You are a remarkable human being who found a brilliant way to survive. I have met with many of the others. You are not alone."

Turning her head away, Roberta sobs, and without another word, she is gone.

Calling Sebrina back to the front, Norma picks up the conversation where they left off. "I know you're set on making it work with all three boys, but that might not happen. For this coming weekend, would you let yourself feel what it's like having them all together? At the end of the weekend, ask yourself, was it worth it? Were they happy? Were you happy? Then we can talk about it at our next meeting. I want you to open to the idea of choosing what is for your highest good, instead of obeying what your mind believes a good mother is supposed to be."

"I know you're right," I acknowledge. "I need to be clear for me, without my guilt controlling me. But I hear Robbie telling me to move aside so he can have time with you. Would you give me a hug before I go?"

"Of course, sweetie." As Norma holds me, I feel her acceptance wrap around me like a warm blanket. Letting go of her embrace, I smile gratefully at her before leaving.

"Hey, you said we would have special time together, remember?" He says with a grin.

"Yes, I remember. What would you like to do, sweetie?"

"I don't know. I just want to be with you." Leaning in, Robbie wraps his arms around Norma. Settling against her chest, he sighs happily. The sounds of their combined breaths mingle with the tinkling of a wind chime dancing in the breeze.

Minutes later, Norma playfully pulls Robbie to his feet. "Would you like to pick some flowers to give to Sebrina?"

"That would be great!"

Collecting her scissors, Norma follows Robbie out into the sunshine.

*****

NORMA'S OBSERVATION

The rush of energy I experienced when Sebrina came today surprised me. I'm grateful for the degree of focus I have. Her comfort level was threatened when I casually suggested she could come into the house without knocking. Her shoulders hunched forward, as her brown eyes grew large with fear.

I could see her thoughts racing. I sensed that she wanted to run away. What seemed so normal for me opened a Pandora's Box of fear for her.

It's interesting when I talk with Robbie; he shows no sign of abuse.

He seems like a confident four-year-old boy. He is eager to touch and eager to please. It's as though he rolls out the red carpet, introducing me to whoever needs to work with me next.

Sebrina was able to carry on a conversation with me despite the interruptions from the others. I made a commitment to her that surprised even me. I'm not clear on why I'm so drawn to committing to her like I am. I'm definitely encouraged by something greater than my logical mind. I know I'm to spend our time together without a plan for how long it will be. I clear my entire day of commitments so I can totally focus on whatever unfolds. The first step is to bring calm to Sebrina so we can begin working. Whenever we are together, I don't dare move, because they view it as a signal to run and hide.

When I suggested we have something to eat, I noticed Sebrina's hesitation. As each child came forward to eat, they displayed signs that they were probably starved and abused with food. That in itself reveals a lot to me. I know at this point I'm not supposed to bring any of this to their attention. It's important that I bring as much normalcy as possible to our time together.

I noticed how rigid Sebrina's body was on the massage table. It screamed at me not to be touched. She has told me a little bit about her history, but I can only guess at the degree of abuse she experienced.

Spirit encourages me to create a safe place for Sebrina and the others. I notice that they don't know what trust is or what it means to be safe. Despite the obvious inability to understand what these words mean, there exists within this person a deep well of faith. Otherwise, she would not have chosen to live through the nightmare of her childhood. We will have to discover what her understandings of spiritual concepts are.

Sebrina seems to be the spokesperson for their faith. I'm aware that there is a greater consciousness involved in the preservation of the whole. I know to hold my tongue because secrecy helps preserve their overall safety. Spirit cautions me to only observe when Sebrina is hysterical, frightened, or ready to flee. It's as though she and I have an unspoken agreement that allows the others to pretend that I don't see them. They slip in and out under the guise of being Sebrina while speaking their truth. For many, I sense it is the first time they have ever been heard.

Chapter 4: WEEKEND WITH THE BOYS

Rocking from one foot to the other, I listen as Norma's phone rings for the third time. *Where can she be? What if I can't reach her?*

"Hello?" Norma answers.

"You have to help me!" I anxiously cry out. "The Hendersons want to talk to me before I take the boys for the weekend. What do I do?"

"Do you know what they want to talk about?"

"Well, no ... but I need to be ready. I know it's going to be bad!"

Chuckling, Norma gently asks. "Why do you believe it's going to be bad when you talk with the Hendersons?"

"I just know it is."

"No, Sebrina," Norma firmly interjects. "You don't know that it's going to be bad. It's your judgment that says it's going to be bad. Would you like to do it a new way?"

"Yes ...?" I nervously answer.

"You and I have been focusing on the breath for the past few weeks, haven't we? As you drive to pick up your sons, I want you to focus on your breath as much as possible. Keep one hand on the steering wheel and the other on your stomach. Every time you notice yourself jumping ahead to what you need to tell the Hendersons, I want you to come back to the present moment and breathe. This weekend is your weekend, to spend with your sons as you want. Stay present, and you can have fun."

"Oh … okay, Norma. I'll try anything, since I'm tired of them seeing me upset so much of the time."

"Remember," cautions Norma, "this is your weekend, too. Be gentle with yourself. Don't have any preconceived ideas of how it should go. I'm here, and you can always call me. Drive with good focus, sweetie."

Hanging up the phone, I race to the car. *I'm going to be late!* There's only one freeway into the valley, and it's always congested. Cars creep, bumper-to-bumper, at speeds of no more than twenty miles per hour.

Hurry up! Hurry up!

You're going to be late!

They will be mad if you're late!

How are you supposed to breathe and keep track of driving at the same time? It's impossible to do!

Turning on the radio, I turn up the volume in hopes it will shut out the voices that are shouting at me.

You're supposed to be breathing!

It'll be your fault if it's not a good weekend.

But it doesn't work. Crying out in frustration, I turn off the radio. Placing my hand on my belly, I try to focus, but the need to escape wins out. Locking my gaze on the horizon outside, I purposely hypnotize myself, creating a wall between myself and feeling. Finally, I'm able to drive the rest of the way free of distress.

*****

As I pull into the driveway of Aaron's group home, he bolts out the front door. Hurling himself into the front seat, he scoffs, "You're two hours late!"

"The traffic was bad. You know what it's like driving here."

"Gees," he mutters, turning his back to me.

"Aaron, I got here as fast as I could. Please," I beg, "don't ruin the weekend by being angry." *If I had been a better mother, he wouldn't be this angry.* Consumed with guilt, I'm barely able to function. I have to do something to make it better. Trying another tactic, I mask my voice in artificial cheerfulness, while asking, "How was school this week?"

"Fine!" he angrily snaps.

Glancing to my right, I try to get his attention, but he's clearly not interested in speaking to me.

What can I do to make it better, I wonder?

It's your fault.

If he had a different mother, he wouldn't be this way.

It's because he's in foster care.

You failed him.

The silence between us is deafening. Invisible cords of guilt squeeze me until I can barely breathe. I know this will be another grueling weekend unless I do something different. Placing my hand on my stomach, I focus on its movement while inhaling and exhaling. Determined to shift my hopelessness, I keep breathing. Finally, my guilt begins to ease.

Encouraged, I try to strike up a conversation once again. "Hey, Aaron, I saw that lady ... remember the one I told you about?" Hoping for the improbable, I wait. Still no response. Realizing that this is futile, I give up and resume breathing.

I get back on the road, headed to the Hendersons' home, where my other two boys live. Exiting the freeway twenty minutes later, I glance back and forth from the road to my rearview mirror. I apply lipstick and comb my hair. My knees steer as I intermittently grab the clutch to shift gears. Multiple conversations run simultaneously through my mind. Each conversation has one objective: to appear stable and be a good parent, no matter what the Hendersons say.

Switching into a parental voice, I sternly warn, "Aaron, stay next to me and don't go running through their house. Please, act appropriately and wait to be invited, okay?" Uttering the last few words in a high-pitched whine, I grimace. *Why can't I be a better mother? I sound like a child, begging for help.* Disgusted with myself, I park, pull myself out of the car, and square my shoulders for what's to come.

The Hendersons live on a cul-de-sac in a large, two-story house. The home sits back toward the far end of the lot, with a large front lawn. The landscape is impeccably maintained, with flowers outlining the perimeter in a vibrant array of colors. Whenever I am here, I'm reminded of how much I haven't been able to provide for my sons. Despite my feelings of worthlessness, I smile bravely. Before I can knock, the front door flings open, and Stephen and Timothy pull me inside.

Yelling over his brother to be heard, Stephen shouts, "I'm glad you're here, Mom! What took you so long?" while Timothy implores, "Come to my room, I need to show you something!"

Astonished by their enthusiastic welcome, I step back, trying to catch my breath.

Coming into the foyer, Carol Henderson takes control. "Please, boys, I know you're excited to see your mother, but we need to talk to her before you go. Take Aaron upstairs, and we will call you when we're done."

Grumbling and muttering, the three boys trudge upstairs. Tim looks back, questioning me with his gaze.

Whenever I'm with Carol and Frank, I can't help comparing myself to them. They seem so normal, and their lives flow in ways I can only dream of. Instead of this encouraging me, I end up wanting to run.

Following Carol into the living room, I tug on my jeans before taking a seat opposite them. Looking around the room, I'm envious. I wish I could give my sons a home like this. Knowing that the interior was recently decorated, I look around me in appreciation. "What is it you wanted to talk with me about?" I politely ask.

"We're having difficulty with Timothy," Carol states. Folding her hands in her lap, she continues. "He is disruptive in class. He talked back to one of his teachers on Thursday. When we spoke to him about it, he said it was no big deal; all the kids talk that way. He told us on more than one occasion that he had finished his homework, but when we met with his teacher last week, we discovered that wasn't true. He's not following through. On his latest report card, he got three D's. We were hoping you would talk to him. He obviously loves you very much and might be more willing to listen to what you have to say."

"Yes," Frank interjects. "I've sat down with him more than once in the past few weeks, trying to address the problem, but he tells me only what I want to hear. Unfortunately, he doesn't follow through on his promises. Carol and I are not able to reach him."

"Well … of course, I will speak to him," I quickly respond. "None of my boys like school. I wish they did. I know he's angry about being in foster care. He begs me to let him come home all the time, but Dr. Barnes says it's too soon."

"Please listen, Sebrina, we're only here to support you. We don't want to take your place, but he needs boundaries and consequences. It's more important to both of us to provide a stable home for him than for him to like us. If the three of us can work together to give this to him, there's no reason why he can't improve in school. If he knows you expect only the best from him, he'll be getting the same message from the three of us."

Are they for real?

What do they really want?

Do they act like this when no one is watching? There has to be something more!

Shaking my head, I try to ignore the voices disrupting my focus. "I will talk to him this weekend. I'll get them back by 7 p.m. on Sunday, okay?" Holding my breath, I wait for their signal to tell me we're done.

With a nod from Frank, I jump up and yell, "Hurry up, you guys, let's go!"

"I'm in the front seat!" cries Timothy, as he races down the stairs.

"No way, I was sitting there first!" Shouts Aaron, as he shoves past Timothy.

Oh God, it's starting already.

Clutching the steering wheel, I try to gather my wits. As car doors slam and the arguing continues, my anxiety swirls out of control. Pulling out of the driveway, I make my way down the street and out of view before pulling over to the curb. Closing my eyes, I rest my forehead against the steering wheel and inhale deeply while trying to contain my hysteria. Between their shouting and the sirens that are going off inside, I feel like I might explode. "Stop!" I angrily shout. "Please … you guys, all week long I look forward to seeing you! I work with Dr. Barnes, the therapists, and Norma, all so I can get you back someday, but when you fight like this, I don't know what to do!"

You're being a drag.

Be nice. They need you to love them.

Caving into my guilt, I cry, "Oh, forget it. Let's go get ice cream!"

"Yeah!" they unanimously shout.

*****

After two and a half long hours of driving, including an ice cream stop, we're finally home. Going inside, I call, "Bill, we're home! Where are you?"

Coming in from the back room, Bill smiles while opening his arms wide. Enveloping all three boys in a bear hug, he laughs good-naturedly. Bill amazes me because no matter how much chaos the three of them create, he never raises his voice. His gentleness has created a special bond between the four of them. His round belly, twinkling blue eyes, and balding head counterbalance how intimidating he could be due to his large size. He's the epitome of quiet. In the two years since I have known him, he has never yelled. Men scare me, so this relationship is unusual for me. I met him in the hospital in 1994, and he has been my friend ever since.

We have lived together for only a short time. We pool our disability checks to pay the mortgage on Bill's condominium. It has three stories and a basement at garage level. The décor is early bachelor. Bill has no interest in decorating, and I feel too uprooted to make it a home.

When my three teenage boys come for the weekend, it's crowded. The living room becomes their temporary bedroom, with duffel bags, clothes, pillows, and blankets strewn everywhere, and with the sleeping bags stacked against the wall to make room to walk. And when they argue, which is often, their shouting, angry voices add to my internal din of chaos, making it easy for me to switch.

*****

"Norma!" I breathlessly exclaim. "I can't handle their fighting!" Gripping the phone, I cry, "All I wanted to do was see my boys, but when I'm with them, I get so overwhelmed! On top of that, there is this horrible crying going on inside of me."

"Slow down and catch your breath. I'm right here," Norma responds. "Are you sitting down, Sebrina?"

"No, I'm pacing," I angrily counter.

"Do you find it hard to breathe as you pace back and forth?"

"Yes, but I have to get away!"

"Sebrina, sit down and breathe."

Shifting the phone to my shoulder, I make room on my bed to sit. "Oh, Norma, I hurt so much!"

"I know, sweetie. Tell me what's going on."

"I see this little girl, and she's crying."

"Do you know what she's crying about?" Norma asks.

"No."

"What are you feeling, Sebrina?"

"I want to smash and get rid of her!"

"Why do you want to smash her?" Norma queries.

"Because she hurts too much!"

"Would you be willing to try something new?"

"Yes, I suppose so," I hesitantly answer.

"I want you to go and sit beside her. Ask her why she's crying, and tell her that you will listen."

Inhaling deeply, I reluctantly walk over and sit down beside her. Living simultaneously in two realities is nothing new to me. In my outside world, my right hand holds the phone to my ear, while my eyes vacantly gaze around the room, fixating on the lipstick plant that is sitting on the windowsill. Concurrently, my internal eyes scan the room in which this small child and I sit. There is a starkness here that I am well familiar with—no furniture, no carpet, dimly lit, props that reinforce feelings of hopelessness and abandonment.

Pulling my knees up, I rest my arms on them, while repeating the words Norma is telling me to say. I notice tear streaks smudged across the child's face, and her shivering body is unusually skinny. She can't be more than four years old. "What's your name?" I ask, genuinely interested.

"Penelope," she replies. "Why won't he leave me alone?"

"What do you mean?"

"He likes to scare me. He laughs when I show him, I'm afraid. I don't know what to do." Banging her head against the wall, she repeats herself over and over again.

"Norma," I anxiously cry, "she's banging her head against the wall! What do I do?"

"Take her head and hold it still, Sebrina. Gently tell her she's not allowed to hurt herself anymore."

"But, Norma, she's fighting me!"

"It's alright. You're the adult, Sebrina. Look into her eyes and tell her you're here to help her."

"Oh, God, this is too hard! I don't like this."

"Do it anyway. This child needs you," Norma firmly directs.

Looking into Penelope's eyes, I try to mimic Norma's voice. "I'm here to help you," I tell her.

"Sebrina, hold her in your lap and tell her she no longer lives with her father. Tell her that she can live with you. Can you do that?"

Nodding, even though Norma can't see me, I do as Norma tells me. I'm learning a new way to help these internal children, which is helping me feel better, and the child is finally at peace. Blinking my eyes rapidly, I purposely return to the outside world. As I rub my forehead, I inhale deeply to feel more present.

"I feel so much better, Norma! Thanks for talking to me!"

"Call me anytime you want. I am here."

*****

Coming down the stairs, I call to the boys. "Did you eat lunch yet?"

"No, we thought we'd wait for you!" Stephen shouts. Bounding up off the couch, he wraps his arms around me. "I'm glad we're here, Mom. I love you so much. Hey, do you think we could go to the movies?"

"I think that's a great idea. Ask Bill if he wants to go with us, and in the meantime, I'll fix us lunch."

*****

Eagerly piling into Bill's van, I sit in the back, watching my sons.

I have failed them so much. Leaning my forehead against the cool window, tears slip down my cheeks unnoticed. The ache inside is intense. It feels like a cavernous hole, right in the middle of my chest. If I could only fill it with something. Consumed by my thoughts, I'm unaware we have arrived at the local cineplex.

Climbing out of the van, Timothy cries, "I get to sit with Mom!"

"I do, too!" Chimes in Stephen.

"That's not fair," whines Aaron.

Feeling the urge to run, I rub my forehead in an attempt to push back the fog that is rolling in. Looking at Bill, I silently plead for his help. I don't want to disappoint them, and if Bill makes the decision, then it won't be my fault.

Smiling at me in encouragement, he silently waits.

Realizing I can't get out of it, I dejectedly cast the verdict. "Aaron, you sat next to me when I picked the three of you up. Let Stephen and Timothy sit next to me now, okay?" Hearing my voice, childishly pleading, makes me angry with myself. Why is it so hard for me to make the simplest decisions?

Sitting in the darkened theater, I'm transported from my own life into the story on the screen. Living vicariously through the characters' emotions, I feel things I would never allow myself to feel in real life. I like this one-sided relationship because no matter what I think or feel, no one gets hurt. Too soon, and the lights come on. As we leave the theater, the conversation flows easily between us.

"Why don't we go get dinner before we go home?" Bill suggests.

"Yeah!" the boys cry unanimously.

"Bill, we can't. I don't have the money for the four of us to go out and eat."

"That's okay, I'll pay for it." Bill's recklessness in spending his own money has no bounds.

"You can't afford it any more than I can," I responsibly reply.

"Oh, come on, Mom, he said it was okay," Timothy chides.

Reluctantly, I give in. I know Bill can't afford it any more than I can, but saying no to the boys is just too hard.

Before entering the restaurant, I caution them to behave, but my warning falls on deaf ears. We explode into the restaurant as though Bedlam herself has arrived. Getting in line for the buffet, the boys impatiently push into each other, which causes Timothy to accidentally bump into the woman in front of him.

"You guys," I whisper, "slow down and wait your turn. Bill, say something, tell them to behave, please!"

Stepping in between Stephen and Aaron, Bill lightly suggests, "Come on, fellas, try and stay quiet while you get your food. It upsets your mom when you act like this."

"Yeah, you guys!" Robbie declares.

"Oh, my God!" Clamping my hand over my mouth, I try to shut Robbie up.

Standing on tiptoe, Robbie whispers into Bill's ear. "Hi, Billy. I is glad we is here. I don't want no broccoli, and I hate those little corns."

"Robbie!" Bill sternly cautions. "Dr. Barnes says you're not supposed to be around the boys. They get upset when they see their mother acting like a child. You don't want to hurt them, do you?"

"Jeez," Robbie gripes, "that's not fair." Stamping his foot, he disappears inside.

"I couldn't stop Robbie," I anxiously admit. "Thanks for helping me, Bill. You stepped in between Stephen and Aaron. I would never have thought of that." Smiling, I squeeze his hand in gratitude.

Getting my food, I proceed to our table. With rapid chewing and minimal talk, our plates are cleaned within minutes.

*****

Awakening to the sound of voices coming from downstairs, I pull on my robe. Peeking my head around the corner, I see their heads sticking out of their sleeping bags. Lying on the floor between them is an open box of cereal. Cartoons are on the TV, and everything is quiet. Coming in from the kitchen with a cup of coffee, I see Bill sitting on the sofa. His half-closed eyes and absent expression tell me he is not fully awake.

Looking around me at these four men, I feel blessed to be with them. Sitting down on the floor amongst them, I smile happily.

"Mom, when do we have to go back?" Stephen asks.

"Shut up. I don't want to think about that," Aaron angrily mutters.

"Wait, you guys," I quickly interject. "We have the whole day in front of us. We don't have to leave until 5 o'clock tonight. The only thing I have to do is talk to Tim at some point."

"If it's about school and the dumb Hendersons," Tim shouts, "I don't want to hear about it!"

"Let's not talk about that right now. Instead, let's decide what we want to do today."

All four of them are silent. Staring at me, they wait for me to come up with the perfect plan. Racking my brains for a solution that won't cost too much money, I laughingly cajole, "Come on, think of something you want to do that will be fun!"

"I know!" shouts Tim. "We could go to the movies again!"

"That's a great idea," I say, chuckling, "but we can't afford it."

Toying with the idea of going to the mountains, I realize it's not a viable option, since Bill's minivan needs a new transmission and my station wagon is falling apart.

"We could rent a couple of videos," Bill suggests, "and lie around all day doing nothing."

"That's a great idea," I say, "but let's make it a video marathon, and all four of you can pick out your own video, and I will make brownies!"

"Yeah!"

Relieved, I race upstairs, grab pants and a shirt, and dress quickly.

This is going to be fun!

Absently, I brush my hair and pull on a baseball cap. Tennis shoes, jeans, a T-shirt, and a cap: unconsciously, the stage has been set for me to switch. Racing down the stairs a few moments later, I hear another voice call, "Come on, you guys, hurry up, what's takin' you so long?"

Uh-oh, Robbie! I can't get back to the front of the body! I'm powerless as I watch him jump up and down, gesturing to the boys.

Turning quickly, Bill asks, "What did you say, Sebrina?" Pulling Robbie by the arm, Bill drags him into the kitchen. "Robbie, Dr. Barnes told you it upsets the boys when you are around."

"I don't care," Robbie says, pulling out of Bill's grasp. Running back into the living room with arms extended out to his sides, Robbie jumps up and down, yelling, "Come on, you guys!"

Instantly, the mood shifts as three angry faces look back at him. Immediately, Robbie withdraws back inside.

Oh, my God, what do I do? Standing there, I am frozen with guilt.

You should have stopped him!

He only wants to be part of the fun.

You're a killjoy!

Picking up my purse, I hastily retreat to the patio. Trembling, I take slow, deep breaths. *What's the matter with me? Did I do that on purpose? I wish I could call Norma, but I never call her on Sundays.*

That's why you can't be trusted with your own sons!

Get them some candy. Then they'll feel better.

Realizing that might do the trick, I absently nod to myself.

The rest of the day is spent in a fog of numbness provided by sweets and movies.

*****

On the ride back to the boys' homes that night, a hasty afterthought surfaces. "Oh no, we were supposed to talk about your behavior at school, Tim!"

"Do we have to?" he whines.

"Yes, it's important," I admonish.

As I drive, I try to reiterate the conversation the Hendersons had with me. Looking at him from my rearview mirror, I can see he is as disinterested as I am ineffectual. The words ring hollow, but I continue on, stressing the importance of him following through.

I play a part with a specific script in mind. I want to be a good mother, but I have no idea what that is. Feeling guilty that I had forgotten to take the time to speak to him, I retreat inward to a place where everything is muted. I interact, but I'm not there. It's the only way I know how to cope with the truth that I failed him again.

NORMA'S OBSERVATION

Sebrina's primary focus is to integrate so she can get her sons back. I have been seeing her for a few weeks now, and whenever I suggest taking one son at a time, her refusal is instantaneous. Her guilt over her supposed failure to protect them drives her beyond reason.

I only know to hold still and continue to make suggestions whenever asked. Her hysteria and switching are constant. This is not only difficult for Sebrina, but also for the boys. She believes that if she tries harder, she won't switch in front of them. I know that's not realistic. I'm available to her on an ongoing basis. The telephone calls help bridge her sense of isolation when she is with them. I have told her to call me on Sundays, but she refuses. Her desperate need to keep the rules dominates her life. She believes if she doesn't call me on Sunday, then she won't use me up. It doesn't matter how often I assure her that I can take care of myself; she does not believe me.

She shares her conflict and feelings about being a mother with me. I am aware there are many mothers. Whenever there is stress, another mother steps in. They lack maturity in handling the new situations that constantly occur. I don't see how she can get her sons back in the foreseeable future. I do not tell her this, as it would be too overwhelming. Much of her life is built around a belief system that is already very fragile.

After every weekend, Sebrina is filled with so much guilt and self-hatred that it's difficult to get her to focus. I know that her guilt is a way to avoid facing the truth that her entire life is in turmoil. If she focuses on "getting the boys back," as she phrases it, she can be okay. She is looking for a quick fix that has no real basis in reality.

I applaud her for continuing to show up and call me. Her need to connect with me is strong. It helps us bridge her inability to trust anyone. I'm sensing that this need to be connected to me is the link that will help her begin to establish trust with me.

Chapter 5: THE MOTHERS

A lot has changed in the few months since I met Norma. With her guidance and that of Dr. Barnes, I stopped taking the prescribed medications I was on. Dr. Barnes was concerned that I might deteriorate and have to be hospitalized again, but I had to take the risk. I knew that as long as I took the medication, there would be minimal healing. Thankfully, due in large part to Norma's willingness to talk to me several times a day, I have been able to stay out of the hospital altogether.

I have mastered the technique of breathing correctly through hours of practiced awareness. I have done as Norma suggested, placing my hand on my stomach and purposely reversing the breath so that the exhale and inhale follow the pattern she taught me. It does not mean I have been able to move any deeper into my body, but at least I'm feeling more comfortable breathing this way.

*****

I get to see Norma today. Arriving in good time, I open the door and happily shout, "I'm here, Norma!"

"Hi, sweetie. Make yourself comfortable. I'll get us some water."

Glancing at the clock, I notice I made good time despite the morning traffic.

With the intention of inviting Spirit to be a part of our session, Norma lights a candle before sitting down beside me on the couch.

"Do you see any other clients today?" I anxiously ask.

"No, sweetie. It's you and me for the entire day. Where do you want to begin?"

"Remember when you suggested I take one boy at a time for the weekend? I've been doing it my way for a long time, but it isn't working! When I think of taking only one of them as you suggested, I feel hysterical. Admitting this feels like I'm betraying them somehow."

"You don't understand," another voice cries. "We can't do that to them!"

"What can't you do?"

"We can't hurt the boys like that!" Doubled over, she begins rocking back and forth.

"We're only talking about how we can help everyone. A decision has not been made yet. What's your name, sweetie?"

Surprised at being seen, the young girl starts scooting off the couch.

"It's alright. I'm here to help you." Laying her hand on top of the distressed girl's hand, Norma smiles warmly.

"I'm Lorraine; I'm one of the mothers. We can't hurt the boys like that. We're already failing them as it is!"

"I hear you, Lorraine, but if we could find a way to help the boys, while helping you and the others, would you be willing to discuss it?"

"Yes?" Lorraine gulps. Her obvious hesitation hangs in the air between them.

"Good, this is about discovery. We won't do anything you don't want to do." Patting her hand, Norma invites Lorraine to move closer. "How old are you?"

"Why?" Lorraine asks defensively.

"I just wondered if you were older or younger than Sebrina. This helps me to understand some things."

"I'm seventeen."

"And how many of you take care of the boys?"

"Oh, there are eight of us, including Sebrina." Face alight, Lorraine continues. "There's Miriam, Mildred, Roberta, Felicia, Diana, Amelia, and me!" Giggling with relief at the change in the conversation, she continues. "When Miriam gets overwhelmed, Diana steps in. She has lots of energy, but if the boys need a mom who is loving and gentle, then Felicia is the one!

Mildred does the mundane things that require no feelings. Amelia is great at cooking and cleaning. Roberta is the main outside mom. She's always there; the others step in only to help."

"And where do you fit in, Lorraine?"

"Oh?" A questioning look crosses Lorraine's face. "I don't know, I just help. I play with them, I love them." Feeling confused, Lorraine disappears without further comment.

Rubbing my forehead, I resume speaking again, unaware of the lapse in time.

"I can't stand the guilt I feel, but I have to do something different. This way isn't working anymore. I want to be with my boys and for us to be happy, but they're always competing for my attention. I get so confused that I don't know which end is up. By the time I take them back on Sunday, we're all disappointed with how the weekend went. That's why I'm willing to do something different."

"Have you ever spent time alone with any of your boys?"

"Yes, and it's wonderful! They're different people. Aaron opens up, Stephen's anger disappears, and Timothy seems more content. All three are happier without each other, but I can't hurt them like that!" Doubling over, I begin crying all over again. "You don't understand, Norma, I've failed them so much!"

"Sebrina, look at me. Getting hysterical helps no one. Breathe, and come back into your body. Before we talk about the boys any further, I want you to become aware of something." Leaning toward me, Norma calmly states, "You are not fear, Sebrina."

"What are you talking about? I know I'm not fear."

"Sebrina, remember we are in discovery. I'm not saying you are wrong. Be still a moment. What do you feel or experience most of the time?"

Rubbing my cheek, I contemplate her question. "I don't know."

"Don't be so quick to answer. Go inside and sense."

Ignoring the internal push to retreat, I look at Norma, hoping she will help me.

"Let's look at this in a different way," Norma coaxes. "When you call me in the morning, what is it you are usually feeling?"

"I'm usually afraid."

"Yes, and when you and I work together, what pushes at you the most?"

"I'm afraid I might not get the boys back. I'm afraid of doing it the wrong way or that I might be lying to you. Oh, that's all fear! Plus, I'm hysterical most of the time, and that's fear too, isn't it?"

"Yes, Sebrina, you're getting it! I invite you to begin to notice that you are so much more than fear. Do you think you would be willing to sense this from a place of non-judgement?"

"Yes …" I hesitantly reply.

"Do you see the palm trees out there?" Pointing in the direction of the golf course that can be seen through the sliding glass doors of her living room, Norma continues. "When the wind blows, the trees bend in response to the storm. They don't become the storm. They are still solidly planted in the earth. As your fear storm blows in, you let go and become the storm. You are no longer tethered in the earth. For you, the earth is your body, and your habit is to leave it. This creates anxiety for you. Could you begin to notice when you're afraid and then consciously choose to help yourself, instead of hurting yourself?"

"Yes, Norma, but will you help me? Most of the time I'm not aware of what I'm feeling."

"Of course I will. Now close your eyes and take a breath. Be very still and sense: is there something here that is just for you?"

After a few moments, I reply, "I do … feel something."

"Breathe, Sebrina. Your breath is an invitation to allow the energy to come closer to you."

Minutes pass in silence.

"The feeling is getting stronger, Norma!"

"Breathe, Sebrina. You can't afford to get excited."

"Okay ... I feel it, but it's hard to describe ..." Audibly inhaling, I remain silent.

"Ask it why it has come, Sebrina."

I hear a melodic female voice say, "I have come to be with you."

Relaying what I am hearing, I add, "Her voice ... it makes me feel safe."

"That's wonderful, Sebrina, but did you hear her tell you that you aren't alone?"

"Yes, I did."

"Feel that: you're never alone. Breathe that truth in, Sebrina."

Nodding my head, I remain silent. I feel comforted by this female presence.

"Now," Norma interjects, "ask her what her name is."

Asking out loud, I hear her reply, "My name is Kuan Yin."

"She says her name is Kuan Yin. Oh ... that's the lady who helps you!" Not waiting for Norma to respond, I quickly add, "I'm not lying, Norma. I really do hear her! Her voice is warm and kind, plus I feel her energy touching me. It's like she's holding me. I feel safe ... do you believe me?"

Smiling warmly, Norma responds, "Of course, I believe you, Sebrina.

Do you know why you can hear her so clearly?"

"No ..."

"You're channeling the energy of Kuan Yin. It's your intuitiveness that allows you to hear her in this way. Would you be willing to ask her for help whenever you need it?"

"Oh, yes!" I exuberantly affirm.

"Breathe, Sebrina, and experience this sweet connection with her. Stay in your body, don't get excited. Instead, allow this gentle experience to fill you and feed you."

"Oh, Norma … I'm not alone. I have felt alone my whole life. It wasn't until I met you that some of that feeling disappeared. This means so much to me, but who is Kuan Yin? I've seen statues of her, but I never thought of her as a real person."

Sitting back against the cushions, Norma's energy transforms as radiant love emanates from her whole being. Her voice resonates with an unusual quality of stillness and strength. "I began to channel Kuan Yin when I was living on the island of Kauai in 1992. She told me she had come to teach me a whole new way of living. Through her, I experienced what true compassion is.

"Kuan Yin lived in China a very long time ago. She was an enlightened being who allowed Spirit to work through her in the flavor of compassion. Many teachers work with different facets of Spirit. Jesus represents one flavor, Buddha another; all serve to teach mankind. Some people can hear one teacher better than another, thus we need many different flavors of teaching the same message. You and I connect deeply with the flavor of Kuan Yin's compassionate love. If you allow her to lead you, you can discover a whole new way of being."

"Oh, Norma, I will. I promise … I will!"

Gently taking my hand, Norma says, "I know you're excited, but let her lead you gently, okay? Now, let's return to the subject of having one son at a time, but this time I want you to put aside your judgments. When you had the boys one at a time, you said you had a moment of sweetness with each of them. Is that right?"

Nodding, I try to adjust to the change in subject. "Yes?"

"Do you think the boys would like to have a moment of sweetness with you, too?"

Dreading the thought of having to tell them, I quickly retort, "But they'll be mad if they lose a whole weekend with me."

"I want you to ask them if they would like a weekend alone with just you. Let them envision what that special time could be like. You have already decided that they're going to be angry. You haven't taken the time to find out whether they might like being asked. Give them a chance for sweetness.

If one child says yes, give it to that child. If one child says no, know that it's okay to have that child accompanied by his brothers. Allow yourself to discover what can be, instead of listening to your fearful mind."

"But who do I pick first, Norma?"

"Make a game of it, and let them choose. You'll be surprised— children are wonderful people. Give them a chance. You can ask Kuan Yin for guidance. She loves you and wants what is best for you and the boys.

Remember, there is no right or wrong answer. Just discover, sweetie." Squeezing my hand, she smiles encouragingly at me. "Will you step back so I can work with whoever else needs to talk to me? But this time, I want you to listen if you can. How does that feel for you?"

Laughing fearfully, I answer, "Uncomfortable, yet I want to listen. It's just that I question everything I hear. Can this person be real? Am I pretending? What they're sharing can't be true, can it? It's easier to dismiss it all. Then I don't have to deal with the uncomfortable feelings they provoke, but I'm tired of running, Norma!"

"That is a profound statement, Sebrina. This is where your choice becomes a powerful tool in your healing. If you choose to stop running and be in discovery, you will be supported in every way. Now breathe, stay centered, and listen."

Before the next breath, Robbie appears. "Jeez, Norma, I want to be with you." Snuggling up to her, with wide-eyed innocence, he asks, "How come Sebina's boys don't like me?"

"It's not that they don't like you, sweetie. They get afraid. They see their mom talking and behaving like a child, and they don't understand that."

"Nuh-uh!" Robbie shouts. "Me, I'm talking about me, Norma!" Jabbing his finger into his chest, he hollers, "It's not Sebina. It's me who tries to be with them! They just don't want me." Bending forward, Robbie cries inconsolably.

"You know that you and Sebrina share the same body, right?" Norma questions gently.

"No!" Robbie shouts. "I is four years old, and I is a boy! I got freckles and short hair. Come on, Norma! This is not Sebina's body!"

"I hear you, Robbie, but the body the boys see is that of a forty-year-old woman. They see their mom. They're not rejecting you. They just don't understand how separate you and Sebrina are."

Wrapping his right arm around his head, Robbie rocks back and forth.

Pulling him into her embrace, Norma holds him close and quietly rocks him. After a bit, she suggests, "Let's get some lunch. Would you like some Fritos?"

Nodding sadly, Robbie follows Norma into the kitchen.

Sitting at the table moments later, the body suddenly stiffens, as another child's voice cries, "Who are you?"

"I'm Norma."

"Where am I? How did I get here?"

Remaining completely still, Norma replies, "I know you're afraid. I will not hurt you. You are in my home, and you are safe." Breathing deeply, Norma fills the space between them with her compassion.

Eyes darting back and forth around the room, the child turns toward Norma and asks again, "Who are you?"

"I am Norma, and you are in my home. Do you know Sebrina?" Shaking her head no, the girl remains silent.

Speaking in a soothing voice, Norma tells the child about her garden and herself. Pointing to her dog lying on the floor, she adds, "This is my dog, Chin Chin."

"Why am I in your house?"

"Your house isn't safe. Your mommy and daddy were hurting you, so the angel brought you to me."

"Oh …"

"What's your name, sweetie?"

"I'm Jennifer."

"How old are you?"

"I'm four years old."

"That is a very good age. What do you like?"

"What?"

"I asked you what you like."

Jennifer fidgets uncomfortably.

"It's okay, Jennifer. What would you like to talk about?"

Momentarily coming to the front, I suggest, "Ask her what she remembers last. I think she just woke up."

I leave as quickly as I can, and the child is unaware of the switch. "What do you remember last, Jennifer?"

Heaving a deep sigh, the body visibly shudders. "I told Daddy I was hungry. I was in the kitchen. I don't know where Mommy was. I made a mistake."

"How did you make a mistake?"

"Because," the voice raises a couple of octaves, "I should never have said I was hungry." Tears begin running down her cheeks. Quickly brushing them away, she repeatedly rubs her leg in nervous agitation.

"It's alright, Jennifer. No one will hurt you now. Just tell me what happened."

"He came up to me. I was standing by the wall next to the table. I only wanted something to eat." As she rubs her eyes, the emotions play across her face. "I was so hungry. I shouldn't have said anything. He comed to me and squeezed me up against the wall. I couldn't breathe. He telled me I wasn't hungry, was I? I made a mistake, didn't I? I shaked my head yes, even though I was hungry. He squeezed me even harder into the wall, yelling at me that I wasn't hungry. I telled him he was right; I was not hungry." Shaking her head no, she slumps forward, completely defeated.

Moving closer to Jennifer, Norma tells her she did nothing wrong. "May I hold you, sweetie?"

Jennifer woefully agrees.

As Norma gathers Jennifer in her arms, the child lets go, sobbing loudly. "I should have known. He never likes me to tell him what I want."

"It's alright. I'm here now. You weren't wrong in asking for something to eat. Your daddy was wrong, but he can't hurt you anymore."

Feeling a subtle shift in Jennifer's body, Norma pulls back to study her face. "Would you like something to eat now?"

"Yes, please."

Norma speaks in a soft voice as she makes a peanut butter-and-jelly sandwich for Jennifer. She senses the children who are behind Jennifer, watching Norma's every move.

Placing the sandwich in front of the girl, Norma sees the all-too-familiar behavior played out again. With bowed head and arms pulled into her sides, Jennifer wolfs the sandwich down in a couple of bites. Looking up, Jennifer cautiously smiles at Norma.

Laying her hand on Jennifer's forearm, Norma asks, "Would you like a cookie?"

"Don't touch me!" Another switch has occurred, as an angry child cries out, "I won't do it!" Collapsing into sobs, the child shouts, "I don't care if I'm hungry. You can't make me!"

"What won't you do?" Norma asks.

"I won't stab my sister, even if I'm hungry."

"Look at me. You are here in my kitchen, and my name is Norma. Your mommy and daddy are not here." Speaking more loudly, Norma repeats that her mommy and daddy are not here.

Slowly, awareness begins to register.

"It's alright. I won't hurt you," Norma promises. "I'm here to help you. I know about your daddy; the other children have told me how he hurts you all."

Sighing, the child looks around the kitchen. "He said I didn't get to eat. He said Julie was having my food because I was bad. Daddy said if I wanted to eat, I would have to stab her for it." Lying her head on the edge of the table, she mumbles, "I'm so tired." Looking up at Norma, she feebly inhales before continuing. "I have to stab Julie with my fork if I want to eat. The last time I stabbed her, I made her bleed! Why can't she stab me instead? Then I wouldn't hurt so much!"

Breathing deeply, Norma grasps even more fully the layers of training this person has gone through. Nothing was left to chance. Quietly speaking, Norma asks, "Would you like something to eat, sweetie?"

Pulling back in terror, the child is gone.

Moments pass.

"I didn't know that!" I exclaim. Bending over, I rub my stomach in an attempt to comfort myself. "I'm so upset. How could these awful things happen, Norma?"

"Breathe with me and help your body, Sebrina. That's it, keep breathing. It helps if you begin to know what happened in your life. Let's move back to the couch so we can be more comfortable."

Getting settled back on the couch, Norma continues, "You heard what they said. Do you believe it? Please, don't answer me quickly. Breathe and sense: does this feel true?"

Breathing deeply, I allow myself to drift inward. I feel an awareness that is hard to put into words, but it feels real. "Yes, Norma, it feels true."

"Keep sensing with me. Can you begin to understand, not from your mind, but from a deeper awareness, why you would have the problems you have with food? Can you be patient with yourself? Being angry and judging only keeps you stuck. Do you sense what I'm saying?"

"Yes, but I didn't know it was this bad, Norma."

"Bad is a judgment, Sebrina. We are in discovery. Yes, these memories are painful, but when you accept them, you will begin to feel the truth. The question of whether you are a liar or not will be answered from a deep knowing within you. Can you sense what I'm saying?"

"I have been denying these memories so I wouldn't feel their pain, but Norma, it hasn't worked. I still feel it! I'll do what you suggest. I feel better knowing there's a reason why I struggle with food. It makes me feel less crazy."

Taking my hand in hers, Norma smiles. "Yes, you are choosing to accept the truth and not run. That is where your real strength is. You have always believed that fighting was your strength. That is the lie. Your strength comes from the truth. I'm proud of you. This is a crucial step in your healing."

*****

Even though Norma wrote only a few observations, I felt it was important to include them in the book. Her observations offer insight into what it was like to work with me. Due to her growing client base and her increasing time commitment to me, she wasn't able to write any more observations.

Chapter 6: SEBRINA INTEGRATES

I am often surprised by how my Soul leads me. Meeting Norma came without forethought or plan. I had read the book, *The End Times*, channeled by Lee Carroll on behalf of the entity called Kryon. The compassion Kryon held for mankind resonated deeply with me. I knew there was an event scheduled for Seattle, Washington, in February of 1996, and I wanted to go. I had no idea how I would get there since finances were tight, but once I recognized the desire and spoke openly about it, everything fell into place for me to attend. It wasn't until years later that I learned this desire came directly from my Soul.

When I got up to the podium to speak, I announced to the hundreds of people in the auditorium that I had been diagnosed with multiple personality disorder. I didn't care what they thought, because I was desperate for help. I told the six-member panel that was sitting on the stage that I felt hopeless, because no matter how hard I worked, I was no closer to getting my sons out of foster care.

That is when Lee Carroll suggested I work with Norma Delaney, who was sitting at the far right of the stage. When he pointed to her, and told me she was the best person to work with, I felt something I can't put into words even now. Despite having never met her, I knew her. It was a knowing that precludes explanation even now.

A couple of hours later, she handed me her business card and apologized that she did not live locally. She explained that she lived near San Diego, California, and offered to work with me by phone. I told her that it wasn't necessary, since I lived only two hours away. The relief I felt was huge. I sensed she might be the person I was looking for to help me integrate and get my sons back home with me.

*****

As Norma settles down on the couch beside me, several months into our work together, we smile at each other without words. I have a quiet resolve about me. "Norma, my job here is done."

"And how do you know that?" Norma asks.

"It's a feeling I have."

"That feeling is your intuition, and it has led you your entire life. But let's backtrack and look at this more fully so you can have clarity for yourself. Do you remember when you were born into the body as Sebrina?"

"Yes, very clearly. I remembered it when I worked with Dr. Barnes at the hospital. Jennifer was eight months old and crying, disrupting the cult meeting. Lois, Jennifer's mother, was trying to keep Jennifer quiet by jostling her on her hip, but this made things worse. In a fit of rage, Jack, Jennifer's father, grabbed Jennifer and put her into a toolbox, closing the lid tight. Then he put the toolbox in a hole that had already been dug."

"When you say you were born, Sebrina, what does that mean for you?" Norma prompts.

"That I came into the body as a separate consciousness."

"I'd like you to close your eyes and go back to that moment when you were born, and tell me what you see."

Settling back against the cushions, I take a few deep breaths and allow myself to drift inward, as I sense. It has nothing to do with my mind; I *feel* where I am going, and with my intention, I am led to the memory. "I can see the lid being closed on the toolbox, and then Jack puts it in the hole."

"Where are you, in relation to the memory?"

"What? I'm in the box, of course."

"Sebrina, please be open to something new. You're telling me you can see Jack pick up the toolbox and then place it in the hole."

"Yes ..." Eyes closed, my brow is furrowed. I'm concentrating on what Norma is asking me, but I really don't get it.

"With your intuition, I want you to tell me where you are in relation to the toolbox and Jack."

Silent moments pass. "Oh, I'm in between them. I'm energy, Norma!"

"Yes, you are conscious awareness. Why are you there, outside the box?"

"To keep the body alive! The air was running out, and moving outside the box allowed the body to shut down and become still.

I was the outside connection to life itself. When the crying finally stopped, Jack bent down and retrieved the toolbox. As he pulled the baby out, her body was lifeless. That's when I moved into the body. Up to that point, I had been a separate piece of consciousness waiting to come into the body so it would stay alive. Wow ... Norma. I just did it. I didn't have to think about it!"

"Yes, Sebrina, because you're a part of Soul Consciousness. As you, the whole being, split in the face of such adversity, you used all of you to stay alive. Your intent was pure. You, the whole consciousness, chose to live no matter what, but ... not only to live, but to stay sane, as well. That choice was honored through your profound ability to split as many times as you did.

"There was a rhythm or pulse within you that said, 'Stay alive.' This constantly washed through you, just like the waves of the ocean wash against the shore. This rhythm led and moved you outside of the toolbox. By slowing your breath, the body could fulfill its destiny: to keep you alive. Do you understand what I'm saying?"

"Yes, and now it's telling me that my job is done!"

"Yes, you have been intuitively led your entire life. And now you are being asked to come home to your heart. Do you know why? Ask Kuan Yin for clarity."

Pausing, I listen carefully. "Kuan Yin says I can serve better from within, as an anchor to lead us back home to our own heart energy."

"Yes, yes ..." Norma murmurs.

"Kuan Yin says that it's necessary to create a new personality that will eventually become the full human—physical, mental, and spiritual. Oh! Now I understand why we changed our legal name to Serena! She says that when we changed our name, we were setting the groundwork for our own integration."

"So stop a moment and sense," Norma quietly prompts. "How does it feel hearing what Kuan Yin has said?"

"I feel warmth ... filling me from the inside out. I *know* I must do this.

Words can't describe how deeply I feel this, Norma. The thought of coming home to my own heart energy fills me with indescribable joy. But I'm concerned about Robbie. Will you talk to him first?"

"Yes, but stay close and listen. He will need to connect with you before you go."

Calling Robbie to the front, Norma laughs as he bounds out, giving her a bear hug. "Oh boy, we is here again!" Extending his arms out to his sides, he laughs. "I missed you this much!" Scooting closer to Norma, he nuzzles his face into her neck.

Returning his hug, she holds him for a moment. "I missed you, too, sweetie. Do you know why you and the others came to work with me?"

"Yeah, cause we want to be integrated so the boys can come home."

"That's right, and do you know what being integrated means?"

"I think so …" His voice trails off as he ponders the question. "It means we is one person, right?"

"Yes, it does, and Sebrina has an important step to take to begin your integration. She needs to go home to the heart, so that true healing can begin. Feel with me a moment. When I say go home to the heart, what am I really saying?" Quiet minutes ensue, as Norma waits for Robbie's answer.

Rubbing his face and pursing his lips, he seriously ponders her question. Looking at Norma, he raises his eyebrows questioningly. "You is saying she gots to go inside, to a special place, huh?" Smiling, he realizes the connection.

"Oh, Robbie, I'm so proud of you! She is the path home, so all of you can be one person. Would you like that?"

He nods yes, but questions flit across his face. "Can I still see her whenever I want to?" he hesitantly asks.

Breathing with compassion, Norma answers honestly. "Not in the same way. She will be right here." Lying her hand against his heart, she adds, "holding a special place for you."

Sadly, he nods his head in acquiescence.

"Sweetie, I'm going to sit here while you and Sebrina talk. She wants to spend some time with you before she goes. I'm here if you need me." Reaching over, she squeezes his hand.

Without further comment, he moves inward. Turning, he runs to Sebrina. "Oh, Sebina, I is going to miss you!"

Holding him tight, I pull him down onto my lap. "I will miss you so much, Robbie."

"Oh, Sebina …"

Holding his hand against my heart, I tell him, "I will always be right here." Rocking him back and forth, I hum softly. Minutes pass, while the body remains slumped against the cushions.

Finally, the eyes open, and Sebrina smiles. "I'm ready, Norma."

"Then let's go upstairs so you can lie down on the table."

Climbing the stairs, I feel an unusual peace. I know I'm coming home to my Soul. I have been the intuitive voice of our Soul, making choices that would ultimately lead us to our goal: to integrate and become an authentic human being. I'm going to lay the foundation for this new beginning.

The idea of integration feels like a promise of new life for us; I do not see it as the death of a personality. To live as separate parts of a multiple system is to exist unconsciously. None of the personalities has ever been connected to the body, which causes us to experience life as cold and flat.

Integration isn't an idea from the mind. It is an invitation from our Soul, and it is filled with warmth and an assurance of peace.

Lying on the massage table, I look into Norma's face. The love that I feel is profound. It speaks of many lifetimes shared. Much is said without words. I touch Norma's face, then close my eyes.

As I take a deeper breath, I relax more fully into my body. I don't need to know how to integrate; instead, my intuitive "yes" guides me. As everything within me slows, my awareness as an individual dissolves. The personality known as Sebrina merges with the Soul, becoming one. The first phase is done. Now, the second phase can begin, with the intent that, in this lifetime, all the personalities will integrate into the new human being formed, named Serena.

Opening my eyes, I'm unaware that I have just been created as a new personality. I'm the beginning of new consciousness being born into the body.

My job will be to hold an energetic space for all the other personalities to integrate into. But for now, I am a small piece of new consciousness living amidst the chaos. I'm to fit in seamlessly. I will go to the mind to know how to act and how to speak. Even though I'm new, I believe that I have always been here. I will share the beliefs held by the rest of the system. I will be the primary person to begin our integration and serve as the body's representative.

Smiling, I look into Norma's face, knowing I like this lady. I know we have been doing work in her healing room. She's the person "I" found to help me integrate. I know all this and more, the moment I open my eyes.

Norma encourages me to breathe. Her voice is soft; the tone is melodic. She is aware of the energy shift in the body. She sees me, the new person born from the Soul. Her job is to remain still and not startle me. She speaks only of the breath and keeps the truth of this moment to herself.

Her breath, her being-ness, fills the room. Gently, she helps me sit up. "Breathe, before you get off the table," she instructs, purposely calling me by my new name of Serena.

Holding my elbow, she walks beside me down the stairs. Entering the kitchen, she guides me to a straight-backed chair. I am detached from everything. The movement of coming downstairs has caused me to leave my body. I see things from a distance. I notice the brightly colored fruit on the counter. I'm aware of the cold floor through my stocking feet. I hear Norma's question about what I might like for lunch, and somewhere, in the background, I hear the hum of internal voices carrying on in conversation. The moment is surreal, captured like a colored snapshot, surrounded in black, for all time.

This is how we live, one moment, separate from the next.

I was born to create a new life for us all. As a house is built from the foundation up, each new experience will build itself, one upon the other, adding to this new human called Serena. My transformation will come slowly, one breath at a time.

Chapter 7: COMPASSION

I wish the drive to Norma's didn't take so long. A memory has surfaced, and the longer I'm seated, the greater my anxiety grows, so driving the speed limit is nearly impossible for me to maintain.

Passing the strawberry fields to my right, I glance at the men, women, and children stooped over in the hot morning sun. I feel sorry for them. *How can they work like that? My back would break!*

Beneath the wondering, another layer of thoughts emerges. It's a rhythmic cadence of words, purposely repeated, to squelch the terror bubbling inside me.

Got to get there! Got to get there!

Go faster!

Hurry! Hurry!

Anxious thoughts, layered one on top of the other, create a wall that blocks the memory from pushing through into my awareness. Reacting aggressively, I tailgate the car in front of me. Gripping the steering wheel, I inch closer. I know I'm driving recklessly, but I don't care.

You could have an accident!

At least you would be out of pain.

You can't. You have three boys who need you.

Oh, yeah. My sons! Backing my foot off the gas pedal, I slowly exhale. Holding the steering wheel with my left hand, I lay my right hand on my belly so I can feel it move with my breath. Inhaling through my nose, I focus on the sensation of my hand moving upwards. As I exhale again, I let my shoulders drop, releasing some of their tension. After long minutes of focusing only on my breath, I feel my anger finally begin to recede. "Please, God, help me drive safely. I'm so uncomfortable, I don't know what to do! I know Norma lives what she teaches. I feel it. She is free! She doesn't need me to like her. She's her own person. Can I have that someday?"

Immediately, I feel an unusual peace fill me, and with it an assurance that I, too, will have in time what Norma has. Feeling grateful, I turn on the radio so I can sing. Within minutes, I've switched again. Gripping the steering wheel, I try to cope with the panic that is building. Feeling angry at the abrupt change in my emotions, I shake my head in frustration. *What's the matter with me? Why can't I be happy without going off?*

Driving too quickly, I take the exit and almost go off the road. Stopping the car at the red light, I shakily inhale. Driving the last few miles to Norma's takes forever. The closer I get, the more anxious I become. Stopping the car in her driveway, I jump out and run for the front door. Entering, I yell, "Norma, it's Serena! Where are you?" Climbing the stairs, I hear her voice through the closed door: "Go into the living room, and I'll be there in a few minutes."

Pacing up and down, I wait for what seems like hours. My thoughts are racing; my skin is screaming. I'm desperate to talk to Norma so I can have relief. Calling to her, I plead, "Please hurry! I feel like I'm going crazy. There's a memory up, and we have to do it now! Are you coming?"

Emerging from the room upstairs, Norma calls, "I'll be down in a moment." As she closes the door to the bathroom, I hold my breath until I hear the toilet flush. I marvel at how peaceful she is; she seems to glide down the stairs.

"I was on the phone with another client when you arrived. I needed to finish with him before we could start." Sitting down on the couch, Norma pats the seat beside her. "Come sit beside me. I want to talk with you before we start working with the memory that is bothering you."

Norma's request pushes at the very core of me. "I have to do this memory right now, Norma! I feel like I'm being swallowed alive!"

"I understand that. Come sit." Gesturing, she pats the cushion again. Begrudgingly, I move and sit down beside her.

"Breathe with me a moment. I promise, we'll begin soon."

The longer I have to wait, the more agitated I become. My mind is racing. I'm resistant to her guidance and only want to dump the memory. If I can say it, I know I can forget it. It seems to be the only release I know, but as I keep listening to her voice, I begin to slow down inside, and my skin stops screaming.

"Now, before we begin, I want to ask you a question."

Immediately, I'm on guard. I know she's going to say something bad; she's just preparing me. My mind races with frantic thoughts; racing thoughts are the gearshift that allows me to switch effortlessly.

"Do you know what real is?"

Responding defensively, I retort, "Of course I know what real is."

Rubbing the couch, Norma continues. She's aware of my defensiveness and ignores it. "This is real, Serena. Feel the cushion; it is solid, and it has mass."

"I know, Norma!" I angrily whine.

Ignoring me, she asks, "When you watch TV, is that real?"

"What do you mean, is TV real?"

"Is the story real?"

"No?" I hesitantly reply. The truth is, I don't have a clue as to what she is asking me.

"So the story you are watching is just a story, right?"

"Yes?" Now I'm really confused.

"I'm asking you this in hopes that you can use it to help you. When you watch TV, you sit here on the couch, view the story on the screen, and it stays there ... on the screen. Now play with me, Serena. As you begin to tell me this memory, try to stay here with me. The couch is real. I am real. The memory is not real—it has already happened. It is just a story. Do you follow what I'm suggesting?"

What does she mean, the memory isn't real? I'm feeling it right now, and I haven't even looked at it. Sighing heavily, I say, "I'll try. I feel so much anxiety, I feel like I'm coming out of my skin."

"Serena, look at me." Voice resonating with strength, she calmly states, "Everyone who can hear me, look into my eyes. I'm telling you the truth. I'm right here, and you are safe. This is a memory that happened many years ago. No one can hurt you now." Redirecting her attention to me, she asks if there is anything I need before we get started.

I switch before answering.

Rubbing her arms in desperation, a little girl cries out, "They're all over me!"

"What's all over you, sweetie?"

Crying hysterically, the child furiously rubs her arms and face. Gently, Norma takes the child's face in her hand so that she can feel Norma's touch.

"Where am I?" the surprised child asks.

"I came to get you. You were being hurt. The angel and I got you away from the bad people. Do you want to tell me what was happening?"

"Daddy said I was bad," she whimpers. "He was punishing me."

"What was he doing to you?"

"He tied me to the tree and rubbed honey all over me. I had no clothes on, and the ants were crawling all over me!" Her voice escalates as she continues, "They were in my pee pee! I couldn't move!"

Another switch, and a monotone voice continues, "I just beed one of the ants; I was crawling up the girl's arm. I was with all the other ants ... nothing bothers me." The face that turns toward Norma is without emotion; it's as though a robot has replaced the child.

"How wonderful you are. You came to help the little girl, didn't you? You aren't afraid. Your job is done now. Would you like to go with the angel?" Gently, Norma calls the crying child back to the front. "I know you can hear me. You were crying and telling me about the ants. You didn't get to finish. When you come back, you'll be here on the couch with me. You are clean, and your clothes are on. You're safe now. There are no ants."

Crying softly, the child returns. "It was bad."

"I know, sweetie. I'm here now. What's your name?"

"My name is Jennifer. I'm this many." Holding up her hand, she shows Norma three fingers. Looking around the room, Jennifer asks, "How did I get here?"

"The angel came and got you. What your daddy did was wrong," Norma affirms.

"I was bad. He telled me." Nodding her head up and down, Jennifer recites the words like a good little puppet.

Taking her hand, Norma says, "There is nothing you could do that would make a loving daddy do that to you. Do you know that?"

Pulling her hand out of Norma's, Jennifer nods her head adamantly, while saying, "I know he loves me."

Changing the subject, Norma asks, "Can you see the angel? She came to get you."

Looking around the room, Jennifer exclaims, "She's right there!" Pointing behind Norma, Jennifer sees the angel clearly. "She's so pretty! Her hair is long, and there's light all around her!"

"She came especially for you. Did you know that, Jennifer?"

Turning toward Norma, Jennifer's face is alight with joy. "She came for me? How come?"

"She has been looking for you. She wants to take you to live with her. Would you like that?"

"Can Julie come? I can't leave my sister."

"Of course Julie can come. Now close your eyes. Can you still see the angel?"

Nodding, Jennifer visibly relaxes.

Norma begins speaking in a quiet tone. "Every child who can hear me and wants to go with the angel can come now. She loves you and wants you to live with her. No one will hurt you anymore. Come. She is here just for you."

After a bit, I come back into the front of the body. Rubbing my face, I remark, "I'm tired, Norma."

"Of course you are, but before you go upstairs to take a nap, I want to ask you a question. When you feel as upset as you were this morning, and are unable to reach me, what do you do?"

"I hang on until I can talk to you. I do the best …"

"Serena, this is not asked in judgment, so would you be still a moment, and go for a bigger truth?"

"Yes."

Speaking slowly, Norma continues, "If you didn't have to hang on, but could feel comfort immediately, would you want that?"

"Yes, but if it is memory …"

"Serena, you're fighting me. I know if it is memory, you will need to talk to me. I'm not rejecting you. Take a breath and stay with me, please. I have a reason for asking this." Norma's tone holds no reproach.

"Okay, Norma."

"So sense with me, and try to hear what I'm asking you. You've had many memories about your past. Is that right?" Raising her eyebrows, she waits for me to answer.

"Yes?" I don't trust where she's leading me.

"Please, don't go to your mind for your answer, but sense: who do you feel kept you alive during all those experiences?"

Brow furrowed, I'm at a complete loss as to where she is going with this. I know she has the answer, and I want her to tell me. "I don't know, Norma. I really don't."

"I don't believe that. I want you to breathe, while being still a moment, and allow yourself to sense the truth."

"I feel it's something other than me, Norma."

"Good. Now close your eyes and sense in the direction of that feeling. Do you see anything?"

"Yes, but it's far away."

"Keep breathing, and invite it to come closer."

"It's a light, Norma!" As the light approaches, I see a woman illuminated by it. "Norma, I see a beautiful lady, and she's smiling at me!"

Chuckling gently, Norma suggests, "Will you ask her why she is here?"

Asking internally, I hear, "I have come to love you."

Opening my eyes, I look at Norma. "What does she mean by that?"

Eyes twinkling, Norma suggests, "Why don't you ask the lady what she means?

Turning inward, I look at the beautiful lady. "I have been waiting for you for a long time," she says.

Opening my eyes, I tell Norma what she said. "How does that feel, Serena?"

I have mixed emotions. I'm happy she's here, and I express that to Norma, but I don't admit that I'm beginning to feel angry as well.

"She's your fairy godmother, and she's been with you always." Norma knows that my maturity is stuck at a very young age, and since children like fairy godmothers, she knows she can introduce me to my Soul through this playful and non-threatening way. The wisdom that has always kept me alive is manifesting as a luminous being. In seeing and hearing the lady, I can begin to connect with my own authentic Soul energy. This is a crucial step in my integration.

"You weren't ready to see her until now. She's here to hold you and give you comfort. She's the mother you've always wanted. Lois was your human mother. Your fairy godmother is your authentic mother. She can bring you comfort and give you an answer to any question you might have."

As Norma speaks, my mind races with questions.

"I want you to practice going within to sense her," Norma says. "This is a beginning. When you can't reach me, you can go to her for help and comfort."

The emotions I'm feeling are uncomfortable. I should feel happy, but instead I'm resentful at *this so-called* fairy godmother and her supposed love for me. Saying nothing, I try to push the bad feelings away.

Norma watches the emotions play across my face. "What is bothering you, Serena?"

"If she has always been with me, then why would she have allowed this horrible life to ever happen?" As I ask the question, I hear my voice shift an octave. It's filled with anger, and that scares me. Everything is hazy. I vigorously rub my forehead, trying to stay.

"Serena, don't leave! Ask her why she would let this life happen, and choose to hear her answer."

I breathe as slowly as I can. My voice trembles with emotion as I ask the question out loud. "Why did you let me and all the others suffer, to go through this horrible life, if you were there the whole time?"

"Why don't we breathe a bit," Norma invites, "so you can hear her answer more clearly?"

Trying to breathe is impossible. My stomach feels like granite rock; I have pain radiating in my shoulders and up into my neck, plus my skin is screaming. Deliberately focusing on the sound of Norma's voice, I try to drop deeper into my body.

After guiding me to slowly inhale, Norma says, "Now exhale through your nose. That's it. Let all the old energy leave. Inhale, and bring your breath deep into your core. Choose to live, Serena."

Finally, my stomach, shoulders, and neck relax. I could fall asleep at any moment. With the next breath, I leave, and my Soul comes forward and speaks through my body to Norma. "It's important that Serena grasp why she chose this life. The willingness to stop living in fear is the crux of this discussion. There are parts of this truth that must be left alone. I know you sense what I'm speaking of. It's still too early in their healing for anything else." Finished, Soul steps back.

I, Serena, move to the front of my body again. I'm unaware of the lapse in time and what my Soul said to Norma. Reciting exactly what I am hearing from my fairy godmother, I say, "Before you were born this lifetime, you decided you would create an experience of fear so big that you could no longer ignore it. You were warned that what you wanted to do would be extremely difficult, but you said you didn't care; living lifetime after lifetime in fear was a waste. You wanted to know the truth and finally be all that you could be in human form." Stopping the flow of awareness, I turn to Norma and exclaim, "I've always felt that being born to Jack and Lois wasn't a mistake, and here it is!"

"Serena, don't get distracted. Stay with what you are hearing, please."

Turning inward once more, I pick up where my fairy godmother left off. "We decided that in order for you to stay alive and sane, your Soul would have to fragment into many pieces to contain the whole. In that way, all that had happened would be contained until you were ready to heal. You were to be equipped with all that you needed to live this life successfully and fulfill your destiny."

"Stop a moment," Norma says, "and ask your fairy godmother if you fully understand what she's telling you."

"She says you need to explain it more fully to me."

Pausing for a moment, Norma asks, "When you go on a trip, what do you take?"

"What? I take a suitcase and clothes and …"

"Right, you take a suitcase, and it's filled with whatever you need to complete your journey in safety and comfort. Is that right?"

"Yes?" Sometimes her examples are so weird.

"When you decided you had to live this lifetime in an extreme way, Spirit provided you with a suitcase filled with the essentials that you would need to stay alive and sane. Are you following me so far?"

"Oh, that's why I'm a multiple personality. That ability was in my suitcase, right?"

When Norma gives us an example, we more often than not take it literally. She knows it's a part of our immaturity and handles it accordingly. "Serena, I'm not talking about a literal suitcase. I'm talking about the fact that in order for you to stay alive, Spirit created what you needed for this lifetime. I've told you before that you're the most psychic person I have ever worked with. That's one of the pieces provided to you in your suitcase."

Envisioning a brown, tattered suitcase, overflowing with items I would need for this lifetime, I answer, "I get what you're saying."

"Being psychic is one of the essentials in your suitcase," Norma states. "When you create a story, you create a psychic package of energy to go along with it. This helps you believe that the story is true. Now, get out of your head and sense: when did you create a story that seemed so real you could see and feel it?"

"It was just a while ago, when Jennifer pretended to be an ant crawling on the arm. That was our psychic energy, but I have to be honest, when I heard that robotic voice say she was one of the ants, I was surprised, because she really believed it, Norma!"

"You're right, Serena. She believed it completely. Now, sense: when Jennifer became hysterical because the ants were crawling all over her skin, what did she do?"

After a moment of reflection, I answer, "She switched, didn't she?"

"Yes, which allowed your fairy godmother to create a new personality."

"Wait, I know!" Laughing, I exclaim, "When you're an ant, you can't feel the sensations of the body! Wow ... that was smart, wasn't it, Norma?"

"It is one more example of your Soul's brilliance. The terror of feeling the ants crawling all over Jennifer's skin was offset by a feeling of calm, because a new personality was created that believed the pretend story that it wasn't being tortured, because it was just one of the ants. That fantasy saved your life."

"What?"

"When you create a psychic package of energy, combined with emotion and a story, your system believes it easily, even when it's not true. Being an ant was a fantasy, would you agree?"

Tell her to shut up!

She's lying.

Shut down, shut down!

Go away!

Concentrating on Norma's face, I try to ignore the voices that are screaming inside me. Rubbing my forehead and jiggling my leg up and down, I feel anxiety taking over. Norma knows I'm being pushed from within. The personalities believe that our internal world is real. Even though it is based on fantasy, it provides a safe haven for all of us to retreat to. This truth pushes at the very core of how our system operates. Norma has no need to push us any further. She knows that disassembling our creation can only be done one breath at a time.

As Norma looks at me, a gentle smile tugs at her lips, which instantly reassures me. "Serena, please allow yourself to feel what I'm going to say. Your fairy godmother was always there for you, creating an inner world that all of you could retreat to for comfort and safety."

Feeling a rush of emotions, I exclaim, "I understand! She created a safe place where we could all escape. A place where Jack and Lois couldn't find us. Wow! She really does love us!" Laughing, I feel relieved.

"Good, Serena. I'm glad you're letting yourself feel that. Now you can begin to go to your fairy godmother whenever you can't reach me. You'll find comfort and an answer to whatever is bothering you. If a child is crying, you can ask her to help you. If you're afraid and a memory is pushing at you, your fairy godmother can contain it until we can talk. Would you be willing to try this in order to help you?"

"Oh, yes, Norma. I can't tell you how this makes me feel." Smiling broadly, I reach out and take Norma's hand.

"I'm so glad, sweetie. Now, I want you to go upstairs and take a nap on the massage table."

"But I don't remember much of what we did these past few hours. Is that okay?" I worriedly ask.

"Of course it is. You'll remember only what you need to remember. Can you trust your fairy godmother that she knows everything, and leave it with her?"

It's easy to let it go, since I'm exhausted. Climbing onto the massage table, I pull the blanket around me and fall into a deep and restful sleep.

*****

What is insanity? It's losing touch with reality. But my Soul, which is the very essence of me, *never* got lost in the pretend. She created the vivid imagery to protect me. From the bubbling brook that ran through the vast meadow to the six-story house painted bright yellow to the trees, flowers, and bugs that lived there, these colorful images helped shut out the insanity of my physical world. They kept me sane, protecting so many of the personalities, until the day I could begin to finally face the truth and live my life for real.

Chapter 8: ROBBIE INTEGRATES

Arriving earlier than usual, I shout, "Norma, where are you?"

Coming in from the kitchen, she wipes her hands on a dish towel before giving me a hug. "Hi, sweetie. Don't put your purse down. I thought we could get a bite to eat. Would you like that?"

Distracted by Norma's outfit of black cowboy boots, black slacks, and an animal-print blouse, I exclaim, "You look glamorous!"

"Thanks," she laughingly replies. "I like dressing up. It makes me feel good."

I wish I could dress that way, but I wouldn't dare.

"Serena, where did you go?"

"Oh ... I was thinking about your outfit," I absently reply.

"It's important for you to stay present if you want to get something to eat. Can you do that?"

"Of course I can!"

"I know of a place that makes the best chai lattes. Would you like that?"

"Yes. This is going to fun!"

"It has that possibility, if you stay here with me," Norma laughingly replies.

*****

The coffee stand sits on the boardwalk only yards from the ocean. Inhaling the fragrance of sea air combined with the aroma of coffee, I giggle happily. I love spending time with Norma outside the therapeutic environment. Standing side by side, we read the painted menu board.

I step back so Norma can order for both of us. That's when I notice the hair on the back of her head is messy! Looking away in hopes I didn't see what I saw, I hesitantly look back, but it's still uncombed!

Holding both our lattes and my chocolate pastry in her hands, Norma guides me to a nearby table to sit.

She's perfect. How could she have messy hair!

What does this mean?

Is something wrong with her?

Don't trust her! You've been fooled before!

"Sweetie, what's the matter?" Sensing the abrupt change in my mood, she knows I could switch at any moment.

Looking at her, I carefully scrutinize everything. Her voice sounds the same, but I'm wary. "I can't talk out here!" I vehemently whisper. Looking back and forth at the people crossing our path, I feel alarmed. "I need to go now!"

Guiding me back to the car, Norma starts the engine. "Do you want Daniel to come to the front until we get home?"

Shaking my head no, I remain silent. Holding my breath, I jiggle my leg up and down. Tears slip down my cheeks as I grip my arms in panic. I wait until the car has fully stopped before I bolt into the house. Making my way to the couch, I grab a pillow and push it hard against my stomach before succumbing to sobs.

Putting her things down, Norma sits beside me. "What happened out there?"

I hesitate, afraid to say what I'm thinking. "I don't want to hurt you, Norma!"

"I've told you in the past that I'm the only one who's allowed to take care of me. Can you trust me enough to tell me what's upsetting you so much?"

As her quiet strength washes over me, it gives me the courage to speak the truth out loud. "When I was standing behind you at the coffee stand, I noticed your hair was uncombed!" Saying it aloud, my voice screeches with hysteria.

"And why did that scare you so much?" she quietly asks.

"Norma, you're perfect. Yet when I saw that your hair was messy, it felt like my whole world came apart. How can it be that your hair is messy?" The face looking back at Norma has many pairs of eyes watching.

Answering in a general way that keeps it simple for the many, she responds with a question of her own. "When Jesus walked for miles on the dusty roads of Galilee, did his feet get dirty?"

"I know Jesus's feet got dirty," a young voice declares, "because the Sunday school teacher said so." Nodding her head up and down, the child recites, "He was perfect, but his feet were dirty." (Jack believed that taking his family to church camouflaged his activities with the cult. What he didn't realize was that he was unwittingly helping Jennifer and the system survive.

Hearing stories about Jesus opened a whole new world of awareness for Jennifer. By feeding her psychic energy into the images she imagined, she created an inner world where kindness, love, and beauty existed. When the horrors of cult life became too big, she would switch into this alternate reality, keeping her hope alive for another day.)

"Yes," Norma gently responds. "When we are human, our bodies get dirty, our hair becomes messy. It's part of the wonderfulness of who we are as humans. I am human, Serena." Norma purposely uses my name so I can come back to the front without pushing the others away. "Is it okay that I'm human, Serena?"

I know I should say yes, but in truth, I don't want her to be just human.

"I can see that you would like me to be more than human, but that's not the truth. I'm as human as you are. Having messy hair does not change who I am. Sense with me a moment: am I any different than I was the last time we were together? Feel your answer, Serena. Then you will know whether you are being honest or not."

She seems the same, but ... energetically, I move out and into her body. I do it without conscious thought, and just as quickly, I know the truth: she's the same as she was before! Relief floods my entire body, but I'm still confused. "I don't understand how you can be so wonderful and have messy hair at the same time."

Laughing with genuine mirth, Norma answers my question seriously. "Messy hair is messy hair, nothing more. It's the story you have connected to it that causes your anxiety. Many children, including yourself, have told me that Lois was obsessed with being pretty. Would you agree?"

"Oh, yes ... she always made sure she was perfectly presentable whenever she went out in public. She would take hours on her appearance. I would watch her pull at her face, imagining what she would look like if she had a facelift."

"Did you see Lois feeling happy with her appearance?" Norma asks.

"No!" I angrily shout.

"You were brought up to believe that being pretty made you in control. It doesn't. It's an outside experience that is inconsistent, because our looks change day by day. It's the experience from within that brings us peace. That peace is consistent and unwavering.

"Lois wanted to hold onto being pretty because she believed that if she stayed pretty, she could make her world work. That was a lie. She didn't know that true peace comes from knowing oneself. That's the work you and I are doing. We're in the discovery of finding out who the real Serena is."

I get what she's saying without having to figure it out! Unfortunately, I hear Robbie yelling in the background. "You're hogging Norma. It's my turn!"

Relaying this to Norma, I laugh. "Before I leave, would you give me a hug?" As her arms wrap around me, I'm filled with a surge of warmth. Without speaking, I step back, allowing Robbie to come forward.

"I gots to sit real close to you." Snuggling up against Norma's chest, he silently fiddles with her necklace. Holding him in a sweet embrace, Norma waits for him to start.

"You know I love you more than anybody else, right?" Pulling back, Robbie scrutinizes her face. "I really wanted to live with you and Garret, but I can't." Nodding his head, he places his hand on his heart. "I have to go home here. I need to, so the other kids will want to go, too. I really love you, but this is what I gots to do."

Norma knows this is an indication of the healing that has already occurred within the system. Despite the years of living through unimaginable horror, this

Being's undeniable strength and joy were so pure that nothing could squelch it. Robbie embodies that joy, and now he is ready to integrate.

Responding easily, Norma says, "If you're feeling it's time for you to go home to your heart, then you must trust that, Robbie." Sensing there is more, she asks, "What's troubling you?"

"I'm afraid you won't see me anymore. I gots to have you see me!" Robbie states emphatically.

"I know, sweetie, and I'll always be able to see you." Holding him, while leaning back, she looks directly into his eyes. "Let's make an agreement. If you place your hand on my heart like this …" taking his hand, she lays it flat against her chest as an example "… I'll know that's our sign that you want me to see you, and I'll take those few precious moments to look right into your eyes like we're doing now. That will be our time and no one else's. Will that work for you?"

"Okay, Norma."

"You're precious to me," she croons.

"All I know is I gots to do this. It's going to help all the other kids in coming home here. Did you know home is here?" Laying his hand on his heart, Robbie raises his eyebrows questioningly.

"Yes, I did, sweetie. You're a brave boy because, despite how you feel for Garret and me, you're willing to do this to help the other children. But let's discover one more thing about what you're about to do, so you have an even greater understanding. Would you like that?"

Nodding, Robbie waits for Norma to continue.

"Imagine that as you take this journey, you will be walking on the yellow-brick road right home to your heart, and in your heart dwells the Emerald City. Then, when the other children come, you and Godmother can have a birthday party waiting for them."

Laughing, Robbie imagines balloons and cake with ice cream. "Can we have hats, too?"

"Yes, you can have whatever you want, but stay with me a moment more, and feel the sweetness that is waiting for you right here." As she lays her hand upon his heart, she invites him to feel the true essence living within him.

Sighing contentedly, Robbie says, "It feels so right, Norma, even if I love you and Garret sooooo much! Will you tell Garret goodbye?"

"Oh, sweetie." Holding him close, Norma promises to tell Garret how much Robbie will miss him.

"I'm ready now, but you will always see me when I do this, right?" Placing his hand against her heart, he waits for her reassurance.

"Yes, I'll always be able to see you, Robbie. So breathe with me and let Godmother lead the way." As the quiet envelops them, Robbie goes inward and watches Godmother approach. As she opens her arms in welcome, Robbie falls into her embrace. Turning, they walk into the Emerald City together.

Chapter 9: LIVING FOR ME

When I was hospitalized, my sister, Julie, took my boys to live with her. She had hoped I would be able to take them back home with me, but as time passed, I became so destabilized that she knew that wasn't an option. Julie kept my sons for only nine months, because the financial strain of single-parenting her five-year-old son, along with mine, plus trying to finish her master's degree in psychology, was too much. Through her perseverance, Julie found a placement home that would take all three of my boys. In its hundred-year history, that had never occurred. The boys lived there for two years, after which Timothy and Stephen were sent to live with the Hendersons, and Aaron was placed in a smaller group home. After leaving Julie's care, my sons' experiences in the foster care system were fraught with so much pain and struggle; I knew I had to do whatever it took to get them back home to me.

The courts stipulated that I needed a job and a two-bedroom apartment in which we could live. In order to accomplish this, I had to return to work, which meant I had to relinquish my Social Security disability benefits. I knew it was a gamble since I was still switching, but I wanted my sons back more than I wanted anything else. I got a job as a server at an Italian restaurant and found an apartment close by.

Concurrently, I began taking only one of my sons for the weekend as Norma suggested. I was surprised to discover that all three boys seemed to be content with this arrangement and opened up to me in ways I could never have imagined. I felt like I was meeting them for the first time. I discovered they were sweet, funny, and oftentimes happy young men.

In May of 1997, I took a three-day meditation course in hopes of becoming more stable. I was inspired by what I learned and decided to offer the course to my sons. To my surprise, they loved it. They chose meditation over TV and video games. Their experience was so authentic that for short periods, they felt content. This motivated me to do whatever I could to offer them advanced classes, no matter the cost.

I stopped going to the hospital outpatient program, but I continued to see Dr. Barnes, since he was my liaison to the courts. I had been working with him for close to five years when he finally recommended that I was ready to have my sons come home. The courts decided that only one son could come home at first. Norma suggested that I let the three of them choose. She said that allowing them to make the decision would help them feel less angry. I expected them to maneuver for first position, but Timothy and Stephen agreed that Aaron should be first, since he lived in a group home. I was surprised by their decision and felt proud of Stephen and Timothy for putting their brother first.

For three months, Aaron and I lived happily in our two-bedroom apartment. He began attending the local high school. Aside from the usual hurdles school presented, the living situation was good. Even on weekends, when either Timothy or Stephen was visiting, the three of us got along quite well. I wanted to believe things had really changed. Norma tried to warn me that things might not always be this easy, but I ignored her warnings.

In June of 1998, the court finally approved Stephen and Timothy's release from foster care. I was elated, but my jubilation was quickly doused. I found that the individual boys I had met on our one-on-one weekends were gone, and in their place were the competitive, angry young men I had known before. I was disillusioned and at my wits' end. I called Norma several times a day. As the boys yelled in the background, I would beg her for help. I felt I was living in one of those chaotic weekends with no end in sight.

My sons had been meditating for over a year at this point. It was a priority for them that had nothing to do with me. At one of their advanced classes, they learned that they could become teachers of this mediation if they were willing to move to North Carolina and live on campus. The staff outlined the type of training this would entail and its cost. All three boys were excited about the possibility and told me they really wanted to do it.

I felt they should get their high school diplomas first; then they could become teachers if that still interested them. I wanted to make it up to them for all the years they'd been in foster care, and if they went away, how could I do that?

Only with Norma and Godmother's help was I able to see this from a different perspective. Norma asked me if I would be willing to look at my sons without judgment. Were they happy? Did they like school? Where did their interests and passions lie? What truly filled their hearts and minds? She encouraged me to let go of the ideas of my mind long enough to allow for an answer that was for the boys' highest good.

I saw their joy and the authentic experience they had with this meditation, and that gave me the courage to do what was best for them.

After a couple of months of communication with the school, the three of them got their tuition paid in exchange for their commitment to work on campus. The arrangement was done on an individual basis, so that if any one of them failed to meet their end of the obligation, that boy's tuition would stop.

They were excited, but I had mixed emotions. I believed I was failing them. I had worked so hard to get them home, and now, only months later, they were leaving again. I continued to share my feelings with Norma while learning to trust something beyond my mind's judgments.

It was decided I would go with them to North Carolina by Greyhound bus. It took us three days of continuous travel to reach the school's campus. What I had hoped would be a fun trip turned out to be very stressful. I returned home, deflated and without direction.

*****

It's the end of November 1998, and as I sit on my bed in my semi-darkened room, the quiet is all but consuming me. Writing my feelings down in my journal isn't helping. Pain is radiating down my neck and into my shoulders. Sitting upright, I slowly look around the room in an attempt to ground myself. I feel desperate. "Please help me, Godmother!"

"Breathe with me, Serena. You're not alone."

As I breathe, a wave of emotions washes over me. Startled by my own outcry, I wonder what's going on with me. I'm jumbled and don't know where to start. Sighing longingly, I wish I could have stayed with my sons in North Carolina, but Godmother was adamant: I was to continue my work with Norma. Looking at the clock, I realize it's too late to call her. Thankfully, I'm seeing her in the morning.

Hearing Godmother call me from within, I write the words she is saying. "Now that your sons are living in North Carolina, who will you live for now?"

Feeling angry, I look away and purposely drift. Ignoring Godmother's question, I put my journal away and try to get some sleep.

Arriving at Norma's promptly at 9 a.m., I find her watering the rose bushes. Waving happily at her, I park the car. Wrapping my arms around her, I feel her love encompass me. Holding onto her a bit longer than I should, I finally step back, hoping she will stop watering.

Turning to me, while continuing to water the rose bushes, she asks, "How are you doing, sweetie?"

Looking around uncertainly, I quickly answer, "I'm fine …"

Sensing my discomfort, Norma turns off the water. Taking my arm, she leads me into the house. Starting a kettle for tea, she asks, "How was the drive?"

Feeling the familiar anxiety start to build, I answer, "It was okay. I'm going to wait for you in the living room."

"That's fine. I'll be there in a minute."

Handing me my tea moments later, Norma states, "I'm glad you're here. Where do you want to start?"

My words tumble out in a rush. "I feel lost, Norma. Everything I worked for is gone. I don't know what to live for anymore." Voice escalating in pain, I add, "I worked so hard to get my boys home, and now they're gone!"

Erupting in a wave of tears, I impatiently rub my face dry. I'm unaware that I've switched. The new voice that speaks is softer and more contained. "I wanted to make it right for them. Do you understand?"

Not waiting for an answer, the body slumps forward, as another switch occurs. "Now that they're gone, how can I show them that I love them?" Ending the sentence with a hysterical cry, she retreats.

Norma watches the switches without comment. She knows that as each mother has a chance to share her piece of the turmoil, it will be easier to work through the jumble of emotions. Sensing that all has been said, Norma calls me back to the front.

I hear Norma calling me from a distance. Moving toward the sound of her voice, I look around the room, rubbing my forehead to clear my thoughts. I feel confused and overwhelmed.

"Serena, I know you're upset, but you cannot help yourself when you are this anxious. Sit back against the cushions and breathe with me."

It takes all of my focus to disengage from the anxiety I am in, but as the minutes tick by, I begin to feel better. Sitting up, I remark, "I can talk now. Thanks, Norma."

Norma's brown eyes twinkle lovingly at me as she says, "The more you can let yourself have this gift of breath, the more you will experience peace even when we're not together.

"Now, let's get back to how you are feeling now that the boys have moved. What I heard you say is that you feel lost without them and that you don't want to live anymore. Is that what you meant?"

"No!" I anxiously cry out.

"Then what did you mean?" Norma quietly asks.

I want to run. A cloud of haze moves in, filling my head with confusion.

"Serena, don't leave! Choose to stay here, and tell me what you meant!"

Struggling to stay, I choose my words carefully. "When the boys were my responsibility, I felt I had something to live for, but now …" Tears flow down my cheeks, unchecked. Saying this much opens a cavern of nothingness within me.

Taking my hand in hers, Norma says, "I hear you saying that without the boys, you don't feel like living anymore."

"That's not what I said!" Internal alarms start wailing, signaling danger to the entire system. Pulling my hand out of hers, I withdraw completely.

That's when Godmother comes to the front of the body to speak to Norma. "What the mothers are feeling involves much more than what we can deal with today. I need you to keep it simple. I want you to help them understand that their feelings are normal. Help them to see that every mother goes through this experience. The more they can realize this is a normal reaction, the easier it will be for us to work through it. What is behind the depression is way too traumatic to be looked at now. I know you sense where I am going with this. What is most important is that they stay safe."

As Godmother continues, her words are direct. "We're at a point with this work where a decision needs to be made, but before Serena can make a decision, I need to know if you will continue working with us once you realize the full extent of what that commitment requires. The work we have done so far has only scratched the surface. What lies ahead will require far more from you than what has been given thus far. What Serena experienced is so far outside the realm of normalcy that it will stretch your capacity to the breaking point. With that said, what do you want to do?"

"Of course, I want to continue working with Serena. I love her and want what is best for her. But she has to decide for herself if she can do this work, once you tell her how much harder it will be."

"Then that is the first thing I would like us to address. After that is discussed, we can talk about this feeling of being lost." Without another word, Godmother sits back against the cushions and closes her eyes.

The room is quiet as Norma waits for someone to come forward.

Sitting up, I look at Norma with a questioning frown. "What were we talking about?" Rubbing my forehead for clarity, I attempt to shake off the feeling that I need to sleep.

"Before we talk any further, I want you to close your eyes and ask Godmother to be here. She needs to speak to you."

Sitting back, I close my eyes, looking within at my internal world. I see Godmother off to my left, walking toward me. Taking my hand, she pulls me onto the soft grass in our meadow. "I want to ask you a question," Godmother says. "It's very important that you listen before answering. Can you do that?"

Hearing how serious she is makes me anxious. I am quiet, though, since I want to hear what she has to say.

"I want you to open your eyes so that Norma can be part of this conversation, please." Godmother's melodic voice is music to my ears.

Opening my eyes, I tell Norma what is happening. "Godmother wants to ask me a question. But she told me to be still and listen first. What does she mean by that?"

"By not answering immediately and allowing yourself to feel what you are being told, you will have a better chance of being honest with yourself."

Sitting upright, I listen intensely, relaying word for word what Godmother is telling me. "You are at a place in your work where you can stop therapy with Norma and live your life somewhat comfortably."

"I can't do that!" I vigorously object.

"Serena, please listen to all that Godmother has to say," Norma says.

Nodding, I remain quiet.

"I ask you to let yourself hear what I'm offering you," Godmother reiterates. "This is a real option. You can stop therapy and live the rest of your life somewhat comfortably, but hear this, Serena. If you choose to continue this work, the journey will be much more difficult. Please," Godmother implores, "be still and feel what I'm telling you. This will be a commitment way beyond anything you have done up to now. That means that what you have felt and remembered thus far has just been a beginning. I know you don't want to hear that, but it's the truth."

"So stop a moment," Norma suggests. "Really, let yourself hear what Godmother is saying. If you choose to continue with this work, it will be harder than anything we have done so far. Are you letting yourself feel what she is saying?"

Nodding my head yes, I remain silent. *How can it be any harder?*

They must be wrong. Looking to my left, I see Godmother. She smiles at me, telling me that whatever I choose, she will always be with me. Feeling reassured, I look to my right, where Norma sits. I love this lady beyond anything I have ever felt before. Feeling their love and this compelling truth from within, I answer, "I can't stop. I have to integrate." Hearing my own voice resonate with unusual strength affirms what I'm feeling. "It's something that I know, and it's not up for debate. Do you understand?"

"Of course I do," Norma responds.

Her smile is the only response I need. "Then let's celebrate with cookies!" I exclaim.

Laughing in celebration, we make our way to the kitchen.

*****

"When we started talking this morning," Norma states, "you shared that you were feeling lost since the boys moved away. Do you remember that, Serena?"

Rubbing my face, I look inside for the specific conversation we had earlier. It's filed away in my mind, complete with pictures, waiting to be retrieved. "Oh, yes. I remember now. I was telling you I didn't know what to do with myself now that the boys are gone."

"Yes," Norma says, "and as we talked, I became aware of a fun discovery. You always want to be normal, just like everyone else. Do you remember telling me this?"

Nodding silently without comment, I listen because I don't trust where she is going with this.

"Missing your sons and feeling lost is quite normal. Almost every mother whose children leave home goes through this. Our society has a name for it: empty-nest syndrome. Have you ever heard of it before?" Smiling at me, she waits for my response.

I don't believe her; the more I recall our previous conversation, the more I remember the anguish I was feeling. I know that's not normal. Lost in thought, I don't answer her.

Sensing my withdrawal, Norma continues. "Play with me a moment, and let yourself remember what it was like before you had your sons."

Realizing that she's helping me toward some greater understanding helps me let down my guard. "I remember how much I wanted to be married and have children. I believed that would make me happy."

"Yes, but don't get off track," Norma counsels. "Can you remember what it was like to wake up every day with only the thought of taking care of *you*?"

"I remember being engaged to Frank; it was a long time ago," I curtly reply. *I don't want to talk about this anymore.*

"Right, it was a long time ago," Norma confidently reiterates.

Unwilling to drop the conversation, she continues. "Stay with me, Serena, and feel what I'm asking you to notice. You had only yourself to take care of. Then one day, after nine months of pregnancy, you came home with two babies. They depended on you for their every need. Every moment, whether sleeping or awake, your focus was on your babies. What did they need? What were they crying about? The change was gradual, but over time, your focus shifted so completely that all you could think about was what you could do for your sons. All mothers go through this. It's a normal part of parenting. Are you following me so far?"

I'm relieved with how the conversation has changed direction. "Yes, I would always think of them first ... even when I was in the hospital, it was my number-one priority to be there for them every weekend, even when it wasn't good for me." Pausing, I struggle to come to terms with these awarenesses. "They always came first, and that hurt me sometimes, didn't it? So, feeling lost is normal."

"Serena, as best you can, let yourself feel what it was like to be their mother for twelve years, and in one day, all three of them are gone. How do you think any mother would feel?"

"Oh! They would feel lost, and that's what I'm feeling!"

"Yes, lost and without direction. Can you understand and celebrate how normal you are? Can you give yourself time and be gentle with yourself? When you're feeling lost or depressed, take a few minutes to breathe and feel. Ask yourself, what would I like to do for myself? No one can do this for you, but you." Norma's voice resonates with unwavering strength and compassion as she continues. "You can't afford to judge yourself. Remember, you're having a normal experience. Can you take a moment and give yourself a hug?" Waiting for my response and getting none, she asks me directly, "How does that sound?"

I don't like her suggestion. "It feels funny, wrapping my arms around myself to give me a hug. Can't I just accept that they're gone and feel better?"

Norma's voice deepens as she shakes her head no. "This isn't going to go away, Serena! You can't switch and hope that it will disappear. As long as you ignore it, the feelings will stay stuck. Only in your willingness to be honest about what you are feeling and then give it to Godmother through your breath can the feelings shift.

"I can see you don't like my answer. When you don't like what I'm telling you, you say no and pretend it's not there. That hurts you, Serena! Part of healing comes from your willingness to own what you are feeling and then pay attention to it. Are you willing to do that?"

Inhaling with resignation, I woodenly answer, "Yes, I will choose to love myself, and not run from what I'm feeling." But in the very next breath, my words betray what I'm really thinking. "It's too uncomfortable to be feeling this way, Norma!"

"Yes, it's uncomfortable. That's the truth," Norma states unapologetically. "The boys leaving home is a part of change. Are you worth the effort it takes to love yourself and not run away?"

Norma's eyes hold me with a love so authentic that I can't turn away, and in that brief moment, my resistance melts, creating a space of yes within me.

Chapter 10: HAMBURGERS AND JOY

The familiarity of my apartment comforts me, offering a safe haven away from the outside world. I work full-time at the restaurant, and on Tuesdays, I see Norma. I usually go to the movies on my other day off. I talk to my sons on a somewhat regular basis, and even though I'm alone most of the time, I'm used to my life working this way.

*****

"I need to talk to you, Norma. Do you have the time?"

"What's cooking?"

"I know we're going to get together tomorrow, but I need to ask you something important. Seeing you once a week isn't enough; I feel I need to move closer to you. Would that be, okay?"

Chuckling good-naturedly, Norma asks, "Why do you need my permission, Serena?"

"Because Norma, I would be living closer to you. I might infringe on your space … you know?"

"Yes, I hear you, sweetie, but take a moment and sense; what do you really mean when you say you would be infringing on my space?"

"I would be closer to you," I repeat. "You know … living in the same area as you and Garret."

Speaking slowly, she repeats her question, but this time she adds, "What are you really trying to ask me?"

Almost choking from the surge of emotions that assault me, I withdraw.

Knowing that I've retreated, Norma states, "Stepping back helps no one, Serena. So, let's look at this another way. Where is this feeling coming from?"

Taking a deep breath, I move more fully back to the front. "It feels like it's coming from my stomach, right below my belly button, Norma."

Laughing with approval, Norma says, "Yes, now go one step further, and ask Godmother why you are feeling this way."

"'It's time we make an even greater shift with our integration work,'" Godmother says. "'Living closer to Norma will facilitate this. Will you trust that all will be arranged for this change?' Wow, Norma, Godmother says that what I was feeling was real! She's asking me to trust that this will facilitate my integration!" Relieved, I laugh giddily.

"Did you hear Godmother say that she would provide the answers on how this move will happen?"

"No, I didn't hear that part."

"I know. When you get excited, you race ahead without hearing what else is being shared; as a result, you shortchange yourself. So be still a moment, and ask Godmother to repeat what she said about the move."

This is moving too fast. I don't know if I can do this. Lost in thought, I'm drawn back by Norma calling my name.

"Where did you go? I asked you to ask Godmother what she said about the actual move. This time, stay and hear her answer," Norma advises.

Inhaling deeply, I silently ask Godmother to repeat what she said.

"I'll be there every step of the way. I will help you find a place to live. We'll find the perfect job for you. All you need to do is trust that this is possible and then let it happen. Can you do that?"

"Do you understand what she's telling you?"

"I think so …" I answer. "She says she will show me where I will live and work, right?"

"Yes, Serena, you will not be alone with this change. I know this is a big step, and it scares many of the children. It will be done gently. Can you trust that this is in motion and put it away for now? Your job is to stay here in this moment."

Feeling overwhelmed, I'm more than glad to follow Norma's advice by pretending the conversation never happened. Everything is as it was before.

*****

Arriving at Norma's house later than usual, I find her in the backyard throwing the ball to Chin Chin. I quickly hug her, while Chin Chin runs back and forth between our legs. Taking my elbow, Norma walks with me into the living room.

"Where do you want to start?"

"It feels like I have a huge hole right in the middle of my chest, and it really hurts. I know that sounds crazy, Norma."

"I believe you, Serena. An internal child has come forward for your help. Will you let her speak?"

Nodding, I quietly step back. Immediately, the face transforms.

Smiling warmly, Norma says hello. There is no response. Again, Norma says hello.

Unmoving, the child stares, frozen in time. Her eyes are open, yet unseeing. Stroking her arm, Norma gently calls, inviting her toward the light. "I can see you, you know. No one will hurt you. The angel is here to make sure you are safe."

Slowly, the eyes shift. Flat, staring eyes swell with pain. The forehead furrows, as awareness begins to dawn. Breathing shallowly, the chest scarcely moves. Mouth slightly open, a quiet whimper is heard. "Please, don't touch me. It hurts too much. Let me go back inside."

"Inside, where, sweet one?" Norma gently asks.

"Inside, where no one can see me."

"Sweetie, the angel and I came to get you. She wants to take care of you. Your daddy and mommy do not get to be your parents anymore. The angel has come just for you." Without saying a word, the child withdraws. Norma waits, knowing that Godmother will take care of her.

"Norma, my chest isn't hurting anymore! Wow ... that really helped!"

"Yes, Serena. When you experience physical pain that seems to have no connection to the present moment, ask Godmother if a child has come forward that needs your help. That will help you. Do you want that?"

"I think so."

"Feel your answer, Serena. Don't think it."

Feel my answer? What does she mean? "Yes," I obediently parrot. "I will help myself."

Norma isn't fooled. She knows I'm not being honest, but she chooses to leave it alone. "Ask Godmother where she wants us to start."

"She says that the child was connected to the issue of abandonment. She says this is a core issue for us. What does she mean by that?"

"Don't get distracted, Serena. Please, repeat everything Godmother is saying."

"Godmother says the issue of abandonment started in infancy and is far-reaching. She wants me to invite the children to come to her." Feeling anxious, I state, "I don't get what she's talking about."

"Stay out of your head, and drop deeper into your belly, Serena. Trust where Godmother is leading you. Will you invite these children to come forward, without having to understand the reason why?"

Although I'm anxious, I do as asked. "Come to the angel, bring her your pain. She is here for you," I murmur. As I breathe, I feel thick dark despair blanket me with its weight. All I want to do is give in to it.

"Breathe, Serena. You're the only one who can move this depression. It's been here a long time, and if you hold onto it, it will stay stuck. When you take out the garbage, do you go through it, examining every piece? Of course you don't." Smiling at me, she continues, "So trust that your breath is your permission to move this old energy to Godmother."

My chest aches with a pain that is vast. Closing my eyes, I intentionally fill my lungs with my breath. Exhaling ever so slowly, I let the energy of despair move out through my nose. It feels as though I'm literally moving tar out of my body. Shuddering with the intensity of my emotions, I continue breathing, and ever so slowly, the despair begins to melt. I actually feel lighter! No matter how deep the pain goes, it always shifts with my breath. Opening my eyes, I smile at Norma. "I really felt it leave, Norma!"

"Do you know why it must shift with your breath?"

Shaking my head no, I wait for her explanation.

"Your choice, combined with your intentional breath, is you giving permission to Spirit to integrate the memories and the emotions with it. The breath is a powerful tool in healing. It's the very essence of Soul. As we breathe deeply into our stomachs, we are consciously choosing to be here. It's our way of saying, 'I choose to live.' That's why when you chose to breathe, the depression had to leave. It didn't have permission to stay, because you were the conscious chooser."

"I get what you're saying, Norma! That's what I was feeling. I wanted to help myself. I was being smothered by the despair, but I trusted what you told me and kept on breathing!"

"Yes, Serena, you created the shift yourself through your breath. I'm proud of you. Now, let's get something to eat before we do any more work."

"Great, I'm hungry!" Before I have a chance to stand, Toby moves forward into the body. "I want to go and have hamburgers with you!"

Not missing a beat, Norma says, "But before we go, you need to promise me you won't go anywhere without holding my hand."

"I promise, Norma!" Grabbing her hand, he eagerly pulls her toward the door.

"Instead of going to a drive-thru, how would you like to go to a restaurant and sit down for a change? I think they might serve chocolate malts. Is that something you would like?"

"Wahoo!" he yells, while skipping to the car. As he scrambles up onto the seat, he excitedly asks, "Can I have ketchup? I love ketchup!"

Toby is three years old. He loves to hop, skip, and climb. He is a stocky little boy with blue eyes and curly, blond hair. He has a sprinkling of freckles that dance across his upturned nose, and just like Robbie, he holds an integral part of the joy within our system. Allowing these joyful internal children to be in the front of the body is like ingesting a medicinal analgesic that fills us with its healing power.

*****

While driving, Norma reminds Toby what it means to be appropriate. "We'll be going to a sit-down restaurant." Glancing at him, she smiles warmly. "Do you know how to behave, Toby?"

"Yeah, I gots to be quiet and not chew with my mouth open, huh." Sitting upright, he proudly puffs out his chest.

"You are a smart boy. It's important you keep your voice down. We have indoor voices and outdoor voices, and I know when you get excited, you tend to get loud. Would you agree?"

Happily nodding his head up and down, Toby whispers, "I know how to do indoor voice real good."

Pulling into the parking lot, Norma turns toward him. "Wait until I come around to your door, please."

Knowing it could be risky to go inside and sit down, Norma has chosen this restaurant for its quiet atmosphere. It's a single-story structure, adorned in stone and wood. Large decorative boulders flank the right side of a cobblestone pathway, leading to the front door.

Norma takes Toby's hand as they walk up the cobbled pathway.

Pulling his hand out of Norma's grasp, Toby races for the closest boulder. Climbing on top of it, he waves his arms and hollers happily, "Look at me, Norma, I'm big!"

Remaining calm, Norma takes his hand and gently guides him off the boulder. "Toby, it's important you stay right beside me. Do you understand?"

Feeling her parental concern wash over him, he nods happily.

As they walk into the restaurant, it appears that two women have come for lunch. The hostess smiles and asks, "Would you ladies like a booth or a table?"

Squeezing Toby's hand reassuringly, Norma requests a booth close to the fireplace.

"Of course," she replies. "Follow me, please."

Norma holds Toby's hand, guiding him to his seat.

"Wow," Toby whispers. "This is a real restaurant, huh, Norma?" Smiling from ear to ear, he waits for her to answer.

"Yes, sweetie, this is a real restaurant, and do you know why I brought you here?"

Shaking his head no, he waits for her reply.

"You are a special little boy, and I thought you might enjoy it."

"I do. Yeah!" Nodding his head repeatedly, Toby looks around the room, studying everything. "Do you think that's a real fireplace?" Pointing to the round, brick fireplace in the center of the room, he raises his eyebrows expressively.

"Yes, sweetie, it's a real fireplace, but let's look at what you want for lunch before the waitress comes."

"I already know, remember?"

Laughing, Norma replies, "Yes, I know, but there could be something else you might like to eat."

Emphatically shaking his head no, he states, "I want a hamburger and fries!"

"Great, then let me look at the menu so I can decide. Then, when the waitress comes, I will order for both of us. Can you let me do that without interrupting?"

"Okay. I don't want to tell her anyway. You can do it." Picking up his knife, he begins carving his paper napkin.

Holding out her hand, Norma waits for Toby to relinquish the knife. Holding the knife close to his chest, he whines, "How come, Norma?"

"It's not up for discussion, Toby."

Reluctantly, he releases the knife. Distracted by the couple, two tables over, he points at them.

"Toby, please put your finger down. We don't point at people. Let me get you a pen so you can draw me something. Would you do that so I can look at the menu?"

Nodding happily, he watches Norma rummage through her purse.

"You gots lots of stuff in there, don't you?"

"Yes, sometimes way too much. Oh, here it is. Handing him a pen, she reminds him to draw quietly so she can look at the menu. Minutes pass quietly without interruption.

"How come the lady is taking so long? I'm hungry now!" Toby implores.

"I know, sweetie. She'll be here soon."

Looking around for their waitress, he spots a young woman across the room and smiles at her. "Remember, Toby, when she comes over, I'll be the only one talking." The reminder comes just in the nick of time.

"Are you ladies ready to order?" the waitress innocently asks.

Looking at Norma with a huge frown, Toby puffs out his chest, implying he is not a lady!

Ignoring Toby, Norma smiles warmly at the waitress. She orders and then remembers to ask if they have chocolate malts.

"Yes, we do. Would you like one?"

"Yes, please, and can you add a cherry to the top of it?"

Bursting at the seams with excitement, Toby can hardly wait until the woman has left the table.

"Oh, boy, I get a real cherry? Thanks, Norma!" Laughing with sheer joy, Toby returns to his drawing.

Norma is filled with gratitude. The system is allowing itself to receive joy through this child. It speaks of the healing that has already occurred. There is no switching into other parts. Instead, there is this joyous child, sharing in a real moment of living. This is a gift for everyone, plus, it's an indication of how far they have come in trusting her. Keeping her thoughts to herself, Norma asks, "Can I see what you are drawing?"

Proudly showing her his napkin, he points out how he has given the kitty a very long tail.

"Do you like kitties?" Norma asks.

"Yes, I lovvvve kitties! They purr and make me feel good. Petunia, the kitty that lives with Serena, is really nice. She sits on top of Serena's shoulders while she walks around the house." Toby's next words come out in a shout. "It's like she's on a ride or something!"

Norma motions for Toby to be quiet. The waitress is approaching with their meals.

"Would you like the malt now or after your meal?" Directing her question at Toby, she waits for his reply.

"Would you bring it now?" Norma cheerfully requests. "And don't forget the cherry, please."

Looking down at his plate, Toby spies the pickles, tomato, and lettuce. Piling them onto his bun, he happily looks up as Norma speaks.

"Would you like some ketchup on your bun, Toby?"

"Oh, I almost forgot!" Toby squeals. As he reaches for the ketchup bottle, Norma intercepts it. With his mouth watering at the impending bite, Toby graciously waits as Norma adds the ketchup to his bun. Grabbing his hamburger, Toby takes a huge bite. "This is great!" Looking up, he's surprised that the waitress has returned with his malt. Smiling widely, with his chewed hamburger in full view, he takes the malt and eagerly gulps it down.

Smiling politely, even though she's a bit surprised, the waitress leaves without a word.

"Toby, would you slow down, please. We have as much time as you need. Eat your food more slowly, so your tummy stays happy."

"But it is soooo good! I love it all."

"Yes," Norma replies quietly. "It's not going anywhere. It's all for you."

While they eat, Norma learns more about the world the internal children live in. As Toby describes the meadow filled with flowers and bugs, and the big, yellow house with six floors in it, his portrayal is so vivid that Norma knows it's as real to him as the hamburger he just ate. She's in awe of this human's Soul brilliance, which created a world so real that it kept the system alive and sane despite the constant barrage of terror from the outside world.

Watching Toby slurp up the last of his malt, Norma gently pries the glass out of his hand. "Are you full, sweetie? Is there anything else you would like to eat?"

Shaking his head no, he urgently adds, "I gots to go potty!" Leaning toward Norma, he grimaces.

"That's fine. I can take you to the restroom here, or would you rather wait until we get back to the house?"

"I want to wait, okay?"

The urgency in his voice lets Norma know they need to leave. She takes his hand as they walk over to the cash register. "I would like to pay for our meal. Would you get our waitress, please?"

Smiling, the waitress approaches and hands Norma the bill. "I'm so sorry. I didn't know you were ready to leave. Is there anything else I can get you?"

"No, we enjoyed our meal very much. Thank you."

Toby runs straight for the car. Fortunately, it's only minutes before they are pulling into the driveway. Bolting from the car, Toby races for the bathroom. Returning moments later, he says, "I had a real good time, Norma." Leaning in for a hug, he wraps his arms around her. "I love you a whole lot, you know?"

"And I love you, too, sweetie. Thank you for sharing lunch with me. It was special. Would you go and find Serena and let her know I'm waiting?"

After getting one more hug, he steps back happily.

Within seconds, I'm back and feeling quite content. I could take a nap if given the opportunity, but Norma asks me a question instead. "Before lunch, you and I were working with Godmother about depression. Do you know where it comes from?"

I'm not sure I'm ready to leave the warm, comfortable feeling I'm having for the work that needs to be done. "No."

"Ask Godmother, and please try to listen to what she says."

"Godmother says the depression is from the abandonment we experienced as a child. She's asking me to relay what I see." Settling deeper into my belly, I close my eyes and watch. "Jennifer is a tiny baby. She's no more than two months old. She's crying, Norma. Her body is cold. She doesn't have anything on, except her diaper, and her bottom is burning! There's no blanket in the crib." Shuddering with the realization that they do this on purpose, I cry, "They leave her for hours on end, alone and crying, and she's still an infant!"

"Don't get lost in the memory, Serena. Stay here, and ask Godmother why she's showing us this."

"She says she's opening the door to our abandonment issues with this memory. She says we will do this gently."

"Take a moment and breathe with the energy of yes, Serena. Allow Godmother to bring it up in her own timing, and don't forget to give this memory to Godmother."

As I breathe, I feel another memory surface. "I'm seeing Jennifer in her underpants outside the kitchen door ... This doesn't seem like a big deal. Why am I seeing this memory?"

"Instead of judging, let Jennifer tell you what she wants you to see. Please, listen from your heart and not your head. You forget, this was an ongoing, twenty-four-hour-a-day experience, and *nothing*," Norma emphasizes, "was left to chance. Every area of her life was specifically altered through the government and the cult's training. This experience impacted her enough that it is here for us to heal. Will you love her enough to listen to her?"

Feeling Norma's unwavering compassion wash over me helps me open my heart to Jennifer. "She's holding onto the doorknob, begging to be let inside. She is sobbing hysterically."

"And is it light outside?"

"No, it's dark. She's so afraid that she's almost incoherent!" Feeling her terror fill my body, I begin to cry.

"Serena, stay here. You cannot afford to get upset. Remember, see it as though it were on a television screen. This will help you, help them."

Determined to stay, I keep breathing; I won't give in to the terror. "She's shaking the doorknob, begging to be let in. The door swings open, and Jack shouts, 'Since you won't do as you are told, then go find another place to live! Your mother and I don't want you anymore!' With that, he slams the door shut. Oh, Norma, this is awful." Feeling Jennifer's terror grip me, I cry hysterically, "It's so real!"

"Serena, I know this is upsetting. I'm not minimizing that, but if you get upset, you can't help Jennifer."

Godmother interjects. "She was thrown outside because she defied Jack. He's intent on breaking her spirit, and he will keep her outside as long as it takes."

"Before going any further, sense, Serena. Can you feel the strength of this child? Do you admire her for telling her father no?"

Nodding yes, I remain silent.

"Ask Godmother what she wants you to see about this," Norma suggests.

Closing my eyes, I hear Godmother say. "Notice, Jennifer said no to her father for a specific reason. He demanded that she stab Julie's forearm for her dinner. Do you remember when we worked with this before?"

Opening my eyes, I'm confused. "I don't remember that, Norma."

"That's alright. It was a memory we worked with before. You're not going to remember all that we have done. Don't start pumping fear. Will you breathe a moment, and bring your breath deep into your belly? You have done nothing wrong. Sense, and see where Godmother is leading you with this."

"Jennifer refused to stab Julie," Godmother says. "Even though he threatened her with no food, it did not sway her. Jack couldn't stand Jennifer's defiance and was determined to break her. This is not the first time he has thrown her outside as a last resort." I feel overwhelmed, as I repeat Godmother's words.

"It's alright, Serena, you're doing great. Now, stay out of your head and notice how Jennifer gets back into the house?"

I'm tired of sensing. I want her to tell me.

"Can you see where Jennifer's energy went, Serena?"

"I see her pulling inside of herself. It's as though she went into the darkness and gave up."

"Yes, by the age of four, Jennifer had learned to switch quite effectively. That child, the one defying Jack, retreated. The terror of being alone was so great that one more piece of the authentic child disappeared. Are you following me so far?"

An unbearable sadness engulfs me. Taking a breath, I ask Godmother for the strength to go on. "The real Jennifer didn't want to stab Julie," I wearily answer.

"Serena, feel your answer. I know you're tired, but you're the one setting Jennifer free to come home to Godmother. The trauma that has been here for many years can be integrated today, because you are present enough to begin to look at it honestly. Jennifer was terrorized by the thought of being thrown out of the house. This was no empty threat. She knew Jack followed through. She had seen him brutalize many people. She was beyond scared."

"Yeah, so why in the world would she want to be let back into the house with him and Lois?"

"That is a question of judgment. Choose, Serena," Norma firmly insists. "Will you see this memory from judgment or compassion? You get to choose."

"Oh … this is so hard!" Closing my eyes, I breathe. Sobs echo painfully from within my chest. Opening my eyes, I tell Norma I will choose compassion.

"Alright then. Notice, Jennifer is four years old. She is defenseless. She loves her parents. All children do, that is the truth. She knows no one else that she can trust. Jack and Lois are her world. Let yourself feel that." Waiting, Norma allows me to really feel what it was like for Jennifer. Continuing, she adds, "Remember that she has no consistent experience of life. Life, for her, is a series of moments. That is how she survives. She has no presence of mind to think about anything beyond this moment. Are you getting the enormity of her life day by day?"

I feel overwhelmed, so I don't respond.

"In order for Jennifer to survive, she retreats into the darkness, allowing for another child to come to the front to do as Jack demands. Over and over, parts of the authentic child are brought home to sleep. And who do you think did that, Serena?"

Knowing the answer is Godmother, I answer quickly. In truth, I just want this to be over. I feel a sadness that defies description.

Sensing that I can't process much more, Norma smiles at me encouragingly. "I can see that you need some rest, but there is one more piece of clarity you need, so we can help not only Jennifer, but you as well. As we worked today, you felt the energy of the depression that Jennifer was in. The truth that Jack and Lois did not want her was loud and clear." Leaning in, while taking my hand, Norma encourages me to feel what she is saying. "Over and over, either through their actions or their words, they told Jennifer they did not love her. Are you following me so far?"

I'm so tired, I don't want to do this anymore. Nodding, I remain silent.

"I know this isn't easy, Serena. Why don't we breathe for a bit?"

Relieved, I close my eyes and listen as Norma leads me in breathing. Dropping deeper into my belly, I continue breathing and begin to feel a renewed sense of purpose. I can do this, I decide.

"I'm proud of you," Godmother says. "It's your courage that is helping these children come home."

"I don't want to accept that Jack and Lois didn't love Jennifer," I admit. "It hurts so much that I feel like pushing it all away."

"I understand. It's not easy to realize that Jennifer's parents did not love her, but I want you to take it a step further. Would you be willing to see the whole truth by staying with me?"

Nodding, I continue listening.

"Jennifer's parents were incapable of loving anyone. It had nothing to do with her. Can you let yourself sense what I'm saying?"

"Wow, you're right, Norma! I can feel it. They were filled with so much fear they couldn't love, could they? It isn't some kind of idea, but a deep knowing within me that tells me they didn't know how to love! I remember Lois talking about her childhood, and it was a nightmare, and Jack was raised in a satanic cult.

They didn't know how to love ..." Repeating the last few words to myself, I feel the truth resonate within me.

"Serena, I'm proud of you. Your bravery is setting you free."

Chapter 11: CHANGES

I moved six months ago and found an apartment within minutes of Norma's house. Then I found a job at a fine-dining establishment a couple of weeks later. Today is New Year's Day, 2001, and I'm getting ready to go to work for the lunch shift.

Staring out my living room window, I watch the eucalyptus trees sway in the breeze. Startled by the sound of steam escaping the iron, I pull myself back to the task at hand. Applying the iron to the crease in my pants, I carefully run it down the leg, pressing hard to take out the wrinkles. It is a meticulous job that requires my full attention; whenever I get distracted, I tend to burn myself.

Feeling restless and not knowing why, I turn on the television for company. As I finish getting dressed, I notice that I look sad. Glaring back at the face in the mirror, I grab my purse and quickly make my way downstairs.

As I drive along the coast, I watch the waves crashing against the shore and listen to the seagulls as they swirl and cry in the updrafts above my car. I purposely drift, letting the beautiful scenery lull me into a sense of complacency.

It's slow just like I expected, so they're letting me go home early. I need to get my check to pay rent. I've been waiting for over twenty minutes, and I still don't have it. I'm told that the manager will hand out the paychecks once he finishes his lunch.

You've got to be kidding! Who does he think he is?

I don't like this man. He acts superior to the rest of us. Wringing my hands, I look in my purse for a stick of gum — anything to help control my anxiety.

You should go and talk to him! Tell him you have an appointment. That will make him move!

As I climb the stairs, my thoughts race. I hesitate to say anything, since I don't like confrontation. But Norma told me that if I got off early, I might be able to stop by and see her. I'm afraid I might miss her if I don't leave soon. The fear that I might not be able to see her is bigger than my fear of confronting him. Cautiously turning the doorknob, I open the door and walk in.

He's sitting cross-legged with a plate of food on his lap. Seeing me enter, he raises his hand. Someone is yelling at him. I hear hateful words being screamed, and I'm shocked to discover that it's coming from me! Clasping my hand over my mouth, I run from the room. Trembling, I race down the stairs and out to my car. I can barely get my key in the lock. Feeling as though I might faint, I back up and tear out of the driveway. I drive with my left hand on the steering wheel while grasping my head with my right. I remember the movie *Alien* and wonder if I might have a monster living inside of me.

Breathing as deeply as I can, I force myself to focus on the road. I rock back and forth. I do whatever it takes to keep the lid on whatever is inside of me.

Pulling into Norma's driveway, I grab my purse off the seat and run. Opening the door, I holler. My voice is riddled with hysteria. Coming in from the kitchen, Norma approaches me with her arms out. Collapsing into her, I cry, "I don't know what happened! I went into my boss's office to ask for my paycheck, and the next thing I knew, I was yelling at him! At first, I didn't even know it was me! The anger was huge, and the words I was saying …!" Sobbing, I'm unable to finish.

"Shhhh, there is nothing too great that you and I, with Godmother's help, can't handle. I'm here, Serena; you're safe," Norma croons. Sitting beside me on the couch, she takes my hand and looks into my face. "I know you're afraid, but if we slow this down, we can have better clarity about what happened at work today. Can you do that with me?"

Nodding, I close my eyes and try to recapture the scenario exactly as it happened. "It was slow just like I expected, so I was told I could leave early, but I needed my paycheck for rent. I waited for a long time. I was told the manager wanted to eat his lunch first, then he would give me my check. Can you believe that?"

"I want to stop you right there," Norma says. "When the manager told you that the boss would bring you your paycheck after he ate his lunch, what were you feeling at that point?"

"I was upset. I had been waiting for a long time!"

"Remember, Serena, no one is wrong." Stating this with emphasis, Norma continues, "We are in discovery. You came here very upset, and if we can slow this down, it will help us discover what really happened. Then we can help all of you. Is that alright with you?"

Feeling out of control, I shudder with my emotions. "I had been waiting," I repeat slowly, "and I thought if I told him I had an appointment, he might give me my check. I was afraid you might not be here if I had to wait much longer." Saying the last few words, I cry uncontrollably.

"Serena, nothing can be accomplished as long as you're afraid. Take a moment and breathe with me, please."

Hearing the steadiness in her voice and feeling the grasp of her hand over mine helps me feel safe enough to close my eyes and breathe with the sound of her voice. As I breathe, I begin to feel that sweet, and now familiar calm take over. Opening my eyes, I smile at her reassuringly. "I feel better now. I want to continue." Sitting straighter against the couch cushions, I begin again. "I remember walking up the stairs to his office. He had on black slacks. There was a plate of food on his lap. He was speaking to someone when I entered." Stopping, I close my eyes to see exactly what happened.

"Serena, what did he do at that point?" Norma gently asks.

"Oh, he raised his hand like this." Lifting my hand upright, with my eyes still closed, I open my palm, facing it toward her. "That's the last thing I remember, until I heard screams coming from me!" Opening my eyes, I look at Norma, expecting her to be surprised, but she is unruffled by this revelation.

"Do you trust me enough not to need an answer right now? I know you want one, but at this moment it's not necessary. Let's go upstairs and work with your body to move some energy. You're upset, so any answer at this point would not serve you." Not waiting for my reply, Norma gently pulls me to my feet.

Dragging myself up the stairs, I feel as though something has changed. I know I'm in trouble, and I don't know why. If I can't trust myself at work, then what will I do? Did I come this far to fall back into such blatant switching?

Pulling myself onto the massage table, I watch Norma light the candle. I wonder if this work with her has been a mistake. By trusting Norma and letting my guard down, did I inadvertently let some dark, evil thing escape from inside me that I cannot put back?

Bending next to my head, Norma strokes my hair while murmuring that it's okay. As she invites me to breathe, I erupt in sobs. "I feel so out of control, Norma! I'm afraid! Maybe I shouldn't have done this much work with you!"

"Breathe with me and choose, Serena. Will you run with the fear or stay here and help all of you? You get to choose!" Bending close enough so that we are nose to nose, I feel her breath upon my cheek. Her warm brown eyes embrace me with a steadiness that defies words. Her very being exudes an unwavering strength. I shudder with every breath I take. In and out I breathe, until after what seems like an eternity, I begin to feel more solid.

Smiling at me, she says, "It's your choice to either run with fear or stay right here to discover the truth. Running will never help you, Serena. We know you switched, don't we?"

Waiting for my response, I nod yes, but remain silent. I know the quiet I am feeling is very tenuous.

"So let's slow this down so you and I can have better clarity. Will you do that with me?" As she speaks, she pulls up a chair so that we are at eye level. Holding my right arm in a tender grasp, she asks, "What was it you were feeling before you went up the stairs to talk to your boss?"

"I was feeling frustrated that he expected me to wait so long just so he could finish his lunch. He could have taken five minutes to come down the stairs to give me my check. I had already waited …"

"Serena, don't recreate what happened. Just tell me what you were feeling. It sounds like you were angry. Is that right?"

"No, I was frustrated with having to wait so long for something that should have been done already."

"Alright, now, sense for a moment. Please, let yourself really feel: what is frustration?"

"It's restlessness and nervousness and … oh, it's anger, isn't it?"

"Yes, it is. Now keep sensing, Serena. As you climbed the stairs, where was your energy? Was it in your body, or was it above your shoulders, floating? What were the thoughts that were running through your head? This isn't to make you wrong. We're in discovery."

Closing my eyes to remember, I see myself climbing the stairs. Realizing I must have been out of my body at that point, I relay this to Norma. Remembering my thoughts, I add, "I was thinking he had no right to sit up there and demand I wait! I hated him and wanted to make him see how wrong he was! Wow ... Norma, I was angry, wasn't I? My feelings were ..." Not knowing how to describe them, I am quiet.

"Yes, now keep sensing: who were you really thinking about? Don't go to your head, but sense the truth, please."

Without warning, my entire body vibrates with the command to leave it alone. I feel threatened and don't know what to do. Closing my eyes, I intentionally shut her out, hoping this will resolve the situation.

"Serena, I know you're uncomfortable with what I asked, but we're going for the truth, aren't we? Now open your eyes and look at me. Who were your thoughts really about?"

"I was thinking about Jack! I wasn't feeling anger, Norma, I was feeling rage!"

"Now keep watching, and tell me what happened next."

"I pushed the door open, and my boss was surprised to see me. He told me that he would come down after he finished his lunch. He had a smirk on his face as he said it. Then he held up his hand, facing the palm out toward me." As I recite these last few details, my voice becomes flat and hypnotic.

Norma knows I've switched.

"So, when he raised his hand, what did that mean?" Norma gently asks.

"Shut down, shut down," the voice repetitively chimes.

"And what does shut down mean?"

"We are done, we are done. Go away, go away."

"And what happens when you are done?"

"The monster comes out."

"Who is the monster?" Norma questions.

"He is …" As the child's whisper trails off into silence, the front of the body is vacated completely.

As the minutes tick by, Norma speaks, "I know you're watching me; I'm not here to hurt you. I want to talk to you. Don't hide; come out and tell me about yourself." Saying this in a loving, yet firm voice, Norma watches.

Slowly, flat, lifeless eyes transform into glaring, rage-filled eyes. Staring defiantly at Norma, he states, "I hate you, and I'm not going to help you. You're a stupid fool to believe you can help them. You can't!" he screams. "I'm the boss, not you!"

Norma isn't fooled by his bravado. She knows this child is the doorway to parts yet to be revealed. "I'm not here to hurt you. I know your job is to protect them."

"I'm not here to protect anyone," he growls. "I hate them all, especially Serena! I will kill her, and there's nothing you can do about it!" With that warning, he is gone.

Norma knows that a critical change has occurred within the system. The children containing the rage are now coming forward. Her priority is to keep the body safe, which will require a different approach to how we work.

I hear my name being called from a distance. Opening my eyes, I see Norma's smiling face. "We have done quite a bit of work today. How are you feeling?"

Rubbing my face, I feel muddled.

"Don't get up, sweetie. Rub your legs and feel your breath as you purposely bring it deep into your body. Did you have lunch today?"

Shaking my head no, I rub my legs as directed. I feel detached. Climbing off the table, I grab hold of the side for balance. Following Norma back down the stairs, I wobble and fall against the wall, dislodging a small wooden display case holding twenty or more exquisitely carved jade animals. Frozen, I watch as they tumble down the stairs, shattering into pieces on the hard tile floor.

Norma turns upon hearing the sound. Looking up, she sees my horrified reaction.

"Oh, Norma, I didn't mean to!" Collapsing on the stairs, I sob uncontrollably.

Quickly climbing the stairs, Norma asks, "Are you okay, sweetie?" Lifting my chin, she asks again, "Are you alright?"

I'm confused by her concern for my welfare. "I didn't mean to do that, Norma! I don't know how it happened. I was coming down the stairs, and …"

"Hey, look at me. Those things don't matter! What I care about is you. Are you alright? Can you stand?"

Totally bewildered by her reaction, I'm overwhelmed by my own condemnation.

What is the matter with you! They cost a lot of money!

You did it on purpose; I know you did!

Trying to ignore the guilt that is smothering me, I respond, "I'm alright, but Norma, how can you be so calm? Those pieces are expensive!"

"Yes, and?" Calmly, she waits for me to finish my sentence.

I repeat what I just said. "They're valuable. You know, they cost a lot of money!"

"Come sit with me." Taking my hand, she guides me around the broken pieces of jade, leading me to the couch. "Serena, you're the one who is valuable. Those are just things; they do not matter." Watching me reject what she said, she continues. "You get to choose. Will you trust what I'm telling you, or will you stay in judgment? As long as you choose judgment, you will be angry with yourself, and you cannot afford that luxury right now." Raising her voice, she asks, "Are you hearing me, Serena?" As she holds me with her gaze and her unwavering compassion washes over me, I erupt into tears.

"Where did you learn that things matter more than people?" she genuinely asks.

"Things … that were not alive always mattered more to Lois than Julie or me! Every Friday, without fail, we had to clean the house. She made us vacuum the shag carpet, insisting we go over the same spot three times to make sure it was clean. Then we had to rake it so it looked good! Come on, rake a carpet that people walk on? She was ridiculous!" Furiously clenching my fists, I continue. "Then she made us comb the tassels on the front area rug on our knees! I'm not kidding you, Norma! We had to clean the ridge between the cupboard doors and the runner in the bathroom with Q-tips! I'm not exaggerating!" Aggressively raising my voice louder, I finish with, "I hated that the house mattered more to her than we did, and if one of us broke something … she had a major fit! She always believed we had done it on purpose!"

Taking my hand, Norma invites me to breathe. "That's a lot of anger you're feeling, isn't it, Serena?" Smiling, she takes my hand, while adding, "What message did Lois give you and your sister by her actions?"

"That's easy, Norma! We were the things in her life, and the house was the …" Stopping mid-sentence, I wonder how to appropriately describe what the house meant to her. "Francie hated her and would come to the front, exploding with feelings the rest of us struggled to repress. She was furious with Lois, so the system did whatever it had to, to keep her quiet. The problem was that most of us felt the way Francie did, so there were times she got through and told Lois off."

"Can you take a moment and thank Francie for her honesty? She dared to express what the rest of you were feeling and were unable to share."

Feeling surprised by this turn of events, I consider what Norma is saying. We had always hated Francie for her anger.

Interrupting my thoughts, Norma continues. "Serena, most of you were unwilling to be honest with Lois about your feelings. Yet this child knew the truth. She was the one who was willing to see how unreasonable Lois was. Can you thank Francie for her courage?"

Closing my eyes, I thank Francie for her honesty. I'm surprised because I feel admiration for her. I watch Godmother approach, smile at me, and wrap her arms around Francie's tall, thin frame. Simultaneously, a sweet, warm peace spreads through my body. Something has healed. I feel it! Opening my eyes, I gratefully smile at Norma.

"You're the one creating a different life for all of you, Serena. Do you want to continue with what Lois taught you and believe that things are more important than people? Or do you *choose*," she emphasizes, "to know that, for you, a person *always* matters more than some inanimate object?"

Her words resonate throughout my body, and I know that the love I'm experiencing is literally melting my pain. How could I want anything else but this new way of living? Leaning in, I hug Norma. "I didn't fall and break your figurines on purpose! I always believed Lois's lies, but no more! I choose to stop believing the lies I learned and to start loving myself!"

"I'm proud of you, Serena. Letting yourself feel it instead of thinking it makes all the difference in the world. When your choice is authentic, you become a loving creator in your life, opening you to so many new possibilities. But enough talk. I'm hungry. Let's get something to eat."

What I didn't realize at the time was this one experience spoke volumes to me. Norma was who Norma seemed to be. She wasn't speaking empty words; her whole being resonated with her concern for me. What had seemed like a bad experience lent itself to my healing more fully than anything we had previously done, because I knew unequivocally that I could trust her.

*****

After lunch, we resume our discussion about what happened at work. "Today, more than ever before, you've discovered how much you trust me, haven't you?" asks Norma.

Immediately, I'm on guard. "Yes, I do."

"I want you to tell me what you feel happened at work today, so we can decide what will be for your highest good."

"What do you mean, 'for my highest good'?" I ask with trepidation.

"Please, don't go to your mind, Serena. You and I agreed that we would do this work to heal and integrate you. My job is to guide you. Is that what you still want? If you don't want that, then I understand."

Interrupting her, I quickly amend, "I want your help. That's not what I said."

Holding my hand, she smiles at me reassuringly. "Alright. Then let's look at what happened today, so we can go forward from there."

"Okay ... I remember feeling angry at my boss for making me wait for him to finish his lunch. Then, when I went to talk to him, I switched. That's it in a nutshell," I casually reply, while shrugging my shoulders in ambivalence.

"Do you think that what happened at work today indicates that something else might be going on with you?" Norma knowingly leads.

"What do you mean?" I warily ask.

"Serena, when we react, we're coming from memory and not from the moment at hand. Over the past few years, you and I have been working with memory and healing those parts of you that were crying to come home. Your move to be closer to me was another shift in your healing process. What I'm hoping you sense is that another change is occurring, and you and I, together with Godmother's help, need to decide what is best for you now. Are you following me so far?" Searching my face for any indication that I've stepped back, she squeezes my hand again before continuing. "I want you to ask Godmother what we need to do next."

I dread what's coming. I would rather go to work and pretend nothing has happened. Not admitting this out loud, I close my eyes to listen to Godmother speak. "It will be best that you don't go to work for the next few days. You need to call your boss and tell him that."

I don't like this ultimatum. Relaying what Godmother said, I quickly add, "I can't do that. They need me, and I'm already on the schedule —"

Stopping me mid-sentence, Norma insists I stop fighting. "Serena, this is for your highest good. Didn't you say you would love you? Were those empty words to placate me, or were you being honest?"

Knowing I had been honest with her, I reply, "No, Norma, I was being honest. I'm choosing to love me, but this is hard."

"I never told you this was going to be easy. The choice to love yourself will take all the courage you have. Are you willing to do that, or do you want to run and continue the old game of fear?"

"No, I'm serious about loving myself, but I'm afraid."

"I'm right here, sweetie. Are you willing not to go to work for the next few days? Can you do that for you?"

"Yes …."

"Good, then I will call them for you," Norma states. "This has been a long day. Would you like to go upstairs and sleep for a while?"

Looking at my watch, I'm surprised to see how late it is. "I should probably go home now."

"I don't want you to drive. Will you trust me and not ask why? I'm doing this to take care of you. A lot has happened today, and I would prefer that Garret drive your car home tonight."

Wondering why she is making such a big deal about this, I shrug and let it go. I'm exhausted as we climb the stairs. Getting up on the massage table, I smile happily as Norma tucks the blankets in around me. I love it when she takes care of me this way.

"Now get some rest, and I will be up to get you in a bit." As the door closes behind her, my mind starts racing.

What's the big deal about driving home?

She's keeping something from you!

Maybe she thinks you're crazy!

Despite my fearful thoughts, my exhaustion takes over, and I fall into a deep sleep.

I wake to the sound of knocking, as Norma pokes her head around the door.

"Were you able to sleep?"

Nodding yes, I sit up, feeling groggy. "What time is it, Norma?"

"It's after dinner, and I know you must be hungry. Garret and I have already eaten. Come down when you're ready, and have something to eat."

What do I do? Garret is home, and he'll think I'm in the way! Making my way into the kitchen, I find Garret at the sink, putting the dishes into the dishwasher. Turning, he smiles at me.

Taking a seat at the table, I look around the room. *Everything looks different in this light.* Taking a bite of steak, I chew slowly. I feel odd.

Listening to the last bit of Norma and Garret's conversation, I realize Norma just asked me a question. I ask her to repeat what she said.

"When we drive you back to your house, I want you to get some clothes and other things that you will need to stay the night. Do you have a suitcase?"

"You want me to spend the night …here? Why, Norma? I thought I was going home after I ate."

"Did you tell me you would follow my guidance and allow me to make the decisions?" I can feel how adamant she is. I feel uncomfortable staying here, but—again, she interrupts my thoughts, telling me I need to stay here and pay attention to what she's asking.

"Do you have a suitcase to put some things in?"

"Yes, there's one ... someplace. It's a huge duffel bag thing ..." I absently reply.

"That's alright; we will use one of ours. Finish your dinner, and then we'll go to your house." Taking a seat at the table beside me, Norma exchanges a knowing glance with Garret before he leaves the kitchen.

"Serena, it's important that you have no plans. I need your full cooperation. Are you listening to me?"

Feeling uneasy, I nod without replying.

"I need you to stay where I can see you. This is not a game. I'm not saying this to scare you, but some things have come up in our work that need to be addressed. Are you following me so far?"

"Yes, I hear you, Norma."

"I have always been honest with you, haven't I?"

"Yes, but you're scaring me."

"I don't mean to, Serena. When we worked on the massage table today, some things became clear for Godmother and me. We've decided that in order to keep you safe, you will stay here with Garret and me."

"What are you talking about?"

"You're not safe. My job is to keep you safe as we do this work. Do you agree?"

What does she mean, "I'm not safe?"

"Serena! Don't go to your head, stay here with me and hear what I'm saying. Will you do that?"

Looking at her in complete bewilderment, I agree.

"Good. Garret will drive your car to the apartment, and you and I will go in and pack a few things. Then the three of us will come back here." Raising her voice, she adamantly adds, "You're not to go anywhere without me, do you understand?"

Feeling something from her that I've never felt before, I agree without further discussion. Trying to finish the last of my dinner, I can barely swallow due to the anxiety I'm feeling.

"Do you want to help yourself or hurt yourself? If you pump anxiety, you hurt yourself. If you trust me and know I only want what is best for you, then you can finish your dinner in peace. Choose Serena. Be here, and don't go to your head for understanding." Leaning in close, she holds me with her gaze, while watching to see what I will choose.

Inhaling deeply, I exhale slowly through my nose. Picking up my fork, I take a bite of steak and chew it; it tastes like sawdust. I should be excited that I get to stay with Norma, but instead of joy, I feel dread, which is strangling my intestines. Angry voices warn me to leave things alone. Ignoring them, I take another bite until my plate is clean.

*****

This marked the beginning of a momentous struggle between life and death for me. If it had not been for Norma and Garret's vigilance, combined with my Soul's determination to live, I would not be here today.

Chapter 12: KEEPING ME SAFE

I have been living with Norma and Garret since the first of January. Norma says I'm not safe to go back to my apartment. She doesn't trust me, so she monitors everything I do. I miss the freedom I had. The trouble is, I really don't know what happened to cause such a shift in my life. Yes, I switched at work, but I've switched so many times before. How is this any different?

Pulling on my robe, I make my way downstairs and into the kitchen.

Norma turns toward me and smiles. "Do you want some eggs for breakfast?" she asks.

"What? Oh, no. I don't want anything now. I have to talk to you, Norma. This is important."

"What's important is that you have something to eat," she calmly responds. "I can prepare eggs or something else, but I want you to eat something solid to start your day."

"I'll have scrambled eggs." Not willing to wait, I implore, "Norma, I know you said that you would tell me when I could go back to work, but it's been four days, and I need to call them, or I could lose my job. Are you hearing me?"

Pausing a moment before answering, she says, "I told you yesterday, and I will tell you today: you're not making the decisions. We will talk about your job later. I'm doing this to help you, Serena. Can you try to remember that, please?"

Glaring at her, I restrain myself before answering. "Yes, but can we at least talk about Petunia being alone all day? I'm worried about her, and I don't think you understand that."

"I understand you're worried about Petunia, and I'm not trying to upset you, but my primary responsibility is you. Petunia is safe, and all of her needs are being taken care of. She is a cat, and cats are used to being alone. If I thought Petunia was in any danger, I would do something about it. I'm asking you to trust me."

Feeling as though I'm existing in two realities at once, I rub my forehead in an attempt to get rid of the sensation. Dejectedly, I take a seat. What is the matter with me? I feel like I'm outside of myself, watching myself fight her at every turn. When I try to repress my anger, it wells up inside me, lashing out at her. It's as though I'm being controlled by someone or something else, and it's unstoppable. I know she loves me. I've never had anyone care for me as she has, but I can't stop fighting her. Engrossed in thought, I absently push the eggs around on my plate. Hearing Norma's voice, I look up expectantly.

"Serena, when you are through with your breakfast and have gotten dressed, then we will talk about your job. If you continue to fight me, it will only hurt you." With that pronouncement, she picks up her pen and begins writing. Knowing that she will not speak to me until I have gotten dressed, I quickly finish my eggs and clear my plate.

"Don't hurry, Serena," Norma calmly states. "It will not change the outcome of my decision."

Leaving the room, I race upstairs to get dressed. Breathing heavily, I'm consumed with fear.

You have to make her understand!

She can't tell you what to do!

Leave! She can't stop you.

Hurry! You have to find out what she will say!

Coming down the stairs a few minutes later, I find Norma sitting in the living room. Taking a seat next to her, I shakily inhale.

"Do you know that my job is to help you?" she kindly asks.

Nodding yes, I remain silent. I'm on pins and needles, anxious to hear what she's going to say, but at the same time, I feel this ominous dread descend upon me. I can barely breathe.

"Good. Then, when I tell you something you don't like, why am I doing that?"

Needing her to get to the point, I repress the scream that is building inside me. Modulating my voice, I carefully answer, "Because you want to help me."

"Yes. I want to keep you safe. Do you understand what I mean when I use the word 'safe'?"

Feeling impudent, I quell the temptation to say, "No, duh," but instead answer, "You feel I'm unsafe because some part of me wants to hurt me. Is that right?"

"Yes, and when you fight me, you feed the rage, making it stronger. Your denial of the rage is keeping you unsafe. Would you let yourself sense the gravity of this situation?" Knowing that she can't force me to face the truth, she waits to see what I will choose.

But I'm not interested in truth. I want what I want, period. "Yes, but Norma, you don't understand."

"No, Serena, it is *you* who does not understand. You obviously want one thing. You would like to pretend nothing has happened and go back to work today. Am I right?" Not waiting for me to answer, she continues. "I made a commitment to your Soul that I would help you integrate, and I don't take that lightly. With that said, I'm telling you that you will not be going back to work. It's not up for discussion. You will not be returning, period."

Staring at her, I'm dumbstruck. Is she kidding? "Why in the world can't I go back to work?" I angrily protest.

"I said it was not up for discussion. I know that I'm not just talking to you; there are others who are listening and know the reason for my decision. They can tell you if they want to, but I will not argue with you. I'll be calling your job today and letting them know. You have nothing to do with this.

"I have appointments with clients and will be on the phone most of the morning. I want you to stay where I can see you. If you need to leave my sight, even if I'm on the phone, you are to tell me where you are going and why. Do you understand me, Serena?"

"Norma, I don't understand. Why are you being so unreasonable?"

"I will not argue with you. Will you please get whatever it is you need before I begin my phone sessions?" Standing still, she waits until I comply.

Begrudgingly, I climb the stairs and gather my colored pencils and paper. In the hospital, the different personalities were taught to use art for self-expression, and to elevate distress so those who can't share are heard.

Returning to the couch, I look at the grandfather clock, and am surprised to see it is only a little after 9 a.m. How can that be? Why does it seem that time is standing still? I can't stand much more of this. Glancing over at Norma, I watch her talking to a client on the phone. I repress the urge to stick my tongue out at her, and instead turn on the TV.

Hoping to find something that will distract me, I quietly channel surf. When I find a movie that's exciting, I start watching it with the volume turned way down.

Within minutes, Norma's voice interrupts me. "That's not appropriate for you, Serena. Change the channel, please."

Her voice, it's so…bossy! I can't stand it! I mouth the words that I have to go to the bathroom. Norma nods, indicating that it's okay.

Walking down the hallway, my legs suddenly go out from under me, and I fall onto the carpet. My body takes on a life of its own. My knees pull up into my chest, as my chin pulls downward into my collarbone. My arms pull in against my ribs, encasing me in a death grip, squeezing me so tightly I can barely breathe. I can't blink; my eyes are frozen open. Terror is coursing through my entire body. I try to call out to Norma, but my mouth is clamped shut. It's like I am solid rock, and there's nothing I can do about it! Making mewing sounds from the back of my throat, I try to get Norma's attention. Lying there immobile, I feel like I will implode from the terror I'm feeling!

I told you to leave things alone, but you wouldn't listen.

You won't ever get rid of me.

Who do you think you are, trying to stop me?

I'll show you who's boss!

Finally, Norma comes to my aid. Bending down on the carpet beside me, she speaks with unwavering strength. "I'm here, Serena." Touching me, she calls loudly for everyone to begin breathing with her. "I know you can hear me. I'm right here. Choose to breathe, Serena. You're not frozen; this is a part of the government's training that you were subjected to."

Feeling her stroke my back and arm, I listen to the sound of her voice, while inhaling and exhaling as much as I can. My ribs are constricted so tightly that I can barely take a breath.

Chin Chin comes over and sniffs my head. "This is a part of the training you went through, Serena. Breathe with me." Over and over, she repeats the same thing in a loving, yet firm voice. Her strength, combined with her unwavering compassion, envelops me. I begin to feel warmth seep into my body. Slowly, the rigidity begins to wane, and my legs relax, allowing my airway to open. Little by little, my body becomes mine again.

Blinking my eyes, I turn my head toward Norma. Gratitude floods my entire being. "Oh, Norma ... thank you! I don't know what happened. One minute, I was going down the hall, and the next, I was on the floor, unable to move!"

"I know, Serena. I told you, you're not safe. They're showing you and me that they're in charge. Will you run or stay here, trusting that Godmother and I are leading you? You get to choose, Serena. This is why I'm as serious as I am."

Taking Norma's hand, I slowly stand. Wobbling back and forth, I grip Norma's hand even tighter, while angry voices urge me to run. *Why can't this nightmare just go away?* Holding hands, we make our way back to the couch.

I feel boxed in, with nowhere to go.

"Do you know what happened, Serena?"

"No!" I angrily shout.

"If you want to be upset, you won't have clarity. Is that what you want?"

Ignoring her question, I cry out. "Why does everything have to be so hard? I have worked with you for almost four years, and now I'm worse? This is not how it's supposed to be!"

"Then how should it be?"

"I should be getting better, but I'm getting worse! And now you're telling me I can't go back to work, and that I'm not safe! I'm afraid, Norma!

I just froze, and that hasn't happened since I was in the hospital. I want to put it all away!" Saying the last few words, I explode into hysterical sobs.

"Getting hysterical is not going to change a thing. Yes, you froze. Do you want to push that away? Be honest, Serena, because we can't move forward unless you're willing to be honest with yourself and me."

Struggling, because I don't want to admit it, I shout, "Yes, I want all of it to go away!" Angrily grabbing my forearms, I dig my nails into my skin.

"You're not allowed to hurt yourself!" Norma sternly insists. "Do you hear me?" Raising her voice, she demands, "Look at me and dare to be honest. The anger you're feeling has waited a long time for someone courageous enough to face it. Are you telling me that you want to quit?"

Tears run down my face unchecked. I feel anger roiling inside me, and I know I can't escape it.

"I want you to do everything you can to stay and hear these children. When you can begin to grasp the level of pain these children have endured, you might choose differently. Right now, all you want to do is run, but in running, you abandon these children, and then no one has a chance to heal, least of all you!"

Calling gently, Norma says, "I know you're angry. I'm here for you. Please, come and talk to me." No response. She calls again, insisting that someone come and talk to her.

Slowly, the head cocks, as the eyes narrow menacingly. "You aren't talking to anyone! Do you understand? I've had enough of your meddling," he warns. "They are mine to do with as I please; I'm the boss, not you!" With that pronouncement, the chin lifts in defiance.

Unwilling to respond to his challenge, Norma breathes, saying nothing. She intentionally fills the air between them with her compassionate breath. As the minutes tick by, his bravado gives way to discomfort. He begins to squirm uncomfortably as his true age becomes apparent. Lowering his eyes, he scratches and picks at his skin. Internally, Godmother has closed the door to prevent him from leaving the front of the body. As he picks and fidgets, the intensity of his emotions becomes too difficult for him to tolerate. Slowly, he lifts his head and looks at Norma.

"Would you talk with me now?" Norma kindly asks. Sensing that many eyes are watching, she waits.

Nodding yes, the child opens his mouth, but nothing comes out.

"I know you can hear me. I'm here to help you. I know the secrets. You're allowed to talk with me. Can you see the angel? She's here, and she works with Jesus. You know Jesus, don't you?"

Waiting for some indication that he has heard her, Norma watches the body visibly relax. Instantly, a switch, and the eyes become cold and lifeless. The voice growls with an unusual force. "I know what you're trying to do, and it won't work. I won't let you in." Crossing his arms over his chest, he looks away in disdain.

"I'm not here to fight you. I know the secrets. I know you were raised in a satanic cult and that the government trained you since you were a baby.

I've been given authority to speak to all that can hear me."

"I won't let you in."

"And who are you?"

"I am the gatekeeper, and I'm here to keep you out."

"I understand that. I'm here to talk to the one behind you. I know you can hear me, and I expect you to come and talk with me and not send out one of your flunkeys."

Norma sees something flicker in the eyes.

Uncrossing his arms, he stands, facing her defiantly. "I have been told that if you come any closer, we will die. I'm not bluffing. There are many fail-safe mechanisms that will be tripped if you keep pushing." As he says the last sentence, his demeanor wavers, indicating the push from behind him. "Please … leave it alone. You don't understand. If you keep pushing, *he* will come out, and then it will be over." Without another word, he sits and closes his eyes. The body is motionless. No one wants to come to the front.

Norma knows nothing can be accomplished from fear. We're at a dangerous crossroads; the years of training to keep the secrets at all costs mean the body is in imminent danger. Only through trusting Soul's guidance can true healing occur. Norma doesn't need an answer at this moment. Breathing quietly, she takes this time for herself. The last few days have been very difficult. As she breathes, her breath fills and revitalizes her. With it comes clarity, Soul to Soul.

"You are doing wonderfully. Continue to be the authority. That will force them to make their move," my Soul whispers to Norma. "Do nothing, and remain consistent. Serena is the doorway for those who want to come home."

Knowing that the time for talk has ended, Norma calls me back to the front. Rubbing my face, I try to focus, but I feel groggy. I don't know what to say. Silence sits between us. Squirming with discomfort, I finally ask Norma what happened.

Ignoring my question, she begins the conversation with a question of her own. "Have you noticed that you're fighting me at every turn?"

"No, I'm not! It's just weird that I can't do anything without your permission!"

"You just fought me. Please, would you notice that your need to fight me at every turn is a push from within. They're controlling you, because you refuse to face the truth that you're not safe!" Raising her voice, she continues, "They want to kill the body, Serena! You're a threat to them! Do you get that?"

Without hearing her plea, I shout, "But you don't understand, Norma!"

"No, it is you who does not understand," Norma wearily states.

Standing up, she moves back to her office. "Nothing has changed," she says. "You're to do nothing without my explicit permission. Do you hear me?" As she turns to face me, her demeanor is formidable. "I expect an answer, please."

"I heard you," I meekly reply, "but can I watch something on TV that is good?"

"What does 'good' mean, Serena?"

"You know, not boring."

"You can watch something that will help you. I know you understand what that means. You're not to watch anything that will cause you to pump adrenaline. We don't need any additional fear right now. This is a crucial time, and your refusal to help me means I can't trust you. I'll be listening to what you are watching, and if I deem it inappropriate, I will turn the TV off. Do you understand?"

Why is she being so hard? Wanting to punish her, I turn on the TV without comment. Finding a program that will pass her criteria isn't easy. I settle in, hoping the show will distract me. Unfortunately, it doesn't. I'm aware of Norma's every move. The minutes drag on, and with each second that passes, the grandfather clock's ticking gets louder.

Getting up, Norma comes and sits beside me. "Would you turn off the TV, so you and I can talk?"

Obeying her request, I turn to face her more fully. She looks more tired than usual. Pushing that awareness away, I wait for her to start.

"You weren't willing to be honest with either of us when we spoke earlier. Would you be willing to stop fighting and look at something with me?"

"Yes, Norma. I'm sorry, but I'm so uncomfortable …"

"Yes, you are. The need to fight me indicates how much you are being pushed from within. If I can't trust you to work with me, then we have a bigger problem than I thought. Would you be willing to close your eyes and breathe a moment? And as you breathe, sense how much I care for you. I'm only doing this to help you."

Closing my eyes, I intentionally breathe. I know she's right, but with every breath I take, the anger grows stronger. "I can't stay still! You don't understand. If I stay still, I might explode!" Beseeching her with everything I have, I shudder forcibly.

"Serena, do you know that people cannot explode?"

"Oh, yes, they do! You don't know," a young voice declares.

Ignoring the switch, Norma calmly responds, "No, humans do not explode. Have you ever seen a person explode?"

"Yes, lots of times," the child emphatically states, vigorously shaking her head up and down.

"Would you tell me about it?"

"Daddy would explode and even spit. His face would get …" Voice quavering with fear, she whispers, "… so ugly, and then he would lose it."

"And when he lost it, what happened?"

"The monster came out."

"Tell me about the monster."

The child anxiously looks around the room before continuing. "It was someone who was so much badder than Daddy. His whole body …" raising her arms, she encircles her body to indicate how big the change was, "would change and become a monster." As she utters the last few words, her eyes become glassy with remembrance.

"So, that's what it means to explode?"

Vigorously nodding her head, the child remains silent. Looking about the room, her agitation is clearly evident. "I sayed too much. I'm sorry," she whispers.

"Who are you saying sorry to?"

Leaning in, she whispers even more quietly, "The watchers."

"You're safe with me," Norma responds. "Can you see the angel?" Shaking her head no, the child furtively looks around the room.

"She's close to you, sweetie. Look inside, and you can see her. I will wait."

Breathing deeply, Norma intentionally fills the room with her compassionate energy. Seeing that the body has relaxed, she begins calling the children home. "All of you who hear me, and are afraid of the monster, can come to the angel. I know you can hear me. Come, sweet ones, she has come just for you. You no longer need to fear the monster. He's not allowed to hurt you anymore." Again, she repeats the invitation to anyone who is listening. "I'm here to help all of you who are afraid. No one," she says with authority, "is going to hurt you. The angel and I are here to keep you safe."

Twenty minutes pass in quiet stillness, allowing the body a brief respite from the destructive anger that has been present for days. Slowly, the body stirs. Sitting upright, I rub my face and forehead. It feels as though a hole has been opened inside my chest. Rubbing the ache, I attempt to connect with something. "What happened? I switched, didn't I?"

"Yes, you did, but that doesn't matter. It's been a difficult morning, and it's time to have some lunch. What do you think you might like to eat?"

Ambivalently shrugging my shoulders, I reply, "I don't really care, but before we eat, can we talk a moment?"

"Of course we can. What's up?"

"Norma, I know you care for me, and I'm not trying to be difficult, but I'm so uncomfortable. I thought by now I would be better. I moved to Carlsbad to be closer to you, so I could finish my integration, but now …"

"When you say 'finish your integration,' what does that mean?" Norma sincerely asks.

"I was almost done, and …"

Interrupting me, she asks, "Who told you that you were almost done?"

"Well, I thought that when I got the boys back, and I was switching so much less …"

"And did Godmother tell you we were almost done?"

"Well, no, but I thought— "

"Right, you thought. That is your mind. That's not where your answers come from. Your mind was trained, and it's not your friend. It's Godmother who wants what is best for you. So, take a moment, and ask Godmother if we're almost done."

"I don't hear anything, Norma."

"Are you willing to hear the truth? Be honest, Serena, because we won't get anywhere if you aren't willing to be honest with both of us."

"I just want this to be over!" Struggling to contain the anxiety that is building again, I purposely take a breath and close my eyes. Focusing on my breath, I decide to face the truth no matter what! Finally, I hear Godmother speaking to me.

"I'm proud of you, Serena. I know this is difficult. It's your bravery that has made the difference so far, but the work that we are doing is very dangerous, and I need you to face it without fighting. Are you willing to do that?"

I nod yes without replying. Godmother continues. As she speaks, I relay her words to Norma. "No, we're not close to done. Your mind wants to convince you of that, so that you will be impatient and continue to fight. As long as you fight, they win. They get your energy, which they desperately need to survive. When you stay in peace, their energy reserves become depleted. Do you understand?"

Opening my eyes, I look at Norma with confusion. "I don't understand what she meant. She said we're not done. That I get, but the rest …"

"Sense with me, Serena. Can you feel the energy of impatience? Is it peaceful?"

Knowing full well how impatience feels, I reply, "It's like a car that is always idling, waiting for someone to come along and gun the engine. It's like … come on, come on, come on! That's what impatience feels like."

"That's a perfect example. So, sense, if you're pumping impatience, what do you think it does to you?"

"I don't know," I irritably reply.

Ignoring my resistance, Norma continues. "It exhausts and drains the body. It makes you frustrated, and that serves anger perfectly. When you pump impatience, you're coming from judgment, which continues to feed the rage."

As she speaks, screams begin to build.

"It's a vicious cycle that you have been living your entire life," Norma states. "As we have been integrating these children, we are removing the anger's ability to keep you stuck in that cycle."

The volume of screams is getting louder. Squirming uncomfortably, I clench my jaw and try to listen only to her voice.

"So the idling engine feeds the anger, and that keeps it all going. Does that help you understand it better?"

I don't care if I understand any of it at this point, because the screaming has to stop. Hoping that it will be enough to end our conversation, I smile faintly and nod.

Compassionately, Norma smiles and takes my hand, pulling me to my feet. She isn't fooled by my silence, but she knows when to quit.

Instantly, the screaming stops.

Following Norma into the kitchen, I sit at the table and watch her make our lunch. I love her so much. She never gets angry with me. Even though I'm with her twenty-four hours a day, she's always the same. She doesn't have highs and lows. She doesn't react, no matter what I do or say.

I trust her implicitly, so why am I fighting her so much? It doesn't make any sense. Heaving a tortured sigh, I'm startled when Norma sets my sandwich in front of me. Looking up, I notice how tired she looks. Knowing that her tiredness is my fault makes me feel guilty. Pushing the awareness away, I pick up my sandwich and take a bite. I chew slowly. It is tasteless. I feel so off. What is the matter with me? Stifling a sob, I force myself to take another bite. Rapidly blinking, I try to repress the emotions surging up inside me.

"What's wrong, Serena?" Norma asks in genuine concern.

"Right, Norma. What's wrong with me?" Fighting the temptation to give in to the anguish, I take a labored breath. I hope Norma has an answer for me.

"Are you willing to hear the truth? You're the only one denying what's going on," Norma states.

"Yes, I'm willing to hear what is wrong," I wearily answer.

"You and I have done a lot of work over these past four years, and in that time, we have brought a lot of children home, haven't we?" Not needing an answer, she continues. "Those children were layers in our journey. Look at your sandwich; it has layers of bread, meat, lettuce, pickles, tomato, and mayonnaise, doesn't it? Your memories are layered, just like your sandwich. We have come to a layer that holds a lot of pain, and that pain is expressed through anger. These children hold anger, and it must come up, or you won't heal.

These children were trained by both the government and the cult. They see you as a threat and want to kill you. They do not know you all share the same body. They see you as someone outside of them. Do you understand what I'm saying?"

"So the anger and pain I'm feeling are theirs?"

"Yes, and our commitment to not leave any child behind means that we're willing to bring these children home as well. Can you try to remember that the pain is theirs and not yours?" Stopping briefly, she smiles at me before continuing. "When you go along with their emotions, you keep them from coming home to Godmother. Sharing your feelings with me helps keep you clear so you can help them. I know this is hard." Leaning in, she wraps her arms around me.

Surrendering to her love, I sob with an intensity that shocks even me. Hiccupping with the release, I reply, "Oh, Norma, I'm so tired. I don't know if I can do this."

"You're not alone. Godmother and I are right here with you. Remember that, will you? After you finish your lunch, you might want to take a nap."

*****

Coming down the stairs a few hours later, I find Norma and Garret sitting on the couch. Before I can retreat back into my room, Norma calls me. "Come sit with us before I go and fix dinner. I checked on you a couple of times, but you were sleeping so deeply, I let you rest."

Reluctantly, I sit in one of the upholstered chairs across from them. I feel like I'm intruding. Nervously fidgeting, I watch as Norma and Garret resume their conversation. Chin Chin is nestled in Norma's arms. She strokes his head as they talk.

Scrutinizing Norma and Garret for any signs of distress, I'm confused. *How can they be so relaxed with each other?*

Sitting down at the dinner table an hour later, I remain quiet while Garret and Norma talk. With my head down, I eat as quickly as possible, so I can retreat back to my room.

"You're not helping yourself by rushing through dinner," says Norma. "Are you listening to your head or to Godmother for guidance?"

How can they eat so calmly and act like nothing is going on? Fighting the urge to run, I look at the grandfather clock and am surprised to see it's only 7 p.m. What in the world am I going to do for the next three hours?

Fidgeting uncomfortably, I wait for permission to leave the table.

"I want you to go and soak in the tub for a bit. See if you can breathe and come deeper into your body; it will help you sleep better. Don't lock the bathroom door. I'll be up to check on you in a bit. Do you understand?"

Feeling ashamed, I nod sheepishly.

You are such a bother!

It would be easier for everyone if you gave up now.

She will end up hating you.

You are a mental case and belong in a hospital.

Fully clothed, I sit on the edge of the tub and turn on the water.

Watching it surge from the faucet, I focus on the water's movement and its sound. As I continue to watch, I lose myself in the experience, which allows me to leave my body. This is hypnosis, and I'm an expert at it.

Rage moves into the front of the body. Leaving the bathroom, the body teeters at the top of the stairs. Standing at the edge, the rage is ready to throw the body down the stairs, but Godmother holds it from within. As an anchor tethers a ship from going aground, she restrains us while silently calling Norma. Seconds pass, the feet inch closer to the edge, but the anchor holds firm.

Norma rounds the corner and sees the body teetering on the edge. Running up the stairs, she yells for Garret. Pulling the body backwards, she holds it tight.

Ascending the stairs two at a time, Garret grabs the other arm, and they move the body into the bedroom.

"I'm alright," Norma firmly states. "I'll call you if I need you." Pulling the door shut, Garret descends the stairs to wait.

Taking the hand, Norma leads the body to the bed. Pushing the shoulders down, she maneuvers the body to sit and face her. Stroking the face, Norma begins calling me. Rubbing the arms and legs, Norma insists I come back to the front. "I know you can hear me, Serena. Do you really want to give up and leave your boys? Are you going to let them win and destroy all that we've accomplished?"

Slowly, the eyes resume blinking, and the breath becomes deeper. The face begins to twitch, indicating someone is moving back into the front of the body.

I'm surprised to see Norma in the bedroom with me. Everything is blank. I have no awareness of what has happened. "Why am I in the bedroom? I still have my clothes on. Didn't I take a bath?" Not waiting for an answer, I cry, "Something bad happened, didn't it? I can feel it." Rubbing my face, I begin rocking back and forth. I feel trapped. *Oh, how I wish this would all go away!*

"You get to choose, Serena. Will you run with fear or stay and find out what really happened? Your denial of what is happening to you is making this more difficult than it really has to be. Do you hear me?" Leaning in toward me, she raises her voice. "Would you face the truth? Parts of you want you dead. Do you hear me?" Staring at me, she watches to see if I might let the truth in. Nodding glumly, I reply, "Yes, I know parts of me want me dead."

"Then let yourself feel it! Don't push it away."

Feeling trapped, with nowhere to go, I honestly begin to breathe. Finally, I'm able to hear what happened.

"You were at the top of the stairs, ready to throw yourself down them. Do you sense the enormity of what I just said?"

Closing my eyes, I sense and feel an abyss of pain envelop me. "Norma, I hurt so bad that I can't describe it to you."

"I know, Serena. It does us no good when I'm the only one who knows the truth. This is what the anger's job is all about: keeping this pain walled off at any cost. You see your anger as bad, but it's what kept you alive. It's a tool and nothing more. When you judge it as bad, you keep it stuck. This anger, segregated off into children, is nothing more than memory. Can you try to remember that?"

"I hear you, Norma, but it's so much more ... than anything I ever thought it was."

"Yes. Your need to deny how bad your life was, has kept you stuck. It keeps children locked in the dark. They can never trust you if your primary goal is to push it all away. You can help yourself only when you are willing to be honest. I want you to get into the tub and breathe. I will be right here waiting for you. Do not rush. This is about helping you, isn't it?" Looking at me, she waits for my response.

Sighing, I follow her into the bathroom. Letting the cold water out of the tub, I intentionally keep my back to her. As the tub refills with warm water, I watch Norma remove scissors, a razor, and other assorted implements she deems dangerous. Feeling ashamed but not giving in, I take a breath. *She is doing this to help me.* Focusing with that awareness, I inhale with determination. Getting into the tub, I gingerly sit down.

Without a word, Norma leaves the bathroom. "I'm proud of you, Serena," Godmother says.

"How in the world can you say that?"

"You continue to show up, no matter how hard this is. I know you want to run, but you keep breathing. That's what is making the difference. I'm here, dear one."

Choking with emotion, I lay back against the bath pillow to breathe. As I inhale, I shudder. As I exhale, I sob. Determined to keep breathing, I keep my eyes focused on the up-and-down movement of my belly. I know if I keep breathing this way, I will feel better.

"Serena, will you let these children come home?" Godmother asks.

"Oh, yes … I'm tired of pushing them away."

"Keep breathing, and stay here. Don't go into the story, but watch so you can help them." As Godmother speaks, I feel her strength embolden me.

As the memory takes shape, I watch Jennifer pull out the dresser drawers, making steps to climb on. She's relentless. Not quite three years old yet, she wobbles and almost falls, but she doesn't give up. Teetering on the edge of the third drawer, she pulls the top drawer open and retrieves a white envelope. Instantly, I know what it is. It's the drug Jennifer's father used to make people unconscious at cult meetings. Jennifer has seen its effects and wants the relief it can give.

Shuddering with the emotions of this memory, I hear Godmother lovingly say, "I'm here, Serena. I stopped Jennifer before she took the drug. I wrapped her in a cocoon of love and put her to sleep. It's through your courage that this child is being freed today. Breathe with me, so I can take her home."

Within moments, another memory surfaces. Jennifer is four. She is alone in the backyard, kneeling by the clothesline. Sobbing, she carves at her arm with a kitchen knife. She desperately wants to die! Her cries come in hysterical waves. Her pain and loneliness defy description. Memory after memory surfaces. I keep breathing, knowing I'm partnering with Godmother, to let these children finally come home to her.

Startled by a knock on the door, I hear Norma asking to come in.

Scrambling upright, I pull my legs up against my chest before answering yes.

"Are you ready to get out? You've been in the tub for almost an hour."

"I'm sorry, Norma. I didn't realize how long it had been."

"There's no need to be sorry, but I want you to get dressed so we can go downstairs. I'll wait for you outside."

Standing too quickly, I grab the side of the wall to stop myself from falling. Feeling unusually shaky, I carefully dry myself off and pull on my nightgown. Leaving the bathroom, I find Norma sitting on my bed.

"I kept seeing Jennifer at different ages when she tried to kill herself. It was awful."

"I know it's hard, but those children were sharing their pain with you. What did you do?"

"I breathed and cried, while inviting them to go to Godmother. Then you knocked on the door."

"I'm proud of you. Your willingness not to fight the pain will allow it to come home much more easily. For now, let's give it to Godmother so you can have a snack and a quiet hour before going to bed. Can you do that?"

"Yes, but I'm not hungry."

"I understand that, but you didn't eat very much at dinner, and it would help you sleep better if you had something to eat. Let's have a snack, shall we?"

Following her downstairs, I pull a chair up to the table.

Cutting up an apple and slices of cheese, Norma brings them to me on a plate with cookies and milk.

Taking a cookie, I chew it slowly. It's tasteless, but I sense my body is hungry. Picking up a piece of cheese and a slice of apple, I eat them together. After a few minutes, I begin to feel more grounded. "I don't think I want to eat anymore. Is that okay, Norma?"

"Yes, you have eaten enough to help you. Let's go watch some TV before bed. If you're afraid or you need anything in the night, you're to come and get me, do you understand?"

"Oh, I couldn't do that!"

"Will you help you or hurt you? This is no game, Serena. They want you dead. Their job is to keep the pain suppressed, and they will do whatever it takes to stop you, even if it means killing the body. So … are you as committed as they are?"

Realizing how serious she is forces me to face the fact that they really want me dead. Reluctantly, I agree to wake Norma if needed.

*****

Lying in the dark, I can barely breathe. Pressure is squeezing my heart, causing stabs of pain to radiate down my left arm. Turning onto my back, I try to alleviate some of the discomfort I'm in. Panicked, I sit up. What was that? It felt like hands touching me! Jumping out of bed, I turn on the light. Looking around the room, I find no one. Am I going crazy? Keeping the light on, I crawl back into bed. What do I do? Biting my fist, I suppress the urge to scream.

Norma pushes the door open, asking, "Why do you have the light on, Serena?"

"Oh, Norma, you came! I couldn't breathe, and then I felt hands all over me …"

Coming into the room, she sits down beside me. "I'm here, sweetie. Why didn't you call me?"

"Because I had just gotten into bed and …"

"Notice the story your mind told you. I told you to call me regardless, and I meant it." Taking my face in her hand, she moves in so close that our noses are almost touching. I can see the gold flecks in her brown eyes. "I'm committed to your healing, which means no matter what. You are worth it to me. Do you hear me?"

I shudder with the emotions I am feeling. Unable to speak, I nod.

"Would you let me talk to the child who was feeling the hands on her? Try and stay, will you?"

Instantly, the child appears, crying out, "They won't let me go!" She climbs over Norma to escape.

"You're not with them anymore!" Norma loudly states. "Look around you, you're not there now." Taking the child's arm, Norma strokes her back.

Startled, the child stops fighting and notices Norma for the first time. Looking down, she sees the pink nightgown she's dressed in. "What happened? I was naked …"

"The angel came and took you away from them. She brought you to me, so I could help you. Can you remember what was happening before the angel came?"

Picking at the cloth of her nightgown, the child is obviously confused. "I was in the chair … you know, the one with the straps. They were putting the electric things on me." Trembling, she scoots farther back on the bed. "Do you work with them?" she fearfully asks.

"No, I work with the angel and Jesus. Do you know Jesus?"

Instantly, a smile replaces her wariness. "Yes, I know him," she says, sighing fondly. "He's wonderful. You work with him?"

"Yes, I work with him and the angel. She's close by. Can you see her?" Waiting for an indication that the child sees Godmother, Norma waits.

"I see her! She's beautiful." Turning toward Norma, she asks, "She came for me?"

"Yes, sweetie. Would you like to tell us what was happening to you?"

"They were putting those wire things on me that make my skin scream."

"And why do they do that?"

"They like to hurt me. They keep telling me I know what they want, but I don't!" she angrily protests.

"Would you tell me more of what happened, so I can help you?"

The child nods, and her face takes on a faraway look. "It hurts, like burning. They don't care how much I scream." Looking down at her arm, she absently rubs it. "They strap down my arms, my legs, my wrists, and even my head. I can't move anything! I get so scared!" As she says the last few words, her voice escalates in panic.

"Look at me. I'm here now. They will never hurt you again, but before we go any further, will you tell me your name?"

"Oh, I'm Lily."

Smiling warmly, Norma continues, "I'm glad to meet you, Lily. Now, can you tell me what happened after they put the straps on?"

Crying with terror, Lily vividly recounts, "I was so afraid. They put the electric things all over me, even on my head! Then they turned it on. I screamed. It felt like I was dying."

Instantly, the body leans forward, and another voice growls, "I know what you're trying to do, and you won't win." Smiling cruelly, he is gone.

Leaning back, Lily cries out, "My skin, my skin, it burns so bad, but they keep telling me that I know what they want, and if I don't give it to them, they will never stop!" Sobbing uncontrollably, she grabs her head in pain.

"I can't stand it! Do you understand?"

Taking Lily in her arms, Norma rocks her, as the child wails in anguish. "It's alright now. I'm here. No one will ever hurt you again. Do you hear me?"

Rocking her gently, Norma murmurs, "I'm inviting the angel to come and take you with her. Then you can be free and have no more pain. Would you like that?"

Hearing Lily mumble yes, Norma calls Godmother to take Lily home. "You can go with her, Lily." As the moments tick by, the body relaxes.

"Serena, come back to the front now. You are needed now." Watching the body sit upright, Norma asks, "Were you able to hear what Lily said?"

"I'm sorry, Norma. I tried, but one moment I was hearing her say that they wouldn't let her go, and then I was here again. I really didn't mean to leave."

"It's perfect, Serena. Can you trust that you weren't supposed to hear any more than that, and let it go?

"Can I ask you something before you leave?"

"Of course you can, sweetie."

"Do you think it's true?"

"Is what true, Serena?"

"You know … the government thing. I really think it might be a lie."

"And why do you want it not to be true?"

"That's not what I said. I asked if you think it's true."

"I understand what you asked, and I'm asking you why you insist on believing it's not true?"

Feeling as though the tables have been turned on me, I look at Norma in total confusion.

"You're choosing not to get what I'm saying. You insist that the government's memories are lies. Have you ever wondered why you don't believe them, no matter how many we uncover?"

Knowing that she won't let this rest until I have an answer, I shrug my shoulders and reply, "I really don't know, Norma."

"You do know, Serena. If you would be willing, you could discover why this always comes up. The words 'It's a lie' are a common theme for us, would you agree?"

Knowing that is true, I easily answer yes.

"Then let yourself sense: where do the words 'It's a lie' come from?"

Breathing deeply, I begin to drift and let my intuition guide me.

"Norma, I see two men leaning in, only inches from Jennifer's face. They are wearing white lab coats, and behind them are five men in uniform. They are laughing at her. She seems to be the butt of their joke. One of the men dressed in a white lab coat is saying, "Watch. We can make her believe anything.""

"Before you go any further, how old does Jennifer seem to be?"

"She is twelve years old." Continuing where I left off, I add, "The man turns back to Jennifer and whispers, 'You know it's a lie, don't you?' Jennifer is nodding really slow ... oh, she's in a trance, Norma!"

"You're doing wonderfully, Serena, but I want you to go back to where this memory started. In that way, we will have greater clarity."

Closing my eyes, I inhale slowly. I feel afraid, but I know I must do this. Within moments, I begin seeing the memory from its beginnings. "Jennifer is fighting them. There are at least five men in a brightly lit, huge room. Lois is there ... in the background, watching. Jennifer screams for her mother, but Lois does nothing." Stopping, I gather myself before speaking again. "Jennifer struggles to escape. They hold her down and take off her clothes before strapping her into a chair. One man, who is wearing a white lab coat, instructs the others on what they are to do. They put a needle into Jennifer's arm. It's attached to one of those poles used in surgery. You know ... the IV thing?"

"I know what you're talking about. Don't get distracted. Notice: what are they doing now?"

"They are strapping her into the chair. There is a pole coming out from the back of the chair. They tie her head to it so that she can't move. She's so angry. She's screaming that she will get them all. Oh, Norma, they're laughing at her." Grabbing my middle, I take another deep breath. Mustering my courage, since I know I must see this through to the end, I continue. "They attach the electrodes to her skin and on her head." Rocking back and forth, I try to keep my agitation at bay.

"Serena, you cannot help this child or yourself if you go into the memory. Your job is to relay what you see. Can you do that, please?"

"Okay, Norma, but this is bad," I anxiously squeal.

"Yes, it is; you're the one who pushes that truth away. Now notice, what happens next?"

Nodding, I gulp for air before proceeding. "They begin by turning on the machine."

"Can you see the machine, Serena?"

Nodding, I don't reply; I'm lost in what I'm seeing.

"Serena, I want you to describe the machine to me."

"It's over there." Pointing my finger at the box that is in the corner of the huge room of my memory, I expect Norma to see it too.

"It's a long, flat, silver box with holes in it. The five holes have multiple wires coming from them. It looks like a stereo of some sort …"

"Alright. Then what happens?"

"They turn it on. They have given Jennifer medicine, so she is out of it. Then, when the electricity is turned on, she screams in pain. That's when one of the men says, 'It's a lie. Nothing is really happening … just go away. You can do that, you know.' Oh, Norma, they do it over and over again, to different parts of the body, including her head. They electrocute her, causing intense pain and burning, and when they turn on the drip, they say, 'You can go away. It is all a lie.' Oh, the pain is so bad!"

"Serena, stay here! Look at me. Come back into this room. Rub your legs and breathe a moment. Do you see me?"

Breathing quickly, I rub my forehead, trying to be present, but I feel as though I'm a million miles away. "I feel weird, Norma."

"Then breathe slowly and deeply, Serena. This is when you get to choose. Who will win, the hypnotic suggestion or you? Is it stronger than you and Godmother?"

Breathing with purpose, I feel myself slowly come back into the room. "Okay … I'm here now, Norma."

"Good. Notice how much power your choice has. The hypnosis is never stronger than you and Godmother. So, what did you learn from this?"

"That the words 'This is a lie' are part of the government stuff."

"Yes, it is part of the training. Can you begin to recognize that thought and breathe it home? It would really help in our work. It was created for one reason: keep the secrets at all costs. All of the training the government did to you was to be forgotten. They were intent on controlling you, and if you had no memory of what happened, or if you began to remember things but pushed them away, telling yourself it was a lie, then their work remained secret. I'm hoping this will help us in our work, so you won't be so quick to deny the truth. Will you let this help you?"

"Yes, but it's bad, Norma!"

"I know, Serena. You don't have to convince me. I've been here the whole time. The brutality you lived through is beyond what most humans can even imagine. But it's you who keeps denying the truth." Leaning over, she pats my arm. "I'm proud of you. You were willing to stay with it despite how uncomfortable it made you. So let's breathe together, so you can get some rest. Remember, if you need me in the middle of the night for anything," she stresses, "then you are to come and wake me. Will you do that?"

"I will, but I'm scared of this thing living inside of me."

"Trust Godmother. She has kept you alive all these years, and she is here now. Remember, the three of us are a team. Now lie back so we can breathe together."

After ten minutes or so of breathing, I'm ready for sleep. I feel safe being here with Norma, and I know I can wake her and she won't be mad at me.

"Remember, if you need me for anything, just come downstairs and get me." She says, closing the door behind her.

*****

The next three days pass in a fog. Norma tells me we are doing great work. I'm glad, because I feel stifled. The regimen remains; I can't do anything without her permission. She is so strict that she won't even let me go out in the backyard to play with Chin Chin. The only time I can go into the kitchen is when she accompanies me. I know she has gone throughout the house, removing objects that I could use to hurt myself.

I'm losing large chunks of time every day. I know others are coming to the front because I have seen the pictures they have drawn. There are pictures drawn in red and black crayon, of things I don't want to remember.

There are other pencil drawings, depicting "rock people." Norma says these people were created because they can't be hurt. The drawings are so literal: small, round boulders attach to one another to form a living person. Do we really believe this?

I have had to wake up Norma every night for help. Last night, I felt I was going to hurt myself again. I called and called for her, since I was afraid to get out of bed and risk going downstairs. This nightmare is ongoing, twenty-four hours a day, seven days a week. It seems to be one perpetual trauma after another. My body hurts most of the time. I have intense headaches, and I'm tired beyond belief.

I wonder if Norma is as tired as I am. I don't know how she can keep this up, since she hasn't left the house for days. I have asked her when she thinks this might end, but she refuses to answer me. Instead, she asks me if I think I'm worth it.

I have never felt such overwhelming sadness. I thought I had been depressed before, but that was nothing compared to this. The depression is so thick, I actually feel smothered by it. Nothing seems to fix this unbearable experience, but Norma keeps inviting me to breathe and celebrate that it is finally coming home for healing. If it weren't for her unwavering confidence that we can accomplish this healing, I would have given up days ago. I watch her all the time. No matter what comes up, she responds calmly. She does not do big emotions. If she doesn't have an immediate answer, she breathes. She has been unflappable, even when I have screamed at her. It's only through her compassionate strength that I have not given in to my despair.

Chapter 13: SUCCESS

How can I face another day of this pain? What if Norma's wrong, and it never stops? Pulling myself out of bed, I wearily descend the stairs. Entering the kitchen, I take a seat at the table. Lying my head on my forearm, I close my eyes. Feeling a tap on my shoulder, I look up to see Norma gesturing at me. She doesn't want to interrupt her client, whom she is speaking to on the phone, so through facial expressions and pantomime, she encourages me to sit up and breathe.

Following her suggestion, I exhale slowly and notice the depression seems a bit lighter. As I inhale again, I actually feel better. Why do I have to be reminded to do this? It always helps, but I forget it so easily.

Motioning to her that I'm going to get dressed, I make my way upstairs. Pulling on my usual attire of sweatpants and a shirt, I go into the bathroom to brush my teeth. Peering at my reflection in the mirror, I notice the eyes looking back at me are lifeless. They belong to someone else, whom I don't recognize. Taking a breath, I square my shoulders and shout loudly that I choose to live! But it doesn't work; the anguish is growing stronger. Drying my face off on my sleeve, I race downstairs. Norma is still on the phone. Motioning frantically, I let her know I'm in trouble.

Nodding calmly, she covers the mouthpiece and whispers, "Go into the living room, and I'll be right there."

Within minutes, Norma is settled beside me on the couch. "I'm here, Serena. What's going on?"

"Something's wrong! I can barely breathe; the pain is so bad!" Finishing the sentence with a scream, I hysterically grab my middle.

"Being afraid helps no one, especially the children who are here to share. Will you step back and let me help them?"

Instantly, the body is up and running for the door. Screaming, the child is incoherent. Norma grabs her around the waist, calling, "I'm here, I'm here! Don't run, the bad men are gone. Can you hear me?"

Trembling, the child gulps for air. "Please, not again. I'll do anything you want, but please—don't take me there again!" Screaming and crying, the child struggles against Norma.

"They're gone," Norma loudly states. "I know how brave you are, so open your eyes and look around you. The men are gone. You're in my house." Slowly, the child relaxes against Norma.

Releasing her grip on the girl, Norma takes her by the hand and leads her back to the couch. Offering her a sip of water, she allows the child to collect herself.

Lifting her head, the girl looks at Norma.

"I'm Norma, and I work with the angel. She's standing right next to you. Can you see her?"

Seeing the angel illuminated in a most beautiful light, the child asks, "She came to help me?"

"Yes, she did. She knew you were being hurt, so she brought you to me, so I could help you. What's your name?"

"I'm Jennifer."

"And how old are you, Jennifer?"

"I'm five." Looking around the room, she anxiously asks, "Where's my mommy?"

"Your mommy isn't here, but she's fine. Do you like your mommy?" Shrugging her shoulders, the child appears ambivalent.

It's okay if you don't like her. Do you know that?"

"I don't like her at all!" Jennifer angrily declares.

"I understand. I've heard of the things she's done, and they were very cruel. Would you like to tell me about her?"

Nodding, the child hesitates and then explodes with anger. "She takes me to that place and makes me go inside. She doesn't talk to me; she just drags me in through the front door!" Wailing, Jennifer digs her fingernails into her forearms.

"How does that make you feel?"

"I get mad!" Dashing the tears off her cheeks, she angrily shouts, "She says she loves me, but she's a liar! I know! I was there!"

"Where, sweetie?"

"In the room with the man with the papers. He told Mommy and Daddy that I could die if they do more experiments on me. They just sat there, smiling, saying nothing! Then he gave them a paper and a pen, and he told them that they needed to sign it so that if I died, it would be okay. I didn't understand what he was saying, but the man told Mommy and Daddy two times that I could die! They didn't even care!" Falling into Norma's arms, Jennifer sobs uncontrollably.

Gently rocking her back and forth, Norma waits for Jennifer's sobs to cease. Suddenly, the body becomes rigid. Abruptly pulling out of Norma's arms, another child shouts, "I know what you're trying to do, and you won't win! Do you hear me?" Jumping to his feet, he glowers at her. "Don't come any closer." Chest heaving with terror, fists curled, he's ready to strike. Godmother is holding the body so he won't hurt Norma. Minutes pass as Norma quietly watches the body, before it slumps to the carpet unconscious.

Kneeling down next to the body, Norma calls my name. Touching my shoulder, she calls my name again, insisting I come to the front.

As I move back into the front of the body, I cry, "Oh, Norma, I hurt. What's wrong? How did I get on the floor?"

"Come sit with me." Extending her hand, she helps me to stand up. "Breathe and consciously choose to come deeper into your belly. What matters now is that you help yourself. We're awakening children that have been asleep for over forty years, and it's being done as gently as possible." With her hand on my back, she guides me back to the couch.

"Oh wow, oh wow, something's really wrong! I feel as though I'm unraveling inside! Oh my God … I'm falling apart! I feel so out of control! I'm in trouble, Norma, I can feel it. Do you hear me?"

"Look at me," Norma calmly insists. "You're feeling memory. Look around you. Is there anything wrong at this moment? You have a roof over your head; you are safe. Godmother and I are protecting you. Will you decide to trust your Soul, no matter how messy it gets?"

Feeling her strength wash over me, I inhale slowly. I'm determined to breathe. Inhaling again, my breath catches in my throat as a wall of anguish almost swallows me alive. Exhaling and inhaling, I breathe through my nose as best I can. I focus on nothing else; it's the only thing I will allow in this moment. Slowly, the terror begins to lessen. Sitting back against the cushions, I take a sip of water. "This is much worse than anything I ever could have imagined!"

"I know, Serena. Few people will ever know the level of horror you lived through, but between Godmother, you, and me, we can do this. Can you stay here in this moment and trust?"

Nodding, I look around the room. I study it, deliberately bringing my full awareness into this moment.

"I want you to go and take a bath. Just soak and breathe, Serena. We have already done intense work today, and it does no good to push it. I want you to rest."

"Okay ..."

"If you need me, just call, and I will come. Can you do that?" Agreeing, I climb the stairs. *I wish I could be anyone but me. Why am I such a mental case? No one can be this disturbed and not be weak in some way.* I'm unaware that I'm spiraling into a dangerous place again. Stepping into the tub, I suddenly feel faint. Grabbing hold of the soap dish, I try to take a breath, but I can barely inhale. *What's wrong now?* Trembling with a fear that seems to have come out of nowhere, I stare at the pink-tiled wall in front of me. Fixated, I feel my breathing slow, which allows me to slip into hypnosis. As I watch, an internal door opens before me. Inside is sweet darkness, beckoning me forward. Startled, I hear my voice calling Norma.

Within moments, she is there.

Speaking emphatically, Godmother states, "She's not safe to be left alone, not even to bathe. Things are escalating."

Norma takes my hand and guides me into a sitting position. Handing me a washcloth to cover my chest, she adjusts the water temperature while reassuring me. "I'm here, Serena. I'm not going anywhere. Breathe ... that's it. Choose to be here no matter what! Come deeper into your body."

Listening to her voice resonate with strength reassures me. Inhaling and exhaling, I choose to fully be here. Finally, I begin to feel like my old self again. "I'm better now. I'll dry myself off and be down in a few minutes."

"No, I cannot leave you alone right now. I'll turn my back so you can dry yourself off, but I'm staying right here."

Sensing how serious she is, I don't argue. Descending the stairs a few minutes later, we both settle on the couch. "Did you hear Godmother say that you aren't safe? She said things are escalating, and you cannot be left alone."

"No."

"Well, I heard it, and I take it seriously. It has already been a full day, and I have some work to do. You are to stay on the couch watching television. I'll be at my desk, so I can see you at all times. Please work with me by letting me know when you're feeling upset in any way. Can you do that?"

"Of course I will." Picking up the remote, I turn on the TV. Turning toward the sound of the opening door, I watch Garret walk in. Going over to where Norma is sitting, he bends down and kisses the top of her head. She tenderly touches his cheek as they smile and make eye contact. There is something in the way they interact that comforts me.

Getting up from the desk, Norma turns to me and says, "I'm going into the kitchen to start dinner. You're to stay there. If you need to move off the couch for any reason, call me first. Do you understand?"

"Yes ... what are we having for dinner?" I absently inquire.

"I haven't decided, but your business is to stay aware. Listen and call me if you begin to feel anxious about anything."

Norma and Garret walk into the kitchen. *I know they're talking about me. What are they saying?* Feeling anxious, I turn the volume down, but I can't hear anything. Turning the volume back up, I find a show that will distract me long enough to ease some of my anxiety. Within minutes, I'm numb.

Startled by the sound of Norma's voice, I quickly turn the TV off, but it's too late. She knows I was watching a stimulating program. She looks at me for a long moment before speaking. "We'll be eating dinner in a bit. I want you to think about something before we eat. You said you wanted to be a part of the solution, but you're not. I don't trust you. Feel what I'm saying, and realize that you're the only one creating this."

I'm stunned. She's never been disappointed in me before. Following her into the kitchen, I try to defend myself, but before I have a chance to speak, she stops me by saying, "I will not discuss it with you. I spoke the truth. Now you can deal with it."

Watching her stir something in the pan, I wait, hoping she might say something more. Feeling guilty, I return to the living room.

You've blown it now!

She's done with you.

You were always bad, and now she knows it, too!

Bands of pain ripple across my shoulders and up my neck into my head. *What will I do if she is done working with me? I'll promise her never to do it again!*

You can't promise that. You know you aren't trustworthy!

You're a mental case, remember?

Why don't you die?

We hate you!

Racing into the kitchen, I shout, "Norma, I was wrong! Please, don't stop working with me. I'll do whatever you say!"

"Who said I was going to stop working with you?"

"Well, I ..."

"Right, you were listening to your mind again. You don't get it, do you? Your mind was trained by the government and the cult; it's not your friend! I'm your friend, Serena. I'm here, committed to your integration, but are *you*? Really ask yourself: do you want to integrate or just find an easy way out? Now go sit, and I will serve dinner."

Norma's strength, coupled with Kuan Yin's guidance, is purposely drawing my rage out of hiding. As long as it stays hidden, it remains deadly. The push to keep talking is how the rage controls me. Norma knows this and is not interested in playing the game. As the internal anxiety builds with no external outlet, the rage will have to reveal itself.

*****

After dinner, Norma hands me paper and a pen. "I want you to make a list of the movies you would like to see, so that Garret can get them at the video store. I need to know that what you're watching will help you. Can you do that?" she kindly asks.

Nodding sheepishly, I try to come up with a list of movies that will interest me. I can only think of two that I would like to see.

"Can I see your list?"

Handing her the paper, I watch as she scratches off one of my two choices. Taking the paper to Garret, she asks him to get children's movies and a few animal documentaries for me to watch.

Sitting down on the couch next to me, she turns on the television. Norma knows that sitting next to me will comfort the internal children and help them feel safe. The rage is doing whatever it can to manipulate her by speaking through me, trying to thwart her at every turn. She remains silent from compassionate wisdom.

"Norma, you need to understand," I urgently implore.

"Serena," she calmly states, "I know that I'm not talking to you. There are many who want to hurt you, and I won't be a party to that. I'm not mad at you. I know that you can't be trusted. That's the truth, so I have to act accordingly. Try and remember that I'm here to help you, and that I'm your friend."

Internal screams intensify within me.

She has to talk to me!

She's being unreasonable!

I have to get out of here!

"Where are you going?" Norma calmly asks.

"I'm going up to my room!" I angrily shout.

"No, you aren't allowed to go to your room until bedtime. If you would like to draw, go and get your things and bring them here."

"I don't want to draw!"

"Then watch television with me."

Sirens wail, adding their din to the internal chaos. The rage is building, but I don't reach out to the one person who has been there for me. Instead, I cling to the rage like a life raft. The right side of my face is cold and numb. Pain radiates up my back and into my head. I'm gripped in something unspeakable, but I don't cry out. Instead, I try pushing it back by jiggling my leg and gouging my skin with my fingernails.

Finally, Garret returns home with a bag in his hand. "I found four movies and a couple of documentaries. I hope these will do."

Taking the bag from him, Norma gratefully smiles at him. "We're watching television, Garret. She can watch these in the next few days. Is there anything in particular that you might like to watch?"

"No, I'm going to work on the computer for a bit. I have a presentation I need to finish." Leaving the common area of the living room, he goes over to his computer and sits.

Darkness envelops me. I feel as though I'm disappearing into nothingness; my head reels, and my insides are filling with an intense pressure. I'm drowning in my own delirium.

The body jumps up from the couch. The voice that bellows at Norma is masculine and filled with rage. "You're not allowed to do this! I'm in charge, and you will not win!" Racing for the door, he grabs the doorknob.

But Norma is just as quick. Grabbing him around the waist, she pulls him back toward the couch, stating authoritatively, "You have no voice here. I make the decisions, and you're going nowhere. Now sit down!" Norma and Garret push the body down onto the couch.

"I'm not your puppet!" he screeches. "You have no power over me, do you hear me?"

Norma holds the body down and asks, "What's your job?"

Silence … the body slumps against the cushions, with the eyes wide open.

"Garret, is she breathing?" Norma shouts.

Leaning close to the face, Garret doesn't hear any breath sounds. Holding his hand under the body's nose, he feels nothing. "She's not breathing!"

Shaking the body hard, Norma looks into the face for a response.

"You have lost," the male voice whispers, and with that pronouncement, the eyes shut.

"Lay her flat on the couch!" Norma yells.

Again, she forcibly shakes the body. Feeling the chest for movement, and feeling nothing, Norma yells. "Someone, anyone, come to the front of the body and breathe!" Norma slaps the face hard with her open hand. Still, there's no response.

Knowing that we were trained to die, Norma leans forward, shaking the body and listening for any breath sounds. She knows that if the human chooses to be done, the body will die. Sensing Kuan Yin's guidance, she immediately knows what to do.

"Toby, I know you're in there. I need your help. Don't you want to go and have hamburgers with me again? If you let them win, then you and I will never do that again! Can you hear me? I need you to come and breathe! You can do it, I know you can! I love you, Toby! I want us to have that sweetness again, but I can't do it alone. I need your help! Please, sweetie, come and breathe! Come right through them. I know you can do it! Godmother will help you!" Coaxing and pleading, Norma keeps calling. All at once, the breath comes with a sudden burst of inhalation. Shuddering with the exhalation, the body bolts upright.

"I could hear you, Norma!" Toby cries. "I was so scared! They was holding me down!"

Pulling him close, Norma rocks him back and forth. "You're my brave little boy. I knew they couldn't keep you from helping me. I'm so proud of you, sweetie."

"Oh, Norma, I'm not going back! It's dark, and there is lots of angry ones. I sawed their eyes. They look like monsters!" Trembling with terror, he bursts into sobs.

Holding him tight, Norma rocks him, crooning, "I won't let them hurt you." Stroking Toby's head, she continues to reassure him. Finally, after holding him for a long time, she calls Godmother to take him.

Lying the body back against the cushions, Norma motions for Garret to remain on the other end of the couch. Calling loudly, she insists that the monsters come and speak to her. "You have no choice. We have broken through your barrier, and now you must do as I say. I'm the new one in command." Raising her voice in authority, she calls, "Do you hear me?"

Slowly, the head turns. The face is void of emotion. Unmoving, he continues to stare.

"What's your job?" Norma asks. Silence.

"I told you: I'm the new one in command, and you must answer my questions."

Still no response.

Calling for the next one in line, she says, "I know you're listening. I can see you. Come forward and speak to me now!" Breathing quietly, Norma watches as another monster moves to the front.

"I'm here," he says, in a low, gravelly voice. "What do you want?"

"I'm your new commander. You're to answer my questions, do you understand?"

Knowing she is dealing with years of governmental training, Norma intuitively moves in a different direction. "Can you tell me your name?"

The eyes flutter with the briefest of reaction, then go flat again. "I have no name, Commander."

"Oh, but you do, and if you take a moment, you'll remember what it is."

"No, I really don't have a name. That would signify my importance. I have no importance outside the greater need."

"And what is the greater need?"

"To protect the inner circle."

"Yes, and you have done that wonderfully," Norma states with genuine admiration. "So, if you have no name, tell me, what are you?"

"I'm a monster."

"And are there other monsters besides you?"

Nodding yes without replying, the monster continues to stare straight ahead.

"I need your help, Godmother. He's convinced he's a monster. I would like you to show him the truth." Redirecting her attention to the monster again, she asks, "Do you see the angel standing beside you?"

Shaking his head no, Norma encourages him to look for her.

As he turns around on the couch in an effort to find her, the monster's face registers surprise before quickly closing down again. "I see her," he answers woodenly.

"Good. Then see what she's asking you to do. I will wait here."

"She wants me to go with her back to the cave. She's not allowed in the cave."

"She's allowed to go anywhere she wants. She has my permission."

Remaining silent, the monster blinks a few times before closing his eyes. Walking with the angel to the back of the cave, he stops in front of a full-length mirror.

"What do you see?" the angel kindly asks.

"Me," he responds.

"Yes, I understand that. Describe how you look."

"I'm big and hairy and very ugly. I have fangs and big yellow claws." Holding up his huge, hairy paws, he shows them to Godmother.

"Yes, I see. Is that how you protect the inner circle?"

"Yes. I keep it safe from harm. No one can get in."

"Yes, and you have done a wonderful job. Part of your job requires you to be brave, and being brave means you're willing to go where most are not. Is that right?"

Nodding yes, he is silent.

"Then I'm inviting you to see something you did not notice before.

Would you do that with me?" Gently, she takes the monster's paw in her hands and guides him to feel up near the back of his neck, right under the fur. "Do you feel the zipper? That's it, right there. That zipper has always been there, waiting for the day when you were ready to discover who you really are. Are you brave enough to do that now?"

Looking perplexed, the monster hesitantly touches the zipper.

Norma watches as the body begins to hyperventilate. Responding intuitively, Norma says, "It's alright. The angel is here to help you. Breathe deeply. You are safe."

Concurrently, the angel speaks, "It's only the brave who would venture to see what is really there. You have done a wonderful job, but your time of protecting the inner circle is over. Can you sense that there is something more for you?"

Feeling compelled to find out who he truly is, the monster sets his claw into the opening of the zipper and begins pulling it down his back. When he reaches the base of his tail, he hesitates.

"You can do it. I'm right here," the angel affirms.

Slowly, he pulls the costume off his right shoulder, revealing human skin. Audibly inhaling, the monster looks at the angel. Slowly, he pulls the costume off his other shoulder and then, inch by inch, he pulls it down, and surprisingly … the body shrinks, revealing a young, naked boy.

With the monster's head still attached, the boy quakes, staring at his reflection in the mirror. Finally, he musters the courage to pull the monster head off, but it won't budge. Looking to the angel, he silently beseeches her for help. Firmly grasping the horns, she jiggles the monster head while pulling upward, and with a loud, resounding pop, the boy's head is released!

Gasping for breath, the boy stares at his reflection. Reaching up, he tentatively touches the skin on his cheek. Marveling at its softness, he asks, "Was I never … a monster?"

Kneeling down, the angel wraps her arms around him, crooning, "No, you were never a monster. You did what everyone needed to keep the body alive, and that took tremendous bravery. You will never have to be alone again. Thank you, dear one."

Feeling safe for the very first time, the boy closes his eyes, welcoming the angel's embrace.

Outside, the body visibly relaxes. Sensing a shift, Norma begins calling to all the monsters. One by one, they make their way to the back of the cave, to be released from the job they have held for so long. It's a miracle: years of government training are being integrated today.

After more than an hour, Norma finally calls me back to the front. Struggling to sit up, I look at her questioningly. I feel sluggish. Rubbing my forehead, I ask what happened.

"That doesn't matter. I want you to keep your focus. You must trust that Godmother and I are taking care of whatever comes up from the others. Can you do that?"

Nodding, I listen. "Good, then I want you to go up and soak. I will sit on your bed and wait. If you need me for anything, call me. Do you understand?"

Feeling as though an invisible force is directing me, I numbly climb the stairs. What in the world just happened? One minute she's telling me to watch television, and in the next I'm being told to bathe?

Sighing, I get into the tub and turn on the water. Startled, I hear Norma knock on the door. "What, Norma?"

"Are you alright?"

"Yes," I wearily reply.

"I'm right here. I can hear everything you are doing. If you need me, call me."

"Norma, why are you acting so weird? I'm fine."

"Please, Serena, trust that I'm doing what is best for you. Keep your focus in this moment, and pay attention to what you are doing."

Sitting down in the water, I exhale, placing my hand on my belly, while looking around the room. *This is reality!* Inhaling, I lay back against the bath pillow. Watching my hand rise and fall with my breath helps me stay focused. *I won't give in to this depression!*

"You are the doorway that can heal all of you, Serena," Godmother says encouragingly. "I know this is hard. Know that I'm here, and I will always be here."

As my head begins to clear, I actually feel better. I climb out of the tub, dry off, and pull my nightgown on over my head. I open the door and find Norma sitting on my bed, just as she promised.

"We're going to bed now. I want you to get some sleep. Today has been a big day, and we have done a lot of work. Is there anything you need?"

Feeling grateful, I wrap my arms around her. "Norma, thank you for this. I know it isn't easy. I was breathing, and Godmother said she was there for me. She said I'm the doorway for all who want to come home to her. I promise I will try harder tomorrow."

"If you can trust Godmother and me, and not fight me at every turn, then that would help tremendously. I know this isn't easy, but when you fight me, it makes it harder than it has to be. Before you go to sleep, I would like to talk with Godmother. Would you let go and step back so she and I can talk?" Nodding, I let go.

"Yes?" Godmother says.

"Where are we at with her safety? I'm only asking because Garret is having a hard time with this. Do you have any idea how much longer this might take? I'm not rushing you, but I have two people to consider."

"I understand that. We have only one more piece to deal with, and then we can go home tomorrow night. Will that work for you?"

"Yes. The level of fear that is always present is exhausting for Garret."

"After this piece of government training is integrated, we'll be able to go home."

"Good …"

"What we have been able to release in these past two weeks is truly miraculous. Thank you for your commitment to us." Squeezing Norma's hand, Godmother moves back inside.

*****

The following morning, I sit down on the couch beside Norma.

"How are you doing this morning, Serena?"

"I'm fine," I respond, absently rubbing my forehead.

"Now, would you like to go for the truth? How are you really feeling this morning?"

Knowing that she has gone way beyond what anyone else has ever done for me makes me hesitate before answering. I feel the urge to lash out at her, but that's the last thing I want to do. Looking into her kind and weary face before responding, I reply, "I'm angry, and I want to run, plus … I want to go home. Is that truthful enough?"

"Yes, I'm glad you could admit that. Would you be willing to trust me a bit longer?"

"Of course, Norma. This isn't about trusting you. It's about how uncomfortable I am every waking moment of the day! It has never, ever been this hard! I know how much you have given me over the past two weeks. I don't take it for granted, but this is harder than anything I could have imagined."

Taking my hand, she smiles at me. "I know, Serena. I have witnessed what we are dealing with, and it goes way beyond what most people can believe. The government was clear with what they wanted; they wanted to control you completely while making sure you kept their secrets. You were not the only one they did this to.

The government wanted to find a way to control people through their minds, and you were a part of those experiments. They did this to many people for many years. They stopped at nothing; they didn't care who they hurt. Really let yourself hear what I am saying. Your life was altered because of what the government did to you." (Norma did research into the government's involvement with mind control, finding numerous reports from professionals in the psychiatric community who had worked with patients over the years, reporting phenomena similar to mine.)

Breathing, despite the panic that is building, I try to repress the "no" that is repetitively playing over and over again in my mind. The more Norma speaks, the louder it gets. Fighting the urge to switch, I hold tightly onto Norma's hand. I'm determined to stay, no matter what. Blinking rapidly, flashes of light start appearing in front of my eyes. It's as though I'm slipping into a deep, cavernous hole. Clutching Norma's hand, I do everything I can to stay.

"Serena, I'm here. I knew it would eventually come up. Can you hear me?"

Nodding yes, I stare at her face through a cloud of haze and flashing lights.

"Good. This is memory. Remember, I'm here, Serena. What do you see?"

"Oh, Norma," I screech, "the eyelids are taped open!"

"Breathe with me and feel my hand. I'm right here, sweetie. Now look around the room. Remember, you can do this. Your eyes are not taped open. Remember, this is memory. Tell me what you see."

"I'm in a room with no windows. It's dark. The body is strapped into a chair; even the head is strapped!" Determined not to freak out, I breathe as slowly as I can. "There's a screen in front of the body and a projector behind it. There are five men in the room. Two are doctors, and the rest are military. The men with the white lab coats are holding clipboards, taking notes." Feeling trapped, I begin hyperventilating.

"Serena, you cannot help yourself if you don't breathe."

Nodding, I stare transfixed at what I'm seeing. Purposely, I bring my breath deep into my belly. Squeezing Norma's hand, I continue staring as the memory takes shape. "Norma, on the screen there is ..." As I begin to find the words, my voice takes on a hypnotic quality ... "colors, swirling in a circle ..."

"Yes. Can you see the swirling? What do they want you to do with it?"

"They want me to go into it." The voice has clearly changed. It's younger and speaks in a monotone.

"And do you obey?"

"Oh, yes ..." The sigh that accompanies the yes is long and drawn out.
"And what do you find when you go into the swirling colors?"

Again, the sigh. "No more pain."

"Yes," Norma croons. "What else do you find there?"

The voice has changed again. "The inner circle."

"And what is the inner circle?"

"It's the library where all the secrets are kept." Continuing, the voice drones on. "Anyone who reveals the secrets will die."

Holding an energetic space of stillness, Norma intuitively allows her questions to flow.

"How does death occur?"

"By thy own hand."

"What does that mean?"

Silence.

"What does 'death occurs by thy own hand' mean?"

Again, silence.

Sensing that this can be left for another time, Norma asks, "What are the failsafe mechanisms that are in place?"

The head slowly turns to face Norma. The eyes flicker, traveling up and down Norma's body. Sneering into her face, he venomously smiles before retreating.

Norma knows my Soul will keep the body safe as this work continues.

"Serena, I know you can hear me. I want you to come back to the front. Follow my voice. I want you to feel my hand. Can you sense that I'm here?"

Shuddering with terror, I recoil as if I've been slapped. Scrambling off the couch, I yell, "I'm in trouble! I'm in trouble! Leave it alone, Norma!"

Standing quickly, Norma grabs my hand, forcing me to look into her eyes. "No one can hurt you anymore. I'm here. Godmother is here. This is the government training you are reacting to. Do you hear me?" Raising her voice to match mine, she pulls me close and wraps her arms around me. "I'm here, sweetie. Can you feel me?"

It feels like my world has been turned upside down. Sobbing uncontrollably, I yell, "Oh, my God, Norma, I'm so scared! I can feel it! Something is really wrong!"

"You believe your mind that was trained through hypnosis. Do you remember seeing the kaleidoscope of colors that was swirling? That was hypnosis. Now sit with me and breathe. You need clarity so that we can help all the children held in this memory. Will you do that with me?"

Agreeing, even though I'm terrified, I sit down and begin breathing. Keeping my focus on Norma's voice, I inhale and exhale slowly. I can feel my blood racing. The sirens are going off, warning me to leave it alone, but I also feel strength filling me from within. It holds me, telling me to trust. I feel the strength begin to grow, becoming larger than the fear. Little by little, the strength takes over, and the terror wanes. "I feel better now, Norma."

"Good, Serena. When you choose, you have the ability to do anything. Now, I want you to breathe, as we begin to get some clarity about this. You were seeing swirling colors on the screen, right?"

"Yes."

"And what did it look like?"

"It was like one of those '60s psychedelic things, swirling inward. You know what I mean?"

"Yes, I know exactly what you mean. So, sense, and watch the swirling. What does it invite you to do?"

Seeing the swirling colors, I begin to feel a familiar listlessness. It pulls me into its center, inviting me to surrender. Relaying this to Norma, I begin to let go into its embrace.

"Serena! Don't hypnotize yourself. Stay here with me. Sense: what is happening as Jennifer watches the swirling?"

"There are words being fed to her through an earpiece. Her eyes are forced open, and she can't move anything! The only way to escape is to go into the swirling and escape the terror and pain." Looking into Norma's face, I open myself to her strength. I feel it emanating from her, inviting me to stay.

"Serena, you're doing wonderfully. Now watch and listen. What are they saying to her?"

"That she is the only one who can enter the inner circle and be safe. No one else can go there." As I relay the words, a feeling of sluggishness overwhelms me. Closing my eyes, I begin to drift inward.

Sensing that this is what I need to do, Norma doesn't interrupt.

As the breath becomes deeper, a quiet, non-threatening male voice says, "I am the caretaker. Who has allowed you to enter?"

Norma looks into a face vacant of all emotion.

Seeing Norma in the midst of his own surroundings, he repeats, "Who are you, and who let you come this far?"

Only through sensing does Norma know how to answer him. "I am here because your days of being the caretaker are over. The government has finished its tests, and the secrets are out. You have done a tremendous job, but it is over."

"Then what is the password?"

"If you look to your right," Norma says, "you will see the new caretaker. She is the only one who has the password. Can you see her?"

"Yes, but she is a woman. Women aren't allowed here."

"That is part of the old regime. I'm the new one in command. Go to her for the password, and I'll wait."

Walking toward Godmother, the caretaker leans in to hear the password. Nodding, he turns and speaks directly to Norma. "She says I'm to go with her, because I have a new job. She says she will be the caretaker of the inner circle. Is there anything else you want me to know before I leave?"

"No, you are free to go. Thank you for the job you did. Is there anything you need to tell us before you leave?" Norma asks.

"Yes, be aware: the left hand knows not what the right hand does."

"Yes, thank you," Norma responds. "The new caretaker will handle that."

Breathing, Norma intentionally holds a space of stillness so that all who were involved with this memory can come home to the Soul. Years of governmental training cannot stop Spirit if the human is willing.

Coming back into the body, I feel weighed down. Trying to remember what we were talking about, I rub my face with the sleeve of my shirt. "Oh, now I remember! Yes, she was strapped in the chair, but Norma, everything is completely controlled; she can't move anything. Do you know how terrifying that is, when you can't even close your eyes? She was being sucked into that swirling thing!" As the memory comes back full-force, I feel the familiar terror.

Not skipping a beat, Norma responds, "Breathe, Serena! You said it yourself; she is terrified. Now sense: what are the words she's hearing?"

"That she is safe in the inner circle."

"Yes, and sense, if everything Jennifer is experiencing on the outside is scary and painful, what would she naturally want to do?"

"Go into the inner circle and find the safety they are talking about!"

"Yes. You're doing wonderfully. Now keep sensing. Is she in the inner circle?"

I'm silent as I begin to sense what is happening. "Norma, there is pain, I mean, real, excruciating pain. The swirling has stopped, and she is stuck. I can't describe it, but she is stuck!" My voice betrays the terror I'm reacting to.

"Serena, remember, you are here with me. Look around you. You are on the couch with me, and Chin Chin is on the floor by my feet. Choose to ground yourself by breathing deeply, and stay focused."

Nodding, I relay what I'm seeing. "Jennifer is terrified that she will be stuck in some kind of no man's land. Everything is dark. There's only pain and words." Grabbing hold of Norma's hand, I let out a groan. I feel Jennifer's experience as if it's happening now. I repeat the words I am hearing. "You will never escape. This is your punishment if you reveal the secrets to anyone. You will always be in the dark, alone, and untouchable. Do you understand? Your only escape is death." Relaying this, I feel isolation and pain that defies description. "Oh, Norma, this is awful!" Sobbing, I grab my stomach, doubling over in pain.

"This is the government's training, Serena! Look at me. Let's slow this down so that we can take the terror out of it. Then we can help these children who are locked in the dark."

Intentionally focusing on Norma's face forces the feelings of terror to recede.

"Let's slow this down, shall we? We know that Jennifer was strapped into one of the chairs we have seen many times before, and that they were using hypnosis again. See how hypnosis was used in different ways?" Calmly stating this fact, she watches, looking for some indication that I'm following her.

"I'm hearing you, Norma, but I felt it, and it doesn't feel that way."

"I understand. They used various techniques combined to create a terrifying experience. They kept her eyes pried open. That in itself would cause anyone to be afraid. They used pain, hypnosis, and drugs to create an artificial experience. They wanted to create an experience that would reinforce the gravity of the situation." Raising her voice, she repeats their warning. "No matter what, do not tell, or you will die."

"I feel the threat. It's more than just words," I argue.

"Remember, this is one of hundreds of experiences, layered, one on top of the other, to guarantee that this form of mind control would remain secret. Feel how wonderfully creative you all were to survive this constant brutality. You're a brilliant human being, Serena, and I'm proud to be able to work with you. Can you let yourself feel what I'm saying?"

"Thanks, Norma. I never thought of myself as a brilliant human being until I met you. I struggled in school just to make decent grades."

"Of course you did. Your energy was used for one thing only: staying alive. School was not a priority, but sense: do you see how wonderfully creative you were? There is this little girl who is being brutalized every day, so she creates monsters, a caretaker, and an inner circle to keep all the secrets within one arena. Every one of these creations was done by a brilliant human being who refused to give up and die. You lived and stayed sane. I'm in awe of you, sweetie. Are you?" Not waiting for me to answer, she pulls me close and wraps her arms around me.

Feeling the warmth of her love and seeing it from a totally new perspective gives me the encouragement I need to keep moving forward.

*****

After lunch and a very long nap, Norma and I sit down to work again. Smiling at me, she takes my hands. "You and I have worked with many different pieces of the government training over the past two weeks, haven't we?"

Nodding yes, I remain silent.

"We have discovered that the government trained you with the intent that no one would ever discover their secrets. Would you agree?"

"Yes?" Raising my eyebrows, I wait for her to continue.

"We discovered that the hypnosis was a key part of the training, didn't we?" Norma waits, watching my reaction.

"Yes, I know that, Norma. What are you saying?"

"Many are listening, so please stay with me, Serena. Your beliefs were created from your experiences with pain, drugs, and hypnosis. The hypnosis worked because you wanted it to work. It seemed to help you escape the pain. Sense with me: what am I asking you to notice?"

"But the hypnosis did work, Norma. It took the pain away."

"That's the belief, but the pain was still there. The hypnosis helped you separate from the pain. You had been doing it your whole life. It's why your multiplicity worked so well. You believed that leaving any situation that seemed threatening worked, *but your body was always there!*"

Feeling panicked, I retort, "I know my body was always there."

"I know this scares many of the children, but if you can grasp what I'm saying, you can begin to help yourself. Yes, the hypnosis seemed to work, but you are a master of it. You have used it your entire life to create pretend stories that helped you stay alive and sane, but pretending is no longer your friend."

Feeling less threatened, I'm able to listen more openly to what she's saying.

"I'm hearing you, Norma. You're telling me that I'm really good at hypnotizing myself."

"Yes, and when you go into hypnosis, you leave your body by switching. That makes you unsafe. I cannot trust you when your primary goal is to leave. Do you understand what I'm saying?"

She is saying a lot, and I'm having a hard time following her.

"Then let's not pretend. In the past two weeks, we've discovered a lot about the training and its purpose: to keep the secrets at all costs. But Godmother, you and I have been more powerful than all the training. Let yourself feel what I've said. All the drugs, hypnosis, and pain could not defeat the power of the three of us. Can you let that truth sink in?" Sitting back, Norma watches to see how I receive what she's saying.

I don't respond.

Taking my hand, Norma tries a different approach. "Do you like Oreo cookies?"

"What?" I ask, laughing. "I love Oreos!"

"Good, then play with me a moment. The Oreo cookie is made up of two solid chocolate cookies, with a sweet vanilla frosting in the middle. Let yourself feel that Godmother and I are like the two solid cookies on the outside, with you as the sweet frosting held completely secure on the inside. Can you feel how safe you are?"

"I like that, Norma. We are the Oreo cookie, aren't we?"

"Yes, sweetie. Now I want you to keep sensing. We are the Oreo cookie, keeping you safe, despite all that has come before, but we need your help. As you choose to stay here no matter what, and you notice you're beginning to feel anxious or upset, what does your body tell you in that moment?"

"What do you mean, what does my body tell me?"

"Sense, Serena: when memory begins to surface, what does your body do?"

"Oh, it gets upset!"

"Yes, and when it gets upset, what kind of signals does it give you?"

"I have terrible anxiety, my thoughts begin to race, and I have this undeniable push that screams for me to go away or leave it alone."

"Yes, that's wonderful, but you also have physical pain. It comes up, telling you memory is here. There are many ways that your body helps you to recognize that something has come up for healing. Would you agree?"

"Yes, but I never looked at it in that way. It just seems to be here all of a sudden."

"I understand, but the more you have clarity, the more you can help yourself. I'm asking you to start recognizing the indicators so you won't hurt yourself as much. We have done a lot of work over the past two weeks, and Godmother says you're safe enough to go home tonight. How does that feel?"

Surprised by this turn of affairs, I admit I'm both delighted and afraid of the idea.

Smiling, Norma says, "Of course you are, but remember: we are the Oreo cookie holding you. But we need your help." Repositioning herself to face me more fully, she continues, "We're going to make a list of rules that you must follow once you go home. I want you to write these rules down, because your safety depends upon it. Do you understand, Serena?"

"Yes, Norma."

"Good. Rule Number One." Raising her voice, she emphatically states, "You're not allowed to go outside for any reason. Is that understood?"

"You mean I can't empty my trash?" I incredulously ask.

"Notice the game player, please. What does it mean, you cannot go outside for any reason?"

"Yes, but …"

"No, Serena, are you going to help yourself or hurt yourself?"

"I will help myself, Norma."

"Good, then write it down." Waiting until I have finished writing, she states, "Rule Number Two. You're not to call anyone. That means not even your sons. Do you understand?"

Hearing the tone in her voice, I know she's uncompromising with what she's saying, so I don't bother arguing. "Write it down, please."

Nodding, I write it down word for word.

"Rule Number Three. You are to call me day or night if any problem arises. No matter what your mind says. This is not up for discussion. Do you understand?"

Again, I nod without reply.

"And this fourth rule is really up to you, and your willingness to be honest: you're to be aware of what you watch on TV. If it's upsetting, stimulating, or sexual, it's not appropriate for you. I can only stress that this is about helping you, Serena. Watching something that gives you a rush floods your body with adrenaline, which hurts you, and keeps the fear game going.

"I will come up every morning and get you. You will spend the day here with me. I'm going to resume seeing other clients, but other than that, nothing has changed. You will spend your days with me. Do you have any questions?"

"No. This is a lot to take in," I reply.

"I know that, but I trust Godmother will keep you safe. Your job is to pay attention. If your body starts giving you signals, you are to call me. Godmother is there all the time. She can help you if you ask. Remember, you're not to interact with anyone. Add that to your list, please. If anyone knocks on your door, you're not to answer it. Do you understand?"

"Don't you think this is a bit excessive?"

"Would you rather be in a hospital?"

"No, of course not."

"Then don't argue with me. These rules are to help keep you safe. I know Godmother will keep you safe, or I could never let you go home." Pausing, she stops to see how I'm reacting to all she has said. Sensing that I'm not fighting her, she continues, "When Garret gets home, we will stop at the grocery store. Garret will stay in the car with you, and I'll go in and shop. Make a list of what you will need, including pet food for Petunia."

I'm still writing when Norma asks, "Did you notice that your body is telling you something?"

"What?"

"These are the signals I asked you to be aware of. You started jiggling your leg and biting your fingernail. Stop a moment and notice what's wrong."

"I don't want to go home with Serena!" Toby wails.

"I know, sweetie, but you'll be safe with Godmother. Can you see her?"

"No! I want to stay with you!"

"I know, but Godmother will take care of you, Toby."

"Please don't send me away!"

"You live in the same body as Serena. She needs your strength to keep all the children safe. Can you do this for the other children?"

With tears running down his face, he says, "I don't like sharing a body with Serena. I want to live here with you."

Wrapping her arms around him, Norma reassures him that she will be there first thing in the morning. Feeling reassured, he closes his eyes and slips back inside.

"I heard what Toby said!" I exclaim.

"Good. That's how you will help all of you. Did you hear Toby say that he wanted to stay here with me?"

"Yes, he's like Robbie, who always wanted to live with you."

"The children feel safe and loved by me, Serena. They don't trust you yet. That's not said in judgment, but with complete honesty. They feel a love from me that they are hungry for. These rules will help them feel safe. Can you help them by promising me that you will follow all of the rules?"

"Yes, Norma, I promise I'll follow all the rules. I really do want to help myself."

"Good. How are you feeling about going home? Please, be still a moment and really let yourself feel the truth."

"I'm afraid, and I don't know why. I have wanted to go home so badly, but now …"

"I understand, Serena. The important thing is that you admit it to yourself. You have depended on me to keep you safe, but you must be involved as well. That means staying aware and being honest with yourself. If you're feeling anxious, you're to call me day or night, it does not matter."

"I promise I'll do whatever it takes to keep us all safe." Feeling a strange connection to the commitment I just made, I tentatively smile.

Wrapping her arms around me, Norma gives me a hug of encouragement. "Then let's get you ready to go home."

Chapter 14: I'M YOUR MOTHER

Norma took me to a psychiatrist so I could get the proper documentation for disability insurance. The doctor had worked with multiples before, so Norma thought he would be supportive. Instead, he took her aside and told her that the work she was doing with me was pointless. He said that I would always suffer from dissociative identity disorder and that she should put me in a hospital. I'm grateful that Norma didn't listen to him, as well as the fact that she waited years before telling me about this conversation.

*****

The money I get from disability only covers my rent, so Norma pays for everything else. I wonder what will happen when the money runs out. Is she going to pay for me indefinitely? How long will it be until I can work again? How long will it take to integrate? These questions constantly torment me. When I try to talk to her about it, Norma tells me that if I didn't do my homework, she would have stopped working with me long ago. She says this work is a gift to her as well; she feels she's in some kind of university program, learning things she never knew before. She tells me my job is to keep the body safe, and that she will take care of the finances. Since I know I would be dead without her, I accept her support, despite the guilt I feel.

Godmother is guiding Norma to do physical exercises with me to rewire my brain. Godmother told us that years of training set up neuropathways in my brain that support my multiplicity, and that, in order for me to truly integrate, those pathways need to be redirected.

When I do the exercises, my entire body reacts as if I'm having seizures. I retch without ceasing, and feel so ill afterwards that I can barely form sentences. Norma assures me this is a crucial part of my healing, and no matter how uncomfortable I get, I must follow through with it.

*****

It's the second week of April, 2001. Climbing up on the massage table, I look at Norma, waiting for her direction.

Godmother comes to the front of the body and speaks. "Start with the eye exercises first," she requests. "It's important that you ask Serena to stay present as much as possible while we do this."

"When we do the eye exercises," Norma tells me kindly, "I want you to breathe and stay as deep in your body as you can, no matter how your body reacts. Can you do that?"

"Okay," I say. "What do you want me to do?"

"Follow my index finger, without moving your head. I need you to sit up straighter, and remember: breathe deeply, and stay focused."

Watching her finger move from right to left, I track with only my eyes, and sure enough, my body starts reacting. My skin crawls, my head aches, and my belly twists with pain. Groans escape my lips. "Oh ... Norma, this is awful!" As my groan turns into retching, I beg her to stop.

"Serena, you're doing much better than you have been."

"This is so hard!"

"No one said it would be easy," she gently reminds.

Watching as she makes horizontal eights in the air, I gasp for breath, as retch after retch takes over. "Stop!"

"Of course," Norma replies. "Take a sip of water."

"Have her lie down on her back when she's ready, so we can do the leg exercises," Godmother requests. "Please remind her to stay. She will connect with something that's important for our work."

"When you're ready, Serena, lie down on your back. Then we can start the leg exercises. Bring your right leg up as far as you can to your left shoulder and try to touch it, while staying as flat as possible."

Bringing my right leg up as far as I can, I lower it back down, as my innards start to shake. As I bring my leg up again, slowly, up and down I go, and with it the retching resumes.

"Stay right here. Serena. Godmother needs you to notice what your body goes through. Now, do the other leg when you're ready. That's it. Bring it up as far as you can."

Convulsions rack my body as I continue retching. "This is hurting me, Norma!"

"I understand, but don't stop! That's it! You're doing great."

I continue moving my leg, despite the pain I'm feeling.

"Stop for a moment and have her breathe," Godmother directs.

Taking my hand, Norma says, "You're doing so much better, Serena."

"Are you serious? I feel out of control!"

"I promise, you are better. Your reaction isn't as intense as it was."

"I'll trust you, even though it doesn't feel any different to me." After a short break, I lie back down and continue the exercise with my legs. Slowly, an awareness starts to form. "It really happened, didn't it?"

"What really happened?"

"I was hurt, wasn't I?"

"Yes, you were hurt," Norma replies. "You're the only one who pretends that you weren't."

Hearing the same response that I've heard so many times before, I inhale slowly, intentionally letting go of any resistance I feel. As awareness grows, grief follows right on its heels. "It was worse than anything I've ever wanted it to be," I whisper.

"Do you know why you couldn't grasp it?"

"No."

"Sense a moment. Can you feel how much you wanted to pretend that it wasn't that bad?"

"Yes, I feel it in every cell of my body; it screams no so loudly, but I won't give in to that. I want the truth, Norma!"

"Then breathe in Godmother's compassion, and allow the truth to ground itself within you. There is nothing as powerful as you and Godmother, so the no does not have permission to stay here." Norma states. "Hear this, Serena, the only way that you survived what happened to you was to pretend that it wasn't that bad. Breathe, with me sweetie, and open your heart to the gift this lie gave you."

"This is what I wanted her to connect with," Godmother says. "The layers of dissociation are deeply entrained in her body and consciousness, so to finally break through so she can finally own this truth is remarkable."

"Serena, would you sit up so you and I can talk?" Taking a seat across from me, she continues. "You have worked your entire life to deny what happened to you."

"Yes … but they really hurt me, didn't they?" I shudder with the intensity of what I'm feeling.

"Yes, and do you know why you've fought so long to deny it? Be still a moment and go for an honest answer."

Holding my head in my hands, I sob quietly. I am shook to my very core. My body is trembling. No wonder I've been in pain for as long as I can remember. *Why have I denied these memories for so long, I wonder?*

"Serena, don't go to your mind, ask the children, they know the answer."

Silently, I ask the children why they pretended it wasn't so bad; instantly, I am inundated with emotions so intense I struggle not to switch, while the cries of individual children flood my awareness. Only by focusing on my breath can I stay present. The message is the same, expressed in different ways, but all agree: our parents never loved us. My heart feels like it's literally breaking apart!

"My parents didn't love me, did they, Norma?" I sob painfully.

"No, Serena. They couldn't love you, because they didn't love anyone or anything. Let yourself feel that truth." Raising her voice in compassion, she continues. "They were unable to love; it had nothing to do with you."

(Norma knows that in previous discussions on this same topic, I've always pushed the truth away through my ability to dissociate. It's like trying to dissolve a huge block of frozen pain, a chip at a time. It's only through her compassionate and loving patience that Norma is able to speak of this as though it were our first time.)

Scrambling off the massage table, I fall into her arms. "I wanted them to love me so badly, Norma!"

"I know, sweetie." Knowing that she's speaking to more than just me, she adds, "It was not possible with the parents you had. It had nothing to do with you, but it doesn't change how much it hurts." Quietly rocking me back and forth, she lets me sob into her chest.

"It hurts beyond anything I've ever known! They didn't love me. Not even my own mother! I really thought she loved me!" Erupting in another wave of sobs, I desperately cling to her.

Soothing me, she croons, "I know, I know …"

With my face still pressed hard against her chest, I cry, "Oh, Norma, I wish you had been my mother!"

"I wasn't your mother then, sweetie, but I'm your mother now."

Pulling back in complete surprise, I exclaim, "What?"

"Listen to what I'm telling you … I am here every day loving you, devoted to your welfare and healing. I love you. I'm your mother, if you will have me."

I study her for an indication that she may be teasing me. When I look into her eyes, they fill me with love, and her smile … it's radiant, melting some of the heartache I feel. "Wow, you're my mom." Whispering it under my breath, I'm totally amazed by this turn of events. Pulling a chair up beside her, I hesitantly ask, "Does that mean I can call you Mom?"

"Yes," she says, smiling at me. "Take a moment and breathe. Let yourself feel the sweetness of this moment."

After a few minutes of silence, she says, "Would you ask Godmother if there's anything else she wants to add to this sweet moment?"

Closing my eyes, I see Godmother off to my left. Her warm, dark eyes smile at me as she states, "She is the human mother you never had. She is your external mother, and I am your internal mother. Remember, we are the Oreo Cookie, holding you securely in our love."

Opening my eyes, I share what Godmother said.

"And how does that feel, Serena?"

Laughing joyously, I reply, "I never knew you were my mom! But you've been my mom for quite a while now, haven't you?" Giggling, I lay my head on her shoulder. Feeling loved like never before, I close my eyes and surrender to its sweetness.

Chapter 15: MOVING TO COLORADO

"Serena, let's play a game. I'm sitting here on the couch, aren't I?"

"Yes?" Eyeing her suspiciously, I wait for her to proceed.

"Good, and when I move over to this chair?" Norma gets up, moves to one of the upholstered chairs opposite me, and sits down. "I'm still in the room, aren't I?"

Feeling angry with her stupid game, I don't answer, but when she doesn't continue, I mumble, "Yes."

"Good. So, when I move across the room, am I still in the room?"

"I don't know why you're asking this, but ..."

"Serena, in all the years that we've been together, have I ever done anything to hurt you?"

"No, but ..."

"Yes, I know. You need to fight. Please, will you listen to where I'm leading you? It would make things so much easier."

Discussions with long lead-ins have always led to heartache, so I'm anxious about where this conversation is going.

"Alright," Norma cheerfully states. "So, I'm still in the same room with you, aren't I?"

Feeling like I might lash out at her, I answer with only a nod of my head.

"The reason I'm telling you this is that I know how upset you get when I move anything in the house. Is that right?"

"Yes, I hate it when you rearrange the furniture. You do it too much!"

"Serena, please don't get distracted," Norma suggests. "Stay here with me. So, when I move across the room, I'm still here, and everything is safe, isn't it?"

Relieved that we seem to be just talking about furniture, I start to relax.

"Yes, Mom, everything is safe."

"Good. I'm asking you to follow this example, because Garret and I are moving."

Internal sirens begin to wail. Remaining seated, I carefully control my voice as I ask, "And where are you planning to move?"

Keeping her voice just as calm, she quietly replies, "We're moving to Colorado, Serena."

Without forethought, I'm up and running for the door. Before I can fully open it, she grabs me by my shirt collar, shouting, "You cannot run, Serena!"

"I don't care. You're moving! I won't make it if you move away! I will die, I will die!" Sobbing hysterically, I struggle to get out the door.

We'll find her, no matter where she goes.

We'll pack our car and follow her, wherever she goes!

"I'm taking you with me, Serena. Can you hear me? Everyone who is listening, I'm taking you with me!" Raising her voice, she invites all of us to listen. "You're precious to me. I won't leave any of you behind. I made a commitment to help you integrate, and that's a priority to me."

Sobbing, I collapse into her arms.

"Come sit, so we can talk. It's okay. I'm here. I tried to do this in the gentlest way possible. I know how scary change is for you, and I didn't want to upset any of you." Holding me around my waist, she leads me back to the couch. "Here, take a sip of water so we can talk." Wrapping her arms around me, she rocks me gently. "We have wanted to make this move for a while now. The opportunity has presented itself, and so we're taking it."

"And Garret is okay with me coming along?"

"Yes, he knows how committed I am to your integration, and he honors that."

"When are we going to move?"

"We're planning to leave mid-June."

"But that's in three weeks! How in the world …"

"That's not your concern, Serena. Now take a breath … that's it. Are you feeling any better?"

Nodding, I remain silent.

"When is your lease up on your apartment?" Norma asks.

"I don't know … wait. I moved here on July first, so … it's up on the first of July."

"Good. That's when our lease is up as well, so that works out perfectly."

"But how will we get there?"

"We will take one or two U-Hauls, depending on how much stuff we have."

"Yes, but what about my car and Petunia and …"

"Serena, today is May 25th. We still have a few weeks before we leave. I would like to speak to Godmother now."

Norma and Godmother speak privately. "I'll need Serena to stay home more, so I can begin to close things down here. I have clients I need to work with, and I also need to pack up the house. Do you have any suggestions on how we can help Serena?"

"She can begin to pack her things to prepare for the move. I will slow things down within the system, so that the move will be her main focus. The timing of this is perfect. If this were even a month ago, it wouldn't have been possible."

Feeling relieved, Norma replies, "I knew this would be easier with your help."

"If we could get some boxes on the way home, she can begin packing today," Godmother instructs. "That will occupy her, and help her feel like she's doing something worthwhile."

"Of course. I know of some places where we can stop along the way."

"I will help the children who can understand about the move, and the others I will put to sleep until we have become settled in Colorado. I would like you to tell Serena that you will need her to stay at home in the interim. Let her know that she can be a help to both of us in that way." With a smile, Godmother is gone.

Calling me back to the front, Norma watches as the face transforms from tranquil countenance to fearful consternation.

"I'm going to need your help with this move," Norma says.

"I'll do whatever you need, Mom."

"Good. The next three weeks are going to be very full for me. I need to take care of some loose ends with my other clients and pack up the house. I will need you to pack your belongings so that when Garret comes, he can pack the U-Haul easily."

"Yes, but you said you needed my help. What can I do for you?"

"I will need you to stay at your place and take care of yourself. I won't be able to work with you like I have been these past few months, but Godmother assured me she would help us both by slowing things down inside. How do you feel about all of this?"

"How many times can I come over in a week?" I anxiously ask, holding my breath.

"In this moment, I cannot answer that. I really need your help if I'm going to accomplish everything I need to in the next three weeks. Can you remain open and see what happens? I know you don't like that answer, but that's the best I can do at this time."

I agree despite not liking it.

"Good. This can be an adventure for both of us if you allow it. Now, before I take you home, I promised Toby I would spend some time with him. Will you go get him, please?"

Leaning in, I quickly hug her before disappearing inside.

"Do we gets some time together?" Toby happily asks.

"Yes, sweetie, but did you hear me speaking to Serena about the move?"

"No, but Godmother told me about it. We're going to move with a big truck, aren't we?" Playfully raising his eyebrows at her, he smiles happily.

"Yes, we'll be driving in a big truck to our new home in Colorado. I'll need you to help with the move. Can you do that?"

"Oh, yes!" Imagining himself sitting high up in the truck's cab, he turns to Norma, face alight, exclaiming, "I can't wait!"

"Toby, what would you like to do before I take you home?"

"I telled you. I just want to be with you!"

"Good. I need to get boxes for Serena so she can start packing up all your things. Would you like to help me find them?"

Running for the door, he hollers, "I'll find boxes with you!"

"Toby, I need your cooperation," Norma firmly states. "That means that you are to stay by my side and not run off. Do you understand?"

"Okay!" Grabbing the doorknob, he impatiently jiggles it, waiting for her to get her purse. "This is going to be fun!"

*****

Boxes are stacked one on top of the other, crowding most of my living space. The furniture is pushed up against the far wall, just below the window. Everything is in one room to make it easier for Garret to pack the U-Haul when he comes.

I have been worried about Chin Chin and Petunia sitting together on the long drive to Colorado, but Mom is unconcerned. She tells me that if I were to stay in the moment and let Spirit guide us, I might be surprised at how things turn out.

*****

Packing the U-Haul with my things took less than an hour. With Petunia on my lap, we pull up in front of Norma and Garret's house. I find Mom in the kitchen. "Put Petunia in one of the rooms before you ask Garret how you can help," she tells me.

Finding Garret inside one of the trucks, I call to him, "What do you need me to do?"

"Bring the boxes that are still in the house outside, and put them close to the truck. I have to rearrange your things so that everything will fit."

Going from room to room, I bring out more boxes than I can count.

After multiple trips, I notice I'm tiring.

Don't stop, you have to keep helping.

They're taking you with them. Show them that you deserve it!

My legs buckle underneath me as I lift another large box. Pushing the box aside, I wipe the sweat off my face with my shirt and lean against the house wall. Closing my eyes, I sigh with satisfaction as the coolness from the wall seeps through my shirt and onto my skin. This is where Mom finds me.

"Are you listening to your body or to your head, Serena? If I have to take care of you because you've worn yourself out, that won't help me at all. Ask Godmother what she would have you do, please." Not waiting for my reply, she walks outside and joins the others.

Going within, I hear Godmother say, "Your body is exhausted. Rest, and let them finish packing. You have done your part. Breathe with me and be still."

That's not what I wanted to hear. Reluctantly, I stop and take a breath, and in doing so, I feel the push to get up and move. Knowing that Godmother asked me to be still, I intentionally take another breath. Lying my hand on my belly, I close my eyes and try to concentrate. Feeling anxious, I pause and listen to the screams coming from within.

"The children are upset with the house being dismantled," Godmother advises. "I will help them not to be afraid. I'm proud of you for stopping to breathe, even though you didn't want to do that."

Taking the time to breathe really helped. I feel refreshed. Wandering through the house, I collect things that seem forgotten. Realizing I have stumbled upon something that I can do without too much exertion, I collect the last remaining objects and put them into a box. Deciding to clean the kitchen, I scrub the counters and sink with cleanser. It feels good to help.

Totally absorbed in what I'm doing, I'm startled when Mom speaks. "Thank you, Serena. I really appreciate how you've helped us, but it's time to go. Get Petunia and meet me in the truck."

Taking the stairs two at a time, I burst into the spare bedroom and find Petunia sunning herself on the window ledge. Pulling her leash from the plastic grocery bag, I fasten it around her middle. Taking her down the stairs, I stop mid-way and look around me. *This is the last time I will go down these stairs.*

"Serena," Norma calls, "please get into the truck. I'll be there in a minute. Chin Chin is already there."

Climbing up into the cab, I put Petunia down next to Chin Chin. Acknowledging her with a sniff, he closes his eyes and goes back to sleep.

Norma climbs in and says, "We need to talk before I begin driving." Turning to face me, she continues. "I have never driven a truck like this, so I'll need to stay focused. Garret is concerned for our welfare, so I'll need your full cooperation. Can you do that by staying aware?"

Hearing how serious she is, I nod in agreement. "Why is Garret so concerned?"

Pausing, she chooses her words carefully because she doesn't want to hurt my feelings. "I have a dog and a cat in the cab with you and me. I do not know how Chin Chin and Petunia will be after a few hours on the road. In addition, I need to maneuver this vehicle and be aware of the other drivers. There's a lot going on. Can you see why Garret would be concerned?"

"Wow, I didn't know that, Mom."

"I know. That's why I need your help. This can be a fun adventure, but I need you to stay aware. If you begin to feel anxious, tell me. I will need a promise from Godmother that no one will try to jump from the truck while it's moving. I need all of you to be involved in this move, so breathe a moment and see if Godmother wants to add anything."

Closing my eyes, I relay word for word what Godmother is saying. "I promise that no one will attempt to jump from the cab. The children who are self-destructive have been put to sleep. I will work with whatever comes up from the system."

Smiling, I open my eyes. "This is going to be fun, isn't it, Mom?"

"It does have that possibility, sweetie." Gently tooting the horn, she motions to Garret that we're ready to go.

Chapter 16: MY NEW HOME

The drive was thankfully uneventful; Chin Chin and Petunia got along just fine. I was the one who struggled with the endless hours of driving, but at the end of each day, we stopped at a hotel for the night. That really helped because I had time to myself.

I was surprised by the beauty of Colorado. The Rocky Mountains are majestic; they span the horizon as far as the eye can see. The sky is vast and brilliantly blue, and I swear the sun shines more brightly here. With the pine and aspen trees, the elk and other animals, it is an amazing place to live!

I spent the first two weeks living with Norma and Garret. Those days passed in a blur. I was anxious about the changes that had occurred over the previous two weeks, plus I ached to live by myself again.

Finally, I moved into my own place the first week of July. From the street, my home looks like a gingerbread house: small and quaint, with forest green shutters and forest green trim running the entire length of the house, against walls painted a bright white. There are multiple windows in each room, which makes it cheerful and bright. The rules are still in place just like they were in California, so I'm still not allowed to go outside for any reason. But at least I can see the view in every direction!

*****

"I'm waking up the children that I put to sleep in California," Godmother says. "For the time being, I need Serena to step back from being in the front as much as she is. I'm awakening core parts of the authentic child, which will bring a greater sense of self into the system. This will help Serena connect to the body in a new way. She will think she's losing ground, but help her to understand this is a crucial part of her integration."

Lying on my back on the massage table, I look into Mom's face and smile. I'm unaware of the conversation that has just taken place. Rubbing my forehead, I'm silent.

"Take a few moments and breathe with me, Serena. Lay your hand on your belly, and feel the motion of your hand as it goes up and down with your breath."

I love the sound of Mom's voice. It's deep and has a rich tonal quality. Sighing deeply, I relax; suddenly, a surge of anxiety pulses through my body, and I switch.

"I knew you were coming, sweetie. My name is Norma. What's your name?"

Shaking her head back and forth, the child remains silent.

"Can I sit next to you?" Pulling up a chair so they're at eye level, Norma asks, "Do you have a name, sweetie?"

Nodding yes, the child remains quiet.

"Can you tell me what it is?"

"Jennifer," the child whispers.

"Oh, I like that name. Do you like that name?"

Shrugging, the child looks away. Tucking her head into her chest, she silently weeps.

"Can I hold you, sweetie?" Holding out her arms, Norma waits for Jennifer to make a move.

Ever so slowly, Jennifer extends her arms and allows Norma to hold her. Tenderly stroking her hair, Norma waits until the child's sobs have subsided.

Calling me back to the front, Norma says, "She's too young to tell me what's hurting her. Will you let her show you?"

Closing my eyes, I see pictures taking shape. "Jennifer's sitting in a highchair. She's crying and crying."

"How old is she?"

"I don't think she's two yet. Lois is in the kitchen, standing with her back to Jennifer, and Jennifer is screaming. Hey, there's no food in front of her!"

"Serena, you can't afford to get upset. You're helping this child tell her story. Will you stay here and be the adult? You can choose to help her or not. It's up to you."

"Oh, okay …" I reluctantly reply, before closing my eyes again.

"As I said, she's crying. Lois goes to the stove and stirs something in the pan. The smell makes Jennifer's hunger worse, plus her diaper is wet, and her bottom is burning."

"Serena, you're doing wonderfully. Now sense: where's Jennifer's energy?"

"It's up close to the ceiling."

"How long has Jennifer been in the highchair?"

"She's been in the highchair for a couple of hours, and she's beyond tired. Being ignored is so much worse than not being fed, Mom!"

"You're right, Serena. That's why I asked you to notice where Jennifer's energy is. So, backtrack a moment. When Jennifer was first put into the highchair, what did Lois do?"

As I observe Lois setting Jennifer down in the highchair, I watch her take an intentional step back. "Oh, Mom, she looks mean!"

"Yes. Now, breathe, Serena. Remember, this has already happened. We're here to help this child. Now watch and sense: when Lois puts Jennifer in the highchair, what does Jennifer try to do?"

"What? I don't …"

"Please stop a moment. Don't argue with me. Sense, what does Jennifer's energy try to do? You'll not see it with your mind's eyes. Let yourself sense with Godmother."

As I feel Mom's unconditional compassion wash over me, it gives me the courage to let go. And as I do, I clearly see what happened. "Oh, she tried to energetically move into Lois, but it was like hitting a brick wall, because Lois was closed off to Jennifer!"

"Yes, Serena! So, what did Jennifer do at that point?"

"She left the body and went up to the ceiling."

"You're doing wonderfully. Can you connect that this isn't the first time this has happened? Remember, this is ongoing, every day and every night. Would you let yourself feel what I'm saying? I know you don't like the truth, but for Jennifer, there was no time when she wasn't being brutalized. This was an ongoing experience, seven days a week, twenty-four hours a day. Now keep sensing, as she floats up near the ceiling: what does she want to do?"

"I don't have to sense!" I angrily shout. "She wants to die!"

"I know this isn't easy, but you can't afford to get upset. This child needs you, Serena. Will you help her?"

Nodding, I shakily inhale while gathering my resolve. "Lois says she doesn't like bad little girls like Jennifer, and she says it with this low, gravelly voice. Then she scowls and looks right at Jennifer. It's like she's on stage, Mom!"

"Don't get distracted, Serena. Tell me what happens next."

"Then she starts speaking in this sweet, high-pitched voice, declaring that she loves good little girls like Lucy Belle. The whole time she's looking all over the room, searching for Lucy Belle. She purposely looks at Jennifer and inhales dramatically, while asking her if she is her Lucy Belle … Wait a minute! Did Lois train Jennifer to be a multiple personality? Not waiting for Mom to reply, I angrily shout, "This is too much!" Clutching my stomach, I begin rocking back and forth to alleviate the shock I feel.

"Breathe, Serena! I'm right here. I want you to ask Godmother what you just asked me, and let yourself hear the truth."

I'm feeling overwhelmed. My mind is racing with screams, but over the din, I hear Godmother say, "We had to let you know the truth gently. Your parents used different names when talking to Jennifer, solely to create multiple personalities. You wanted to believe it was only Jack, but that's not true. Breathe, and let yourself feel the truth. It's how you will help the children who are listening."

I'm stunned. "But how can this be true?"

"Serena, do you want to help yourself or hurt yourself? You get to decide," Norma says. Raising her voice, she continues. "You don't like the truth, and that keeps you stuck. Will you breathe with me?"

After a few minutes of focused breathing, I sadly say, "It's true, isn't it?"

"Yes. It takes courage to stay and look at how your life was. I'm in awe of how brave you are." Taking my hand, she squeezes it gently. "Now, let's see where Godmother wants to go with this."

"See what Jennifer does as Lois asks if she is her Lucy Belle. Watch how creative she was in staying alive," Godmother suggests. "Remember, she's hungry and cold. She's been sitting in wet diapers with her bottom burning for hours. On top of that, being neglected has traumatized her deeply."

Closing my eyes, I watch Jennifer nod yes to Lois's question, and instantly, another child is born. Lucy Belle looks up into Lois's smiling face, holds up her arms, and says, "Mama." Gone are the feelings of hunger, pain, and despair, and instead, a new child is born, waiting to be imprinted. As the truth of this realization hits me, I shudder, consumed by an inexplicable sadness.

"Breathe, Serena. Help these children come home. You cannot afford to keep this pain. Bring it home with your breath."

"I am, but it hurts!"

"I know. I'm not minimizing that, but breathe so it can keep moving."

Breathing and crying, I wrap my arms around my waist, hoping this will give me some comfort. The level of brutality Jennifer lived through is unfathomable. As I continue breathing, the tears finally begin to subside.

"Will you let Jennifer come back so I can help her? If you can, please listen so this can help you as well."

"I will, Mom, but …"

"I'm only asking you to choose. If you're not able to hear, then that is okay. I'm not judging you. Can you remember that?"

Closing my eyes, I slip to the back, making room for Jennifer to come forward. Hearing Mom coax Jennifer to the front, I breathe, knowing that my choice, combined with Mom's compassion, will help bring Jennifer out. After a couple of minutes, Jennifer rubs her face, silently watching Norma.

"Invite her to live here. Tell her this is her new house," Godmother states quietly. "She is part of the core child, the beginning that is crucial to connect with the body. I will help take care of her, but Serena will need to be involved as well. I will guide this every step of the way."

"Hi, sweetie, how do you feel?" Smiling gently, Norma breathes compassion, enveloping her.

Without responding, the child bows her head.

"I'm glad you came back. We've been waiting for you for such a long time. Can you see the angel? She is standing near you."

As she lifts her head, Jennifer's eyes roam around the room, furtively moving from place to place until she sees the angel. Slowly, a smile transforms her troubled face. Looking behind Norma, she nods while pointing her finger.

"Good. She brought you here to live with her and the lady, Serena. They will take care of you. Can you hear the angel talking to you?" Nodding her head, Jennifer closes her eyes.

"She's exhausted," Godmother says, "and needs rest. It's important that Jennifer and others begin to feel that this is their experience. Serena, I know you can hear me. I'm asking you to let these children experience the body. Serve meals and let them eat. Take baths and let them feel the warmth of the water. Intentionally invite them to be here. I know that some of this will feel foreign to you, but none of the internal children ever got to know what it felt like to be safe and in a body at the same time. You can be this connection for them. Are you willing to do that?"

Hearing Godmother's words, I turn to Mom. "I don't understand."

"What is it you don't understand?"

"I thought I was supposed to stay present and be in the front. Now I'm being asked …"

"Why are you afraid? Don't you know Godmother has kept you safe your whole life? She only wants to help you. She's asking you to let these parts of the original child be here as well. She is the wisdom guiding this adventure. Can you continue to follow her guidance?"

Feeling guilty for doubting Godmother, I grudgingly agree.

"I know this isn't how you want it to be, but if you let Godmother lead, you will discover a gift with this."

Chapter 17: CONNECTIONS

"I don't like having these core children here!" I angrily declare.

"You didn't have a problem when Robbie or Toby were here. What's different about these children?"

"I don't know," I irritably reply.

"I won't fight with you, Serena. Ask Godmother why you are feeling so angry."

I know Mom's right. I'm upset for no apparent reason. Going within, I ask Godmother for help.

"You don't like seeing how severely wounded these core children are," Godmother responds.

"Do you understand what she's saying?"

"Yes, but you don't understand, Mom! When I see them, I physically hurt!

I feel that if I stop fighting, I might ..." I shakily inhale.

"I understand, Serena. The anger you're feeling lets us both know there's something else going on. Before we go any further, I want you to drop deeper into your belly and breathe."

Choosing the breath over my anger, I take the next several minutes to breathe.

"Would you allow yourself to see these children through Godmother's eyes? Don't think your answer, feel your answer instead."

Nodding, I allow the experience of last night to come back to me, and in doing so, I grasp more fully how catastrophic Jennifer's world was. Compassion fills me as I see her tremble in the tub. "When you said nothing was left to chance, that everything was distorted by the training, this is what you meant, isn't it? Even a simple bath was tainted with cruelty."

"Yes, every moment of Jennifer's life was distorted. She couldn't eat, sleep, go to the bathroom, play outside, have relationships, or take a bath without being constantly terrorized. Please, breathe this truth in, Serena. When you face it without resistance, you become the doorway for these children to come home. But I would like you to take this a step further. Would you be willing to see why Jennifer reacts so violently to being in the tub?"

Closing my eyes, I let the memory surface. "Lois is scrubbing Jennifer's skin so viciously! Oh, Mom ..." sobbing uncontrollably, I open my eyes and look around the room. I'll do whatever it takes to stay present, but the pain I'm experiencing is pure agony. Maintaining a deep and steady breath allows me to stay with the memory as it unfolds. "Jennifer is screaming and screaming, and the water is red with her blood."

"You're doing great, Serena. Where is the blood coming from?"

"From her vagina ..." Grabbing the pillow off the couch, I push it into my stomach.

"And how old is Jennifer?"

"She's only two years old, she's so little." Clenching my jaw. I'm overwhelmed and can barely handle the emotions that are flooding my body.

"Breathe, Serena!"

"You don't understand! Jack raped her, and Lois is mad at her for having sex with him! Is she crazy or something?" Not waiting for a reply, I shudder as pictures continue to flood my awareness. "Jennifer fainted, right there in the tub!"

Bolting off the couch, I run into the bathroom and slam the door shut. Rocking back and forth on the toilet seat, I try to cope with what I'm feeling.

"Serena, I'm right here. Breathe with me, sweetie." Hearing the kindness in her voice through the closed door makes me sob even harder. "I hurt so badly!" Taking deep breaths, I try to gain control. My head feels fuzzy, and my body is screaming in pain. Opening the door, I fall into Mom's arms. "I don't know why this is bothering me so much. I've seen things much worse than this.

(Separating into different personalities created layers of insensitivity to traumatic experiences through dissociation. But at two years old, it wasn't as developed as it would be in later years, so the impact of Jennifer's abuse hits me hard.)

"Look at me," Mom says, holding my face. "When you try to figure out why, you don't help yourself. The truth is, this memory hurts. Can you accept that and breathe?"

Walking back to the couch, I'm struggling to stay. Taking determined breaths, I settle deeper into my belly before opening myself to the memory again. "Lois is scrubbing Jennifer's vagina, telling her that if she were a good little girl, this wouldn't have happened to her. Oh, I hate Lois so much!" I angrily scream.

"I understand, Serena, but notice: what does Jennifer do?"

"She wants to die! I can feel an energy beckoning to her."

"Tell me about it," Mom quietly suggests.

"It's calm and dark, it seems familiar somehow …" As my voice trails off, numbness fills my entire body.

"Don't go into the energy, Serena. Choose to stay here." Saying it loudly, she invites me to come back into this reality.

Blinking and rubbing my eyes, I inhale deeply, trying to brush off the feeling the darkness was giving me.

"Can you sense what that energy was about?" Mom asks. "What did it allow Jennifer to do?"

"It felt peaceful, and it seemed to take her pain away."

"Ask Godmother what that energy was."

"It was the energy of death," Godmother says. "By the time Jennifer was two, she wanted death more than anything else."

"Really let yourself feel the truth … that Jennifer wanted death more than anything else." Stating this fact quietly, Norma adds, "Are you letting yourself feel it?"

Inhaling slowly, I intentionally open myself to the truth, and as I do, the death energy fills me again. Feeling pleasantly numb, I blankly stare at Mom.

"Breathe more deeply, and let it come home to Godmother. I know it seems comforting, but if you really want to heal, you cannot afford to play in this energy." Calling my name, she continues, "It is not your friend, Serena! Breathe, and let Godmother have it!"

Taking a deep breath, I let it move to Godmother. After several minutes of breathing, I feel lighter. "What am I supposed to get from all of this?"

"You told me that you didn't like seeing Jennifer wounded, but these core children are severely wounded, and they don't trust you. They feel your anger. You have watched me accept them unconditionally, but they need that from you, too. You tell me you want to integrate, but when it gets difficult, you run. Do you hear what I'm telling you?"

I don't want to feel how badly they were hurt. I must admit that is how I really feel. The urge to go numb beckons me, but I don't give in to it. Instead, I breathe until I don't want to run anymore.

"What else bothers you about these children, Serena?"

"You don't understand. I physically hurt when I see them."

"I understand that, but it isn't your pain. The more you stay close to Godmother, the less the pain will affect you. I'm not saying it won't hurt, but the intensity will be tempered by Godmother's love. Would you be willing to let yourself feel the love Godmother has for you?"

Willingly, I open myself to Godmother, and a comforting warmth fills me from the inside out. It's like warm honey, smooth and thick. Closing my eyes, I continue to breathe. Sinking deeper into the cushion of the couch, I sigh contentedly.

After several minutes of silence, Mom speaks. "You can have this sweetness anytime you want. Godmother is always here, offering it to you. She loves you more than you can comprehend. Do you want that kind of love, Serena?"

"Of course, I do."

"You're the only one who can give it to you. If you go to Godmother instead of running, you can have a different outcome. Now ask Godmother if there's anything else she would like us to work with."

"I want to begin working with the infant energies that were created from the trauma in the first few months of Jennifer's life," says Godmother. "There was never a chance for Jennifer to connect to the body in a normal way, so Serena experiences the body as though it belongs to someone else. Doing specific activities that normal infants experience will help Serena feel more connected to her body. Before we begin, I would like you to explain some basic facts about the body and what we're going to do."

Pulling pen and paper from her purse, Mom draws a tiny, stick-figure baby with a cloud hanging above it.

Laughing, I point at her drawing. "Is that supposed to be a cloud?"

"I know ... I'm not the greatest artist, but you get the idea. When a baby is born, the first thing it does is cry. The baby inhales, bringing a bit of her soul energy into her body." Pointing to the large, circular image above the baby, Norma continues. "The soul comes into the baby's body with each breath she takes. Are you following me so far?" Scanning my face for some indication of my understanding, she waits.

"I didn't know that!"

"That's why we're having this conversation," Mom replies, chuckling. "In a loving household, the mother and father hold their new baby. When the baby cries for food, she not only receives warmth from her parents' touch, but she also feels ..." Norma raises her voice for emphasis, "the milk coming into her belly, filling her. Her cry does not go unnoticed. Instead, her cry is met with a loving response. Don't go to your head, Serena, but let yourself sense: how would the baby respond to this experience?"

Visually seeing what she has described, I watch as the imaginary baby is picked up and fed by her mother.

Interrupting my train of thought, Mom invites me to sense how the belly might feel when it's warm and filled with milk.

Purposely creating a feeling of warmth in my belly from the imagined milk, I exclaim, "Wow, the baby feels good. She inhales, receiving her soul into her body because it feels good ... and safe, doesn't it?"

"Yes, she responds to the experience naturally, thus coming into her body and into her life without fight. The baby builds trust through her body's feelings. She doesn't have to think about feeling safe or loved; she just is. But your parents didn't allow this natural connection to form; they deliberately distorted it. That's why Godmother is asking us to help these little ones."

"Of course, I'll help," I eagerly respond.

"Good. Then ask Godmother what she wants us to do."

"Godmother says she wants you to wrap me in a blanket. She says you will know what to do after that."

"Will you stay behind these infant energies, so that you won't disrupt them?" Mom asks.

Nodding enthusiastically, I get up, ready to do whatever I can.

"Come sit on the floor and breathe, while I get a blanket out of the closet. Godmother will bring them to the front. Just let yourself fall back into your body so that they can move forward."

Sitting cross-legged on the floor, I close my eyes and let myself drift toward the back of my spine. That's when I feel another energy move out in front of me; she's little, she can't be more than a month old. Her body is lifeless.

Coming back into the room, Mom says, "Lie down in the middle of the blanket, Serena." Wrapping my body end over end, she snuggly wraps me up in the blanket like a burrito. Smiling, she looks into my eyes, speaking quietly. "I can see you, little one. It's okay ... I'm here." Her compassion emanates from a deep stillness within her. She is unhurried. With a rhythm borne from intuition, she responds from a place outside of the mind. Crooning, while touching my face and arms, she invites each baby to come forward and into Soul's arms.

For over an hour, we work, taking each energetic piece of me into the greater embrace of my Essence. There is reverence for what we are doing, and I know that my participation makes a huge difference in my healing.

Chapter 18: BECOMING AUTHENTIC

I can barely catch my breath; my heart is beating so rapidly that my chest hurts. Rocking back and forth, I try to find comfort in any way I can. What will I do? Mom won't be home for another three days! Rubbing the couch, I concentrate on how real the fabric feels, but the feelings of terror won't abate. As another child's scream rips through me, I shout for Godmother to help me.

"I am here, Serena, breathe with me."

Sitting straighter, I intentionally focus on my breath. I've been doing this long enough to know that if I stay with the terror, I won't be able to help myself. Finally, after long minutes of determined breathing, I feel Godmother's compassion calm my aching chest.

"Give the memory to me, Serena. Don't let any of it stay. I will keep it safe until Mom returns home."

Visualizing the memory broken into pieces, I pick them up and put them into a large drawstring bag, closing it tight until I can talk to Mom.

*****

Mom got home last night. I can't wait to see her!

As I watch the cars come over the ridge, I can barely contain my excitement. She should be here any minute! *Is that her car? Why is it moving so slowly?* When her black Jaguar finally pulls into the driveway, I fling open the door and holler my greetings to her.

Coming into the kitchen, Mom says, "Let me put the bags down. Then I can give you a real hug." Lying the grocery bags on the floor, she smiles before taking me in her arms.

Sighing with relief, I stand still, letting her love fill me. Finally, I step back and inspect her from head to toe. "You look pretty, Mom!" Dressed in slacks and a flowered blue blouse, she looks beautiful to me.

"Have you had lunch yet?"

"No, I was waiting for you, Mom."

"I'll make us sandwiches while you put the groceries away. We have a lot to talk about, I bet."

"We do. We really do!"

Moments later, as we sit side by side on the couch, Mom says, "I got you something." Putting a little paper bag in front of me, she smiles.

Pushing aside the brightly colored pink tissue paper, I find a gold necklace, inset with various colored stones, nestled in the bottom of the bag. Putting it over my head, I finger the stones appreciatively.

"I saw it in Sydney and knew you would enjoy it."

Hugging her enthusiastically, I exclaim, "I love it, Mom. It's just like your jewelry. Thanks!"

Swallowing the last bite of my sandwich, I look up expectantly and ask, "Are you ready to work?"

"Ask Godmother where she wants us to start."

"Please read your entire list first," Godmother requests.

"What? That makes no sense," I object.

"Serena, please don't start arguing," Mom says. "Would you trust Godmother and just read your list? She's been doing pretty well up to now." Gently chuckling, she motions for me to start.

"Why are you laughing? I don't think it's funny, Mom."

"Godmother has the sweetest sense of humor, and I can hear her laugh sometimes, that's all. I'm not laughing at you, Serena. We both love you and honor how wonderfully you are doing. There is a reason that Godmother is asking you to do this, so please read your list."

As I read the list aloud, my thoughts wander. *What is Godmother up to? I need to talk to Mom about each one of these things. They're important.*

Feeling Mom's touch on my arm, I look up in surprise.

"Didn't you hear me, Serena?"

"What?"

"I asked you three times if you could see a common denominator in what you have written."

Looking down at my paper, I frown, confused. Looking at the list, I try to find the common thread that she is talking about. To me, it seems to be separate items with no commonality.

"Ask Godmother what she wants to show us, will you?"

"But I need to talk to you about each one of these things. I've been waiting —"

"I understand, Serena, but Godmother has led you up to now. Would you be willing to trust her in this?"

Nodding, I hesitate, because I know this can't be good. Asking Godmother for guidance, I repeat her words aloud. "Serena has trouble handling things because she pretends to be older than she is. I know that you understand where I'm going with this. As long as pretend is allowed to stay here, we are stuck. Do you follow what I'm talking about?"

"Yes, so where do you want me to start?" Mom asks.

"With the truth, please. I will step in whenever it is needed. Ask Serena to be open and not fight where we're going with this. It's crucial for her integration."

Taking my hand, Mom scoots closer to me. "Do you remember when we discovered the monsters in the cave?"

"Yes."

"And when we found the monsters, what did they believe they were?"

"What?" I'm confused.

"Did they believe they were monsters?" Mom gently asks.

"Oh … yes! I remember that Godmother helped them take off their costumes. That's when we discovered they were just little kids!" I'm relieved with this line of questioning. At first, I felt threatened by what Godmother was asking, but this is easy!

"Good, and when the children discovered they weren't monsters, do you remember how they felt?"

Shaking my head no, I'm silent.

"I didn't think you remembered. At first, they were afraid. Their costumes seemed to keep them safe and away from pain. Letting go of their costumes took courage, didn't it?"

Uh-oh, I'm feeling anxious again. I don't like where this is leading. "I don't have a costume on!" I angrily deny.

"Would you be willing to stay with me and not rush off to your head?"

My anxiety has increased tenfold, and my body is hurting. Repressing the urge to fight, I inhale slowly and listen.

"Can you sense the courage it took for them to let go of their costumes?"

"I didn't know it took courage," I quietly reply.

"I know you didn't. What do you sense allowed them to do this courageous thing?"

Knowing the answer, I reply without hesitation. "It was Godmother, wasn't it?"

"Yes. And sense: why do you think Godmother would be bringing this up now?"

Feeling defensive, I shrug. I feel the darkness beckoning to me.

"Serena!" Mom commands, "Don't leave! After all this time, don't you trust Godmother and me?"

Feeling ambivalent, I watch Mom through a cloud of haze as she and Godmother talk.

"It's alright," Godmother says. "Whether she likes it or not, this must be confronted, or we cannot move forward. I will hold a space so that she cannot leave."

Feeling cornered, I notice my feelings are no longer muted. Mom's too close. I'm frightened and feeling angry, and I want nothing to do with this conversation.

"You tell me you want to integrate, but when you are asked to look at the truth, you withdraw." Slightly raising her voice, Mom asks, "What do you choose, Serena?"

Squirming uncomfortably, I clench my jaw. I'm tired of being in pain, but this work just keeps getting harder. I never imagined what it would require of me, but I can't quit now! Clutching the sides of the couch, I face Mom squarely and say, "I'll do whatever it takes!"

Smiling, Mom leans in and gently asks, "Have Godmother or I ever done anything to hurt you?"

Feeling the tears slip down my face, I shake my head no.

"Let yourself feel that, will you? Breathe with me, and feel how much we both love you."

As I lean back against the cushions, Mom leads me in breath. Encouraging me to settle deeper into my body, she reminds me of how sweet my breath can be. As my determination surrenders to peace, my breath becomes my only awareness, and I know without reservation that whatever I am being asked to do will be perfect for me. Opening my eyes, I look at Mom with gratitude. "I'm okay now."

Patting my hand, she smiles warmly at me before continuing. "I know how courageous you are; I watch it. I've never worked with someone who is as committed to their healing as you are. So, tell me what you understand so far."

"I understand that the monsters in the cave were not really monsters. In fact, they were children hiding in costumes to keep them safe."

"Good, but I want you to take it one step further. Really let yourself feel how much they believed they were monsters. They believed it completely, or it wouldn't have worked otherwise. Can you let yourself grasp what I'm saying?"

Remembering how the monster that had stopped Mom at the mouth of the cave was huge and threatening. This was no game to him. He was clear about what his job was, and he would do whatever he had to do it. Relaying this to Mom, I squeeze her hand and grit my teeth. I sense where this conversation is going, and I don't like it a bit.

"Even though the child wore a costume, he never once dreamed that it wasn't real, did he?"

"Just say what you are going to say!" I anxiously cry.

"It's okay. She's as ready as she is going to be," Godmother interjects.

"Yes, Serena, you're wearing a costume of sorts. Will you let yourself feel the truth of this, or will you fight, only delaying the inevitable?"

Pursing my lips, I nod silently.

"The costume you wear is that of an adult. We repeatedly discovered that every adult in the system was only a child trying to keep the life moving forward by pretending to know how to handle things. Do you remember that?"

"Yes, I remember …" *I know what she's saying is true, but how am I supposed to keep this work going if I'm a kid?* Lost in thought, I don't hear what Mom just said. "Will you say it again, please?"

"As long as you keep pretending, you're lying to yourself. You can never fully integrate as long as you stay a child in maturity. So, sense with me: what does it mean to be a child?"

Repressing the anger I'm feeling, I concentrate on Mom's face. Studying her eyes, I count each line that surrounds them, hoping I can distract myself long enough to keep the anger at bay. Tight-lipped, I answer evenly. "I really don't know, Mom."

"I know you don't. Then ask your mind what it means to be an adult."

"I know that! It means you act mature and have answers for problems, and you take care of yourself …"

"Yes … so breathe with me a moment and do not judge!" Raising her voice, Mom looks squarely at me. "Do you take care of yourself, Serena?"

Silently, I shake my head no.

"Please let Godmother's compassion fill you. This isn't said in judgment. This is to help you heal and allow for complete integration. Can you remember that?"

Nodding, I breathe, asking Godmother to help me face the truth.

"And when a problem comes up, do you know how to handle it, or do you get afraid and withdraw?" Taking my hand, Mom smiles at me, waiting.

"I get afraid."

"Do you know why you get afraid?"

Shaking my head no, I'm feeling overwhelmed and defeated. Refusing to give into my emotions, I inhale deeply.

Sitting back, Mom smiles at me before continuing. "You have no experience to draw upon. If everyone in the system ran whenever the going got tough, how could anyone have a chance to grow up? There isn't a vast wealth of experience just lying there for your awareness. Can you sense how this works?" Not waiting for an answer, Mom continues. "When I was a child, I had experiences. These experiences layered themselves, one on top of the other. As I grew into an adult, I experienced both success and failure that I learned from, preparing me for future events in my life. Are you following me? Tell me what you understand before we go any further."

My chest is weighed down, and I can barely breathe. "I understand that because you grew up without running away, you grew into an adult …?" Unsure of my answer, I sadly shake my head while shrugging my shoulders.

"This is a perfect example, Serena! You're ready to give up and hide, because this seems too hard. You've been pretending to be an adult when, in truth, you react to most situations like a small child. Can you feel this truth without judging yourself?"

Drawing on the courage I know Godmother has, I breathe and let myself fully grasp what Mom is saying. Slowly, things start to connect. "Oh … that's why I get afraid when you leave on a trip! It's not that I'm wrong, I just don't have experiences to draw upon, do I? I don't trust I can take care of myself!"

"Yes," Mom happily responds. "It's because you feel safe when I'm at home. Are you courageous enough to let go of your old ideas in order to discover a way of living that comes from truth?"

Hearing only snippets of what Mom is saying, I struggle to stay. Pulling myself away from the voices warning me of doom, I breathe deeply and reply. "So, what would you have me do? I am a child living in an adult body," I robotically parrot.

"Yes. Feel that statement without any judgment. It's just a fact." Facing me, she sits in complete serenity. "Ask Godmother how she would like us to proceed with this, please."

"Ask Serena," Godmother says, "if she would breathe with us and let go; have no idea, no plan, just trust us more than the fear that is warning her to hang on."

As I inhale, I consciously lower my shoulders, releasing some of the anxiety I'm feeling. Focusing on Mom's voice and nothing else allows the fearful swirling in my mind to settle down. As I inhale and exhale, my breath becomes slower. I begin to feel a sweet, rhythmic vibration pulsing ever so gently in my fingers and toes. As I inhale again, my body warms. I feel safe, with not a care in the world.

"Serena, can you feel the warmth of your body as you breathe? You don't need to answer me. Just open yourself to this sweet vessel that kept all of you alive these many years. Despite your body continuing to grow, every child remained stuck. Allow this truth to fill you." After a few moments, she adds, "Would you be willing to ask Godmother how old you are in maturity?"

Nodding, without opening my eyes, I hear Godmother tell me I'm only three or four years old.

Whispering aloud, with eyes closed shut, I watch Godmother smile at me. I feel her strength holding me. Knowing that integration and full healing are what I want more than anything else, I keep breathing.

"Sweetie, I'm right here. Ask Godmother what she would have us do, please."

"Feel this first before we go any further," says Godmother. "This is the key that will allow us to discover the authentic person locked behind the façade."

Opening my eyes, I ask, "What does she mean, locked behind the façade?"

"First, let yourself feel the truth. Your maturity is that of a three-, maybe four-year-old child. How does that feel?"

"It feels awful!" I cry.

"You get to choose," Mom warns. "Will you stay in judgment, or will you face the truth? Godmother has never lied to you."

Mom's compassionate strength inspires me. Closing my eyes, I breathe more fully, while opening myself to the truth that I'm a child in an adult body. (Being raised in an environment of terror meant the personalities were always on guard, watching the people around them for cues on how to behave. Our life was lived from the mind. No one in the system felt safe or had an authentic connection to the body. Each personality had a specific job to keep the life moving forward, so that the outside world would see "us" as normal. I'm being invited to live differently by feeling and connecting authentically to the body. But it can only be done from truth and not from the mind.)

"Ask Godmother to help you feel it, Serena."

I feel the truth that I have been a kid playing an adult game. What an exhausting way to live! Knowing I can't do this alone, I ask Godmother for help. As I take a deep, slow breath, awareness washes over me. My mind is no longer in control. I have the sensation of being little in this big body. But in the very next moment, I feel Godmother's presence in a way I've never felt before … so intimate, so close. I'm not alone.

Mom invites me to speak from this new place.

"I feel weird." Hearing my voice come out like a child's, I clamp my hand over my mouth in surprise. "I feel different, and I can't say how." My pronunciation is incorrect, but I'm feeling something that is hard to describe. I'm more solid, and my mind, which is usually loud, saying cruel things, is unusually quiet.

I see tears glimmering in Mom's eyes.

"How come you are crying?"

"Your bravery touches me, sweetie. Ask Godmother where she wants us to go with this."

"It's important that she begin to connect with this authentic feeling," Godmother says. "When you speak to her, and she responds with an adult voice, this will tell you that she has stepped back into her familiar façade. Invite her to breathe and let go of her pretend. She is to be a child all the time; that means in every respect. The more she surrenders to her authentic self, the more this transformation can occur. This is not like a baby that is born and grows incrementally by days. This will be done differently, from the inside out. The more Serena surrenders to this space, the more I can do my work from within. Do you sense what I am saying?"

"Yes."

"Then be very clear with her," Godmother stresses. "In all areas, she is to be an authentic child."

"Did you hear what Godmother said?"

Nodding, I prefer not to speak, as I feel unsure of myself.

"How do you feel about what Godmother said?"

I wonder how in the world I will be a child alone in this house. I don't think she understands. There is no one here to cook and clean …

"Serena, did you hear me? How do you feel about what Godmother is asking you to do?"

I hear my adult voice answer loud and clear. "I don't think it will work. You don't understand …"

"No, it is you who doesn't understand. With Godmother, everything is possible. She can take care of you, but you must be willing to give up control and discover what it means to be authentic. Do you understand why she's asking this of you?"

Shaking my head no, my mind races with fearful, angry thoughts. One moment I'm feeling peaceful, and in the next, I'm panicked. I want to be integrated so I can have a life, but this is asking too much! As my panic builds, I shout in an adult voice, "I can't do it!"

"I know, Serena. Remember when Godmother told us that this journey would be harder than either of us could imagine? You said you would do whatever it took. No one is making you integrate. You can quit right now if that is what you really want to do. Breathe, and decide. I'll love you no matter what. I do not need you to change. This is your decision."

"I can't quit, but what you're asking me to do is impossible!" I angrily shout.

"Who are you listening to? Godmother has never led us astray. Do you think I knew how this integration would work? I did not, but I trust Godmother implicitly. Will you breathe with me and let yourself feel the authentic peace that Godmother is asking you to stay in? I'm right here. I won't go anywhere."

I would do anything to integrate, so if this is what I'm being asked to do, I will do it. As I listen to Mom's voice lead me in breath, the tension drains away, and peace returns.

"Let yourself feel the difference between what a pretend adult feels like and what it's like to be the authentic child, Serena."

Sighing happily, I remark. "I like how this feels."

"You can have this anytime you want. Ask Godmother if there is any part of this you don't get."

"Your feelings will be your indicator," Godmother says.

"What?" I ask. It seems that with this change, even my reasoning is limited."

"It means that if you feel anxious," Mom states, "or if you're trying to figure out what to do, then you are listening to your mind and not being authentic. And if you're not sure, speak out loud and listen to what you are saying to yourself. The minute you hear yourself speaking in an adult voice, you will know you are not being authentic. If you ask for Godmother's guidance, you can have a different outcome.

"Now ... I know you wanted me to be here the entire day, but this morning a client called me with an emergency. She is very upset, so I made time for her. I know you're disappointed, but will you accept that I have to leave earlier than you would like?" Not waiting for an answer, she continues. "It's important that you ask Godmother to help you with cooking meals.

Let Godmother be in the front of the body as much as possible. When you're watching television, you are only allowed to watch age-appropriate shows. This will help your mind stay still. If you watch a show created for an adult, it will feed your mind, and that will not be for your highest good. Do you follow me?"

Feeling upset and a bit overwhelmed, I lean in and give Mom a hug. "I'll do whatever it takes," I reply.

Leaning back so she can see my face, Mom smiles and gently suggests, "Do it because you love you, Serena."

Chapter 19: MOMENTS OF REAL HAPPINESS

Feeling restless, I channel surf, hoping to catch a glimpse of anything that might be more interesting than stupid cartoons. "This is boring!" Startled at hearing my adult voice, I realize I'm pretending again. Rubbing my forehead, I turn off the TV and try to breathe, but after a few moments, I give up.

You're a mental case!

You're forty-nine years old! That's no child!

She'd never find you if left now.

You have a suitcase; pack your things so we can leave!

Staring at the front door, I imagine myself walking down the street, suitcase in hand. How would I do it? I could hitchhike, but that could be dangerous ... and since Mom is paying for everything, where would I get the money I need? Shaking my head, I try to refocus and let go of the fantasy. I ask Godmother for help.

"Breathe with me," Godmother says. "I'm right here. Notice how you're feeling as you pretend to be an adult. What are you feeling, Serena?"

"I feel anxious, and my stomach and back hurt. My head is pounding, and I feel like I'm coming out of my skin!"

"Breathe, I am here."

Hearing her soothing voice, I inhale, releasing some of my fear.

"That's it. Bring your breath deep into your belly."

I purposely slow my breath; it takes a long time before the fear begins to lessen. Shuddering with frustration, I wipe the tears off my face. I'm tempted to give up.

"Focus and let your feelings move, Serena," Godmother says. "Don't hold onto anything. Let it all come to me. That's it. I am here. I won't ever leave you."

I burrow into the couch cushions with resolve. Focusing only on my breath allows my body to quiet. I'm so tired. Head dropping forward, I'm almost asleep when I hear Godmother ask me to speak out loud.

"What do you want me to say?" I ask in my child's voice.

"Describe how you feel, and say it aloud, please."

"I feel calmer and warmer," I murmur.

"Good, and notice, where is the anxiety?"

"It's gone," I answer.

"Sense with me. What is different about what you are feeling now, compared with what you were feeling in your body before?"

"In my body?" The more she questions me, the less tired I feel.

"Don't go to your mind, Serena. Feel what is different. Where is your energy? Is it up in your shoulders or down in your belly?"

Forcing myself to focus, I answer confidently, "I'm in my belly."

"Yes, your mind is quieter because you let yourself drop down into your body as you breathed. This is the gift of breath. When you help yourself, you help the other children feel safe, too. Now, keep feeling … and describe how the rest of your body feels."

"I feel solid, like the body is fuller."

"As you go about your day, pay attention to how your body feels. It will be your signal as to whether you're being authentic or not. Do you understand what I've said?"

"Yes."

"Good. Then tell me what I'm asking you to do, please."

Sighing in frustration, I instantly feel stupid and want to retreat. *All she ever says is 'pay attention!'*

Obeying Godmother, I repeat exactly what she said.

"Try again," she prompts, while gently laughing. "Did you notice you're not being authentic? Take a breath and come back down into your belly. That's it … breathe deeply and slowly, Serena."

After a few minutes, I'm able to try again.

"Say it in your own words," Godmother prompts.

"You want me to notice what my body is telling me, right?"

"Yes … The more you connect the feelings in your body to the thoughts you are reacting to, the more you will be able to help yourself. Notice where your energy is in your body. Are you up in your shoulders, feeling anxious, or are you anchored in your belly, feeling more solid and full, as you described just a moment ago? Speak out loud to help you connect the two. I'm here always. Can you feel me?"

Closing my eyes, I look for Godmother.

"No, don't look for me in that way. Instead … feel me." Her voice is comforting, filling me with sweet warmth that extends throughout my body. "Will you allow me to come even closer, Serena?"

I let go, with no idea of what will happen. As I breathe, I feel an energetic vibration fill my entire body, wrapping me in a cocoon of love. Nothing is as important as this. Inhaling in sheer bliss, I respond, "This is so …"

"Shhhh … Don't go to your mind. Just breathe and allow me to keep filling you."

But I don't stay with it. Instead, I pick up the phone to share the experience with Mom, and just that quickly, I leave my Soul's sweet embrace to go to my mind. When Mom doesn't answer, my anxiety returns. Shaking my head in frustration, I speak aloud, and sure enough, my adult voice is back. I don't let it deter me. I bring my energy back into my belly while inhaling slowly through my nose, and finally, after minutes of focused breathing, my anxiety disappears. And when I talk out loud, my child's voice has returned!

"I'm proud of you, Serena! You didn't give up. It will get easier, I promise!"

Godmother's words of encouragement motivate me to keep trying.

Angry voices warn me to leave it alone. They say I shouldn't trust it, but I feel something that is different. I don't understand it yet … but when I'm the child me, I feel more real. I decide to trust Mom and Godmother and ignore the others' warnings.

*****

I notice that Mom looks tired. "How are you doing, Mom?"

"I'm going to be leaving on a trip in four days, so we will need to make a list of the things you will need while I am gone." Keeping her voice purposely light, she adds, "Bring me your calendar so we can mark the days of my trip on it."

"How long will it be this time, and where are you going?" I angrily ask.

"Have you noticed you're not being authentic?"

That is the last thing I want to hear. Instead, I answer no, and obediently begin breathing. But my obedience doesn't pay off. Clenching my jaw, I ask, "How long will you be gone?" Trying to keep the emotion out of my voice, I try to convince her that I'm being authentic, but she isn't fooled.

Remaining unruffled, Mom says, "You get to choose, Serena. I can go home, and we can work another day, or you can breathe so we can work now. It's up to you." Remaining calm, she waits for my response.

Instead of answering, I close my eyes. I don't want her to go home, so I honestly begin to breathe, and after ten minutes or so, it pays off. I'm not upset anymore. Just as I'm about to open my eyes, Godmother asks me to keep breathing.

Following her suggestion, I feel a shift happen. Instead of the empty awareness I was feeling a moment ago, genuine peace fills my entire body, causing me to involuntarily shudder with relief. As I open my eyes, I smile: now I'm ready to work.

"I don't come here to fight, Serena." Leaning forward, Norma clasps her hands together before continuing. "I don't go on trips to cause you upset. It's a part of our life, and when you can accept that, you will be happier. Now, where is your calendar?"

Pulling it out from under the couch, I hand it to Mom so she can mark off the days she will be gone. "Ask Godmother what we can do to help you while I'm gone. I know cartoons don't interest you very much, so I would like some suggestions from her."

"If you can find some crafts that she could do and maybe a movie or two that are appropriate for her, it would be helpful," Godmother says.

"I know ... the movie *Elf* just came out on DVD. I would love to see that!" I excitedly exclaim.

"I will see what I can do, Serena. Don't get distracted. Ask Godmother what kind of crafts she would like you to do, please."

"If she can use her hands to create something, it will help her to stay more present," Godmother responds.

"Alright. Then I will bring over what I can find when we work on Friday. I will need a grocery list as well, since we leave very early Saturday morning. It will need to cover at least two and a half weeks." Stating this, Norma waits to see how I will respond.

Feeling overwhelmed, I nervously pick at my skin. I don't want her to be gone that long. Taking a breath, I make a different choice and drop deeper into my belly, choosing to stay with the peace I was feeling. "So how long do we get to work today?"

"We have as much time as you need, sweetie."

*****

Friday has come too fast. I want Mom to come because I miss her, but at the same time, I want her to stay away, so she won't leave.

Seeing her pull into the driveway, I swing the door open and happily holler, "Hello!" As I watch her pull bag after bag out of the back of the car, guilt consumes me. *How can she spend that much money on me?*

Noticing that I've withdrawn, Mom kindly takes my arm and suggests that I begin putting the refrigerated items away. "Have you had any lunch today?"

Shaking my head no, I remain silent.

"Serena!" Mom calls. "Where have you gone? Who are you listening to?"

"Huh? I don't know."

"You get to choose. Will you help you or hurt you? Please, put the refrigerated items away while I fix us something to eat. What kind of sandwich do you want?"

"I want peanut butter-and-jelly," I woodenly reply.

"Get yourself a glass of water, and go sit on the couch. Purposely focus with your breath, please."

Settling down on the couch, I take a breath and put my hand on my stomach. I'm extremely upset, and my skin is screaming. Focusing on my breath, I stay with it until Mom comes into the living room.

"Do you feel any better?"

Nodding absently, I reply, "I don't know what happened."

"That's alright. You are here now. Eat your sandwich so you can feel more grounded."

"Why is everything so hard, Mom?" Feeling angry with myself, I wait, hoping she can give me a reasonable answer.

Ignoring my question, Mom asks one of her own.

"When you breathe and feel peace fill you, is that something you would like more of?"

"Of course, I would. Don't you know that?"

"You can have that if you stay aware and don't go to fight."

"I didn't go to fight. I was asking you a question," I defensively reply.

Deciding not to pursue it any further, Mom invites me to move closer to Godmother. After a couple of moments, she asks, "Where does Godmother want us to begin, Serena?

"She says she wants us to go over the rules while you are away."

"Alright then." Leaning forward, Norma says, "Do you understand that you are not to go outside for any reason, or open the door, nor answer the phone to anyone but me? And you're only to watch television that Godmother says is okay?"

"Yes, I know that, this isn't new."

"When Godmother asks me to go over the rules, there is a good reason for it. When you ignore them, then you're not safe."

I have forgotten that I was tempted to pack a suitcase and leave just a few days earlier. "I'm hearing you, Mom. I promise: I will pay attention."

"That's all I ask. I'm not trying to be difficult, but when Godmother says we need to look at something, I know and trust her implicitly without having to question her motives. If you would stay aware and not go to fight, it would make it so much easier on both of us." Sitting back, Norma crosses her hands. "Now, ask Godmother if there's anything else she wants us to discuss."

"She says that I need to be authentic first. Then she wants us to talk about working with my hands."

"Then breathe so you can be the authentic you."

Nodding, I start breathing again. I'm like a yo-yo, going back and forth from façade Serena to authentic Serena without any consistency. After long minutes, I feel myself shift as the stress leaves my body.

"So what does Godmother mean when she says 'working with my hands'?"

"Don't look to me for the answer," Mom states. "Go inside and ask Godmother what she means."

Closing my eyes, I hear Godmother's words clearly. Repeating them verbatim, I say, "If Serena creates things that bring her joy, she will have an easier time staying authentic."

Hearing her cue, Mom gets up and retrieves the bags from the kitchen. Feeling the weight of unworthiness fill me again, I switch back into the pretend adult.

"Will you receive these freely?" Godmother whispers.

Lying the bags down in front of me, Mom steps back, smiling happily.

"I asked the lady at the store if she could help me find some crafts that would be fun for you, and this is what she showed me!" Pulling out a plastic container filled with brightly colored pink stuff, she hands it to me and sits back down.

"What's this?" I excitedly ask. Examining the picture on the container, I notice a variety of items can be made from this material.

"It's called Floam," Mom explains. "Evidently, you can make things from it, and when it dries, it will be lightweight, and you can play with it."

"Oh, this is so cool, Mom!" I've switched back into being the authentic child. Dumping the packages out onto the floor, I find they come in green, blue, yellow, pink, and white. Reading the label out loud, I struggle to pronounce some of the words. "It says Floam is a gooey substance mixed with bits of Styrofoam that can be formed into anything I want to make!" Voice raised in anticipation, I grab another bag, giggling. "This is neat. I can't wait to play with it." Pulling out hard balls of Styrofoam, I look at Mom quizzically.

"I bought those in case you could use them with the Floam."

"What a great idea, Mom!" Jumping up, I hug her tightly.

"I know when I go on a trip, it's hard for you. That's why I'm happy I found something that looks like it can be fun. Would you invite Godmother to do these things with you?" Not waiting for my reply, she continues. "I look forward to seeing what you create. Now I have one more gift for you." Pulling a small bag from her purse, she joyously laughs.

"You found it! Wow, *Elf* is mine, and I can watch it as many times as I want! This is great!" I'm so excited, I feel as though I may burst from joy. Rocking back and forth on the couch, I try to contain my enthusiasm.

"Put the bags to the side. Sit back and breathe with me so that you can calm down." Leading me in breath, Mom's calm, sweet voice soothes me. "Now ask Godmother what she wants to talk about."

Godmother's answer comes easily. "It's important that while you are gone, she allows herself to discover what it's like to play. Living only in memory creates heartache. I know you understand where I'm going with this."

"Did you hear what Godmother said?"

"Yes, but I don't understand."

"Are you aware of what you think about most of the time? Are you in fear, thinking about what has happened, or are you afraid, thinking about what will happen tomorrow? How much time do you spend in this present moment?"

"What?" Feeling guilty, I withdraw, retorting, "I don't know what you're asking."

"Notice, Serena, you're fighting me. So, take a breath and settle deeper into your body. Are you being authentic or are you listening to your mind?"

I know I must stop letting my mind control me. As the minutes tick by, and I keep breathing, my anxiety finally wanes.

"Okay … I'll say it again," Mom states. "Do you stay in this moment? Look around you. This moment is the only thing going on in your life. There's you, there's me, and there's Petunia at the end of the couch. There's no one else in this house but the three of us."

"Okay …"

Mom knows I'm not following her example, so she tries a different approach. "Today, I brought you different things to play with, didn't I?"

"Yes."

"While you're playing and having fun, would you be willing to notice how much of that time you spend in fear?" Smiling at me, she continues. "Notice without judgment, and then ask Godmother to help you come back to be in the present moment. Breathe and feel what you are doing. Allow yourself to enjoy what you are creating. Notice: are you in your mind listening to the others, or are you deep in your belly, being authentic? The more you stay in each moment authentically feeling, the more you will begin to feel joy. Would you like that?"

"Of course I would," I earnestly reply.

"This is where you get to choose, Serena. This is your life and no one else's. When you are afraid and choose something other than fear, you win. Godmother will help you with this. Can you begin to become aware?"

"I'll try, Mom."

"That's all I ask. Now, I have to go. I hope you have lots of fun with the Floam. I look forward to seeing what you create."

"Oh, Mom, I know you have to go, but will you hold me for a minute?"

"Of course, sweetie." Getting up, she sits beside me on the couch and wraps her arms around me.

Sighing happily, I respond, "Thanks, Mom, for all that you do for me. I don't take it for granted."

"I know that. I love you, Serena. You're worth it to me."

*****

Cutting the package with scissors, I release the Floam from its tub. I rub a small amount of it between my fingers. I love how it feels; gooey and bumpy, and it doesn't stick to my fingers. But I want more colors than this.

"Godmother, is there a way for me to make more colors?"

"You can use food dye, but only put a small portion of the Floam into the bowl, so that if it doesn't work, you can try something else."

"That's a great idea!" Pulling out all the bowls I have, I place a dollop of each Floam color into them, adding drops of green, yellow, red, and blue food dye to make the colors I want. *I'm like a wizard making a magic potion!* Giggling, I step back to admire my creation. I've made nine more colors to play with!

"Would you notice how you're feeling?" Godmother invites.

Can't I just play, I wonder? Impatiently, I answer, "I feel good, Godmother."

"And what does that mean, you 'feel good'?"

"Why do you ask such weird questions?"

"It's important that you begin to connect with how you are feeling, Serena. Right now, you're excited to play with the Floam, aren't you?"

"Yes ..."

"Then how is your body feeling?"

I notice that my arms and legs feel quiet, without anxiety. My stomach isn't clenched, and my shoulders, which are usually tense, are relaxed and free of pain.

"As you play with the Floam, if you would stop every half hour or so and notice how your body is feeling, that will help you to become more aware."

Nodding, I promise Godmother I will do as asked.

Emptying the contents of the bag Mom bought onto the floor, different-sized Styrofoam balls roll off in different directions. *I know what I can make; this is going to be fun!* I can barely contain my excitement as I look through the stacks of holiday cards I have saved over the years. I'm envisioning what I want to make with the Floam, and it's going to be wonderful! Gathering aluminum foil, toothpicks, wire, and liquid glitter, I begin playing.

*****

The time has flown by. Mom is coming home tomorrow! Christmas ornaments shaped like reindeer, snowmen, doves, and candy canes hang on lampshades and the backs of chairs. I am delighted with what I made.

I watched the movie *Elf,* and when Buddy the Elf cut out paper snowflakes to decorate the department store, I replayed that one scene a dozen times to learn how to do it myself. I made over forty snowflakes and decorated them with glitter. Then I attached a string to each snowflake and hung them from the ceilings of my kitchen and living room. Whenever a gust of heat bursts through the air ducts, the paper snowflakes twinkle and twirl in the breeze. I also made strings of paper garland, which I hung from every corner of the living room. My house looks like a winter wonderland, and I love it!

Laughing joyously, I hear Godmother say, "Do you know what's even more important than all of this? You're allowing you, the authentic Serena … to be created. You've had a series of connected moments in which you've been here without switching. As each one of these moments moved into the next, allowing you to feel and be here in a new way. These collected moments are creating the real you, and that is the real miracle, Serena."

*****

As I stayed in my body and felt what it was like to be authentic, I connected with the truth in a whole new way. Truth had always been an elusive idea in my mind, disconnected from reality. But as I felt the truth resonate in my body, it helped me differentiate the trained person from the authentic one I was becoming. As the weeks progressed and I became more authentic, my need to speak and act as a child slowly disappeared.

Chapter 20: I AM THE DOORWAY

"Do you realize how long a day is?" I anxiously ask.

Smiling at me, Mom replies, "Yes ... why do you ask, Serena?"

"Because a day seems to go on forever! I'm not kidding, Mom!"

"Oh, Serena, I know you're serious, but it's music to my ears to hear you say this." Laughing merrily, Mom adds, "You never experienced what a full day felt like, because you were always switching into other personalities. I celebrate your awareness. Do you?"

"I didn't look at it that way."

"I know. You went to your fearful mind that told you something was wrong. Your awareness shows us both how much you've changed. Can you allow different to be okay?"

"Of course I can."

"Great." Squeezing my hand, she prompts, "Then ask Godmother where she wants us to begin."

"Godmother wants us to talk about the energy of fight."

"Great, so what does the word 'fight' mean to you, Serena?"

"It means you have your fist up."

"Yes, that's a perfect description. Ask Godmother why she wants us to talk about this, please."

Listening, I repeat her words exactly. "Serena always goes to the energy of fight first."

"But that can't be true!" I object.

"This isn't said in judgment, Serena. Your reaction just now was from the energy of fight. Godmother is asking us to talk about this to help you open to a new awareness. Now, take a breath, and tell me how your body is feeling."

"My shoulders and neck are hurting, my head is pounding, and my stomach is tied in knots."

"Yes. And would you say your body is a representation of what your closed fist is?"

Silently nodding, I'm afraid to say anything because I might lash out at her.

"What are you so afraid of, sweetie?"

Her compassion invites me to open and let go, but I'm overly anxious and can barely breathe. "I feel threatened by what we are talking about. I know it's unreasonable, but I want to scream at you to leave it alone!"

"You're not the energy of fight, Serena. We're talking about this so that you can become aware. You told me that your shoulders and your neck are crying. That pain is you ... hitting you." As she says it, she starts gently punching herself in the shoulder for effect. "I want you to pick up the Kleenex box and start hitting yourself with it."

"What? I can't do that!" Feeling self-conscious, I resist her suggestion.

"Would you be brave enough to discover something I'm asking you to notice?"

Leaning over, I grab the Kleenex box that's on the floor, and gently start hitting myself on the upper arm. After a couple of times, I ask her if I can stop.

"No. Keep hitting yourself. I want you to notice something."

Leaning back in the rocking chair, she quietly watches me hit myself over and over again.

After the umpteenth time of doing it to myself, I angrily shout, "I'm not doing this anymore!" Slamming the box onto the floor, I angrily glare at her.

"Who gave you permission to stop hitting you?" she calmly asks.

"I did! I didn't like hitting myself! It felt awful!"

"I hope so," she calmly responds. "Because every day, of every hour, your fist is up, hitting you. Whether you do it from your thoughts, or through energetically pounding your body, it's you doing it to you."

"Aren't you exaggerating?" I angrily interrupt. "It's not every day, all day long."

"Notice: you're fighting me even now. You cannot have integration and still fight. The two cannot coexist. Do you even sense what I'm saying?"

I know I'm overreacting, but I feel threatened. Closing my eyes, I breathe, focusing on the rhythm of my breath. After a long time, I begin to feel less afraid.

"I know this work is difficult, Serena, but when I bring up a subject, and you fight me with this level of resistance, it's hard on both of us. Now, I want to ask you a question, and it might seem to be off-topic, but I want you to be open. Can you do that?"

"Yes, I can."

"Then, sense: who is Godmother, really?"

"You want me to tell you who Godmother is?"

"Yes, and instead of going to your mind for the answer, why don't you ask her?"

Closing my eyes, I see her off to my left, bathed in a beautiful white light. "So, who are you really?"

"Sense with me, dear one. I am your Heart. I am the love that you truly are," says Godmother.

Opening my eyes, I repeat the words exactly as she said them. "She says she is my Heart, and that she's the love that I truly am …? I don't get what she's saying."

"Stop a moment and breathe. Feel … Godmother is your own Heart, leading you and loving you, asking you if she can come closer to you than ever before. You believed that Godmother was outside of you, as a separate entity that had come to lead you. You weren't open to the truth that Godmother is really your own essence, leading you in every moment. We're not talking about the organ in your chest that pumps your blood. We're talking about your Soul energy, Serena." Leaning toward me, Mom adds, "You have believed you were the energy of fear so completely, it has kept you stuck. Now we're telling you that you're the energy of love. How does that feel for you?"

"I feel what you're saying is true right here." Lying my hand over my chest, I continue. "Remember how you taught me that love wasn't pain? I had always believed that if I let love in, I would be hurt. But you proved to me more than any words could that you loved me no matter what, and that felt good! I like the idea that Godmother is my own Heart energy."

"It has taken a long time for us to get to the place where you can trust yourself enough to feel this truth, Serena." Getting up, she comes toward me with her arms open.

Standing in the middle of the living room, we hug tightly before taking our seats again.

"Now, before we leave this subject, ask your Heart if there is anything she wants to add."

"Go back to the topic of fighting," says Heart, "and help Serena connect to the feeling of why she fights all the time."

"Would you be willing to face the truth that you fight because you're afraid all the time?" Mom asks.

Closing my eyes, I sense why I need to fight all the time, and in an instant, terror radiates throughout my entire body. I want to run so badly! Only through my Heart's compassionate strength, combined with my breath, am I able to remain sitting.

"Repeat these words exactly as I say them," my Heart requests. "Your multiplicity worked because you were disconnected from the truth of what was really going on in your life. Each traumatic event was contained in multiple parts, so that you would not be overwhelmed by the enormity of what was really happening to you."

"Do you get what Heart is saying?" Mom asks.

"More than ever before."

"In your willingness to stay and not to run," Mom adds, "you allow these frightened parts to come home to your Heart, which is what integration is. Imagine a strand of pearls breaking and falling to the floor in every direction. You have been like that strand of pearls, and as each part came forward to share their story, they felt heard and, from compassion, they naturally came home to your Heart. Each new integration was like a pearl being added to the string called *you*. Let yourself feel that what we're doing is creating a new strand of pearls called *Serena*, this authentic person that I'm talking to today."

"Even though this work is hard," I reply, "the gifts I receive from it far outweigh the discomfort I go through."

"I'm glad you feel that, Serena. Now ... I want to ask Heart something. Will you sit back and let go, please?" Waiting a moment for me to comply, Norma asks, "Is part of her denial her resistance to the truth, or is it something more?"

"It's both. We can only take this a breath at a time. When she starts realizing how often she fights and that it's hurting her, this will empower her, putting another chink in the wall of her denial."

Calling me back to the front, Norma asks if I have any questions.

Feeling a bit muddled, I shake my head no.

"If you notice how often you fight, and begin to connect that it's you hurting you, then we all win. Now, I have to go. I know we didn't have as much time as you'd like, but you get to decide: will you fight or stay with Heart? I'll call you later tonight."

Following Mom to the door, I wave goodbye.

*****

It is days later, and I'm sitting upright in a straight-backed chair, gently hitting myself with the Kleenex box. My lower back is in pain. Heart says it's because I'm angry at myself, but I don't feel angry. So, I'm hitting myself with the Kleenex box. I feel stupid doing this, but I don't stop. "I'm doing this to me," I say aloud, "because I'm soooo mad." I pause, but still, I don't feel angry.

"Would you notice that you're the one blocking it and let it go?" my Heart suggests. "Just be willing, and I'll do the rest."

Nodding, I choose to let the block go. Within seconds, anger radiates up my spine and into my chest. I clench my jaw, inhaling abruptly. This is uncomfortable!

"Why are you angry with yourself?" Heart asks.

"Because … I hate being alive!" Exploding with anger, I double over, crying.

"Don't be afraid. I'm here, Serena. Let the child who is holding the anger tell you why she hates being alive."

"I hurt so much. Don't you hear me?" The child's anguish stabs at my heart, but I don't give up. I continue breathing, and as I do, different children come forward to share their stories with me. In the background, I hear Heart reminding me that I am the doorway for them to come home. Finally, after an hour or so, things quiet down, and my pain is completely gone.

"This is the first time you've helped these internal children when Mom wasn't here. I'm proud of you for staying with it. Can you sense why they were so angry?"

"They needed me to hear them, didn't they?"

"Yes, and no matter how much you ignored them, they didn't go away. The next time you're feeling pain, you will know it belongs to them. Then you can do it differently, and that will be a gift you give yourself."

Chapter 21: THE DREAM

"I had a bad dream last night, and I can't seem to shake it; it feels real somehow."

"Did you ask Heart what's going on?"

"Heart says there was a part of the dream that reminded me of drowning."

"So breathe, and let yourself remember: but stay present no matter what feelings come up, can you do that, Serena?"

"Okay … I'll try, Mom." Taking a breath, I close my eyes so I can remember the dream. "I was on the beach, looking for something ... Oh, that's right, I was blind, unless I forced my eyes wide open, then I could see. That was scary! I was forcing my eyes open, looking for something in the sand; I was totally absorbed in it when, all of a sudden, I was swept up by a huge wave. I couldn't breathe, Mom!"

"Serena, come back to this moment," Mom commands. "Look around you! We're sitting in the living room. The dream is not real!"

Breathing slowly through my nose, I study my surroundings while rubbing the fabric of the couch. I purposely concentrate on feeling my breath as it comes in and out of my body, and slowly the feelings of terror subside. But once I start speaking again, the terror hits me with renewed force. "You don't understand how hard this is!"

"I do understand, Serena, but when you choose hysteria over staying here, it's because you don't want to know the truth. You must choose to stay!"

"Okay, Mom. I'm not trying to be difficult, but this is terrifying … just give me a minute." Closing my eyes, I breathe, choosing to stay present as best I can. "Heart says I need to let the sensation of drowning come up, without fighting it." Grimacing, I bravely take a breath and let myself feel what it's like to drown. "It's awful, I couldn't breathe, no matter how hard I tried." Taking a deep, slow breath, I close my eyes, letting myself remember.

"Open your eyes, Serena, so you can remember that you are in this present moment, safe in your house."

Eyes open, I see both worlds simultaneously. "Jennifer's in that huge warehouse—you remember, Mom—the place that is large enough to store an airplane?"

"Yes, Serena."

"She's being dragged up these wooden steps …"

"How old is Jennifer?"

"She's five."

"Alright. Go on."

"She's begging the men not take her to that … thing!"

"Describe what you are seeing, Serena."

Hesitating, I look at the ugly monstrosity. It's enormous. "It's oblong-shaped and lying on its side. There are four men in white lab coats, and a few military men standing on the platform next to this thing." Apprehension over shadows all thought. Focusing on Mom's face, I do the best I can to stay present. "I'm afraid."

"I understand, Serena. Anyone would be afraid, but it's not happening now; can you try and remember that?"

"Okay … Jennifer is being dragged up the stairs to the platform. They don't care that she's terrified!" I cry out hysterically.

"Would you stop a moment and hear what you just said?"

"What?"

"You said that the men don't care that Jennifer is afraid," Mom states. "Do you think, at this point in their experiments, they would start caring for her?"

"No, but —"

"Be honest, Serena. Don't give me an answer you think I want to hear. Do you think, after all this time, they would care? These men are disconnected from their authentic selves, which allows them to do horrific things to a child without remorse. Do you get that?"

"I never thought about it in that way."

"That's why I'm telling you this, it's important to have connected awareness, Serena. Now keep watching. You're doing great!"

Reconnecting to the memory, I watch it unfold. "It has latches on one side, so that opens completely. Two of the men are attaching electrodes to Jennifer's body. Oh!" I moan, "I don't want to do this anymore. I just don't!" Rocking back and forth, I'm so afraid.

Raising her voice, she calls, "Look at me, Serena! Bring your breath all the way down into your belly, so you won't be as afraid. Now try this: hold your arms out straight in front of you, cross your wrists, put your palms together, interlace your fingers, then bring them to your chest and hold them there. Extend your legs and cross your ankles. That's it! Can you feel how that helps anchor you in your body?"

Trying this unusual technique, I'm surprised by how calming it is. Focusing on the memory again, I continue. "They're talking among themselves as though Jennifer weren't there."

"What are they saying, Serena?"

I repeat their conversation, word for word.

"How can you be sure she won't drown, sir?"

"That is none of your concern!" the officer barks. "You are to follow orders."

"I understand that, sir, but when it fills with water ... " the younger man questions.

"You will follow orders. Is that understood?"

"Yes, sir."

"The younger man was upset!" I remark, surprised.

"Yes, Serena. He wasn't disconnected from his authentic self as much as the other men were. But please: stay with the memory so we can keep helping you. What are the men doing now?"

"They're putting electrodes all over her body."

"Do they give her instructions, Serena?"

"Yes, one of the men tells her it's up to her to stay alive. Wow ... that was a mean thing to say."

"No, Serena, it was honest," Mom calmly states. "They don't care if Jennifer dies; they're doing a job. Now watch what happens next."

Comforted, I continue watching. "They lift her into that thing, and all the while she is kicking and screaming. There is water at the bottom of it. The sides are slick, there's nothing to hold onto!" Shuddering with intense emotions, I continue. "They close the lid. The interior is dark, except for two tiny windows on either side of the enclosure. Oh … they're filling it with more water!"

"Serena, look at me. Stay here while you tell me what's happening."

Whimpering, I continue. "The water is filling. Jennifer is beyond scared. I don't know how to describe what she is feeling."

"Is she struggling or lying on her back?"

"She's struggling."

"Remember, Jennifer did not drown, because you are here."

"Oh, that's right!" Relief floods my body as I laugh at how funny that is.

"So, the tank is filling with water," Mom prompts.

"Jennifer is floating on her back. I think she's unconscious."

"How does Heart help Jennifer stay alive?"

I intuitively open myself to the memory. "At first, she is hysterical as she screams and thrashes in the water, but as the tank continues to fill, it's like she passes out."

"Don't think, Serena, sense, what happened?"

"Oh, she switches! Heart comes fully into the body, and her energy moves out, becoming larger than the tank that she's floating in. The body is in a state of deep peace, where breath seems absent." Speaking quietly, I continue. "Heart is no longer just of the body; she has become one with the water, and her energy matches that of the water's vibration." Looking up, I'm surprised by my own awareness. I feel the truth of this resonate deeply within me.

"You're doing wonderfully, Serena. You said that Heart is so still that she's almost without breath. Sense: what does that really mean?"

"The breath is intentionally slowed ... as the breath slows, so does the mind. Only Heart's presence is there in the tank. Heart holds the body in a place of alive deadness. I don't know any other word to describe what I am aware of."

"It's a great description, Serena. Keep sensing: how did Heart's energy keep Jennifer alive?"

"Her energy holds the body, so Jennifer won't drown. Her heart slows, as well as her breath. It's as though the experience of having a body disappears, and she becomes one with the water ... and the tank." I feel the awareness of that moment fill me. I *see* the memory from a place beyond my limited mind. "Heart's energy holds the body still."

"Yes, Serena."

"The electrodes that were jumping are now still," I quietly reflect.

"When you go to Heart," Mom kindly states, "instead of coming from your limited mind, the possibilities are endless."

My mind is still. I know the reason I'm alive is because Heart stepped in.

"Ask Heart if there's anything she wants to add to this."

"Heart says that when you reminded me that the men did not care, she wants us to discuss what's really going on ... she says ... the bigger picture? Do you understand?"

"Yes, Serena, what do you understand so far?"

"I know this was another experiment, but for what purpose?"

"Sense: don't go to your mind. Serena. What have they been doing with Jennifer?"

"Hurting her and making her life a living hell!" Instantly angry, I shout, "They did it to control her!"

"And why did they want to control her?" Mom quietly asks.

Without thinking, I blurt, "Because they couldn't!"

"Yes." Chuckling at how honest I just was, Mom smiles at me, encouraging me to continue.

"Wow, they couldn't control her, could they?"

"No, they couldn't. Now notice: Jennifer is five, isn't she?"

"Yes …?"

"And the men have been doing experiments on her for a long time, haven't they?"

"Yes."

"And Jennifer continues to step up and perform in the face of whatever they throw at her. This test had a specific purpose. Can you sense what that was?"

"No."

"Serena, you are not stupid! Let yourself know, would you?"

Closing my eyes, I watch the whole experience from beginning to end. I know the men have done lots of experiments on her before. This was just one more, but there was something different about this one. Voicing that thought out loud, I continue. "This experiment could have killed her."

"Yes, but the other experiments had that potential, as well." Leaning forward, Norma continues. "Remember, they do not think in terms of Spirit as we do. They are looking to see how her mind responds."

"Can't you just tell me, Mom?"

"They're watching to see how Jennifer transitions from one sphere of reality to another. They want to control her, and so far, they haven't been able to.

They will do anything to accomplish that. So, take a breath and let yourself sense what really happened. Your Heart will show you, if you are willing."

Sitting back, I close my eyes, releasing the fogginess with every breath I take. The terror Jennifer felt floods my awareness. Breathing through my nose, I remind myself it has already happened. Exhaling slowly, I relay what I see. "Heart takes over, the mind is no longer involved. Heart energetically moves out, touching the sides of the tank. Fully immersed, the body floats near the surface, where a bubble of oxygen is.

"As Heart surrenders even more fully to the experience, she matches the body's vibration with that of the water, slowing it until the two are as one. This is the alive deadness I spoke of earlier." There is no internal dialogue to distract me from the awareness I'm having. Instead, my entire being resonates with a deep sense of knowing.

Listening, Mom infrequently murmurs yes. As I finish, there is silence between us.

"That was brilliant, Serena. When you try to convince me you are stupid, I don't buy it. I have seen who you really are. Take a breath and feel what I'm saying. You are quick to tell me you don't know. Instead of replying with that automatic answer, could you begin to let yourself sense the greater truth within you?"

"Yes ... I will."

"Good. When you go to your mind for the answer, you remain limited. This memory shows you what Heart and you can do in partnership. I'm proud of you for letting yourself see this so clearly." Standing up, she hugs me.

"We have done a lot of work today, and I want you to rest."

Following Norma to the door, I wave goodbye as I watch her drive out of sight. Something has changed for me, and it feels good. "I really am strong, aren't I, Heart?"

"Someday," she quietly whispers, "you will know who you truly are."

Chapter 22: NEW FREEDOMS

I began taking unsupervised walks in the spring of 2007. I don't wander far, but to be outside, on my own, for the first time in almost seven years is liberating! With scissors and plastic grocery bags in hand, I cut wildflowers wherever I can find them. As I walk along the streets with sacks overflowing with flowers, drivers honk their horns and wave happily at me. Coloradans are a friendly lot, and I have learned to enjoy these brief interactions. I like how my body feels after I come home. It's alive with sensations I've never felt before. I ache from the exertion, but it's an ache born from movement, not of memory.

*****

The restlessness I feel is exaggerated by the fact that today is July 4, a national holiday. People are outside having fun and celebrating, while I'm inside watching television again. Pacing from room to room, I can scarcely contain my anxiety. Sitting down on the couch, I close my eyes and ask Heart for help.

"Would you breathe with me?" she lovingly invites.

I focus only on my breath, but no matter how much I focus, my anxiety continues to grow. "I'm tired of living this way. Show me what to do, Heart!"

"Look into my eyes while you breathe, Serena." Raising her voice, Heart adds, "Don't look away. Keep looking at me, no matter what you feel!"

I surrender more fully into my breath, and as I do, something happens: a vibration in my core that moves outward, engulfing my entire body.

"Don't be afraid, Serena."

The feeling intensifies as I breathe, and as it grows, my body starts to shake.

"I'm here, Serena. Don't be afraid."

Looking into Heart's eyes, I continue breathing. I don't know how long I've been breathing this way, but it doesn't matter. I am firmly held by Heart's gaze, as my body forcibly shakes; I can barely remain seated on the couch.

"We are changing the polarity of your body from fear to love. Keep breathing, Serena. Everything is alright."

I trust Heart, even though my body is shaking uncontrollably.

Her eyes assure me all is well. "I'm claiming this body to be a vessel of love from this point on!" Heart declares.

Even though my body quakes, there is no fear. I know that something miraculous is happening. This continues for almost half an hour before things calm down.

"Get in the tub and breathe, Serena. It's important that you rest. I want to continue to work from inside. Thank you for trusting me."

"Can I ask you a question?"

"Of course, you can," Heart replies.

"What did you mean when you said we were changing my body's polarity from fear to love?"

"Do you know what polarity is?"

Drawing a blank, I shake my head no.

"Polarity is two contrasting energies within one body that produce unequal effects. Would you agree Jennifer pumped fear almost all the time?"

"Yes."

"Jennifer experienced fear most of the time, but once in a while, she experienced extreme joy. Authentic joy is the pure energy of aliveness, and it is gentle to the body. But her joy came from the energy of fear and her trained mind, which was extreme and put her body in danger. When she pumped this extreme joy, she would become catatonic. Do you know what 'catatonic' means?"

"I think I do. It means you just sit there staring out into space."

"Not exactly. It means the body is near death. No one in your body wanted to live, so your body was vacated of its life energy even more, to such an extreme point that it was unresponsive and cold.

In order for me to keep your body alive, I had to put Jennifer's extreme, artificial joy to sleep. The joy that replaced that, for example, when Robbie or Toby was in the body, was an artificial, gentler version created from what the mind believed was happy. It had witnessed people laughing who seemed 'happy,' and copied them to survive. But it was not authentic. At that point, any type of emotional experience that was not hurtful to the system was gratefully received, since Jennifer's life was an abnormal experience of survival and pain.

"The work we have done has culminated in this shift today. You are no longer a vessel of fear; love has permission to be here! But don't be fooled, we are not done yet. Your mind will try to convince you of that, but it is a lie. This is just one more step in our journey of integration. Breathe with me, dear one, and feel the gratitude for what we have accomplished today, because this is a miraculous step in your healing."

Chapter 23: RETURNING TO WORK

"Serena, we're at a remarkable place in our work. Heart says it's time for you to get a job."

"What?" I ask incredulously.

"This isn't about making money to support yourself. It's about discovering how you will behave in the outside world; can you stay authentic, or will you run in fear? Will you feel safe? This is an opportunity for you to grow stronger," Mom states. "I didn't know if we would ever get here."

"Yes, but what will I do? Where will I go?"

"Ask Heart, and she will show you."

Closing my eyes, I inhale deeply, determined not to freak out. *This is scary!*

"You are safe," Heart croons. "Sense a moment: what do you like doing that brings you joy?"

Relaying Heart's question to Mom, I fearfully answer, "I don't know."

"Serena, look at me. You are listening to your mind, which is telling you that you aren't ready, but Heart and I are telling you that you are!" she joyfully declares. "Who do you want to trust?"

Deciding to trust them instead of my fearful mind, I take a more honest breath. My thoughts are racing. *I still switch. I don't know if I can do this.* Turning my attention to Heart, I wonder. *What is it I like to do?* Drawing a blank, I hear Heart whisper, "You like to bake cookies, don't you?"

"Oh … that's right. I like to bake cookies!" I happily reply, but my joy is instantly replaced with concern. "Can baking cookies be a real job?"

Leaning toward me, Mom earnestly replies, "From the day you were born, Heart has been there. If baking cookies is what you like to do, then trust and discover where Heart will lead you. Did you think that when Sebrina asked me to help her integrate, I had any idea what to do?" Not waiting for a response, Mom continues, "Of course I didn't. I trusted I would be led … and look at where we are today! We're talking about you returning to work." Smiling, she continues. "Can you trust that if you weren't ready, Heart would not lead you in this direction?"

The shifts I've made have come so gradually that I didn't realize how much I've changed. I've been staying present like never before, and when I do switch, I have co-consciousness more often than not. Is it a gamble? Of course it is, but Heart promises she will be there every step of the way, so I decide to take this next step.

*****

Baking cookies at the grocery store isn't fun like it is at home. They come frozen, ready to bake. I make hundreds a day, laying them out on cookie sheets, cooking, cooling, and packaging them. I'm also required to bake a variety of breads. I put frozen loaves in pans to thaw, and once they are baked, I wrap them in cellophane and lay them out on display tables for customers to buy. It's a monotonous process of defrosting, cooking, and packaging an endless array of baked goods daily.

I've been here two months, and I'm ready to quit. The one benefit I've received from this job is that my confidence has grown tremendously, and I feel ready to try something different.

*****

"Where do I go to find a new job, Heart?"

"Go down the street and be open to discover, Serena. Don't have a plan. Can you do that?"

I had thought that with Heart leading, I would be told where to go to get my new job. Evidently, that's not the case. Taking a breath, I enter a real estate office and ask if there are any part-time jobs available. Hearing no for the umpteenth time, I leave unperturbed.

Walking up the street, I walk into a business center and go door to door, finding nothing. Entering the bank at the end of the complex, I walk up to the next available teller. "Do you know if there might be any part-time jobs available?"

"There aren't any at this branch, but do you know the branch by the freeway? They have a couple of openings, but you'll need to apply online."

Excited, I return home and start the application process.

*****

Arriving ten minutes early for my interview, I look around the bank's interior. I like the large bay windows on the north wall that let in the sunlight. Large plants are located throughout the branch, which add color to the bland décor. There's a woman seated across from me, quietly typing on her computer. Tellers are helping the clientele. The bank's interior is spacious; I like how it feels in here, unhurried and safe.

A young woman approaches me, holding out her hand. "Hi, I'm Alice, the assistant manager. Jeanette is running late. Come into the conference room with me." Taking chairs across from each other, we sit down. Before we have a chance to talk, the branch manager enters. "Did you start the interview?" Jeanette asks.

"No, we just sat down," Alice states.

"I'm glad to meet you, Serena. Do you want to work part-time or full-time?"

"I'm interested in the part-time position," I calmly reply. I want to sound mature. I was concerned that they might have a problem with me taking the bus, so Mom and I practiced what I would say. It's important that I don't explain why I take the bus or apologize for who I am. I'm to keep breathing, and trust that I can be honest without over-explaining.

"Why do you want to work at a bank? I notice from your resume that you did sales before," Alice inquires.

"I did outside sales for years and lived on commission, which was stressful. I want to try something new." Sitting with my hands in my lap, I answer their questions easily. Even though I'm nervous, I feel I'm coming across well. "Do you feel I'm right for the job, because I would love to work here."

"I have four more applicants to interview," Jeanette replies, "and then I'll let you know sometime early next week."

*****

I got the job! I start the first Monday in January.

*****

There are two branches in town, and I'm working at the smaller one. I'm one of six employees, five of whom are women. I feel safer with women, so this works out perfectly for me.

I have never seen so much money before. When we get our weekly shipment from Loomis, thousands of dollars lie in neat, tight bundles awaiting verification before we put them away in the vault. I follow their lead by pretending that having piles of money lying in front of me is normal.

I'm one of three tellers, and when people have to wait, I get overwhelmed. I rush through whatever I'm doing with the person in front of me, so the one waiting in line won't have to stand as long. Rushing causes me to make mistakes, so at the end of the day, I'm off in my cash drawer more often than not. Jeanette reminds me that we aren't a fast-food restaurant, but it doesn't help when I get panicked. I don't like anyone having to wait for more than a minute.

Yesterday, an elderly gentleman came up to my station, and I couldn't stop staring at his eyebrows. They were white and bushy, hanging over his eyes like patio awnings. Before I knew it, I heard myself telling him that his eyebrows were the most glorious things I had ever seen. As the gentleman laughed with genuine delight, I was horrified. I knew a child had come forward to speak. Clamping my hand over my mouth, I apologized profusely, but he didn't seem to mind.

I feel inadequate most of the time. I feel I'm walking a tightrope, straddling two very different worlds simultaneously: the outside world where I go to the bank and pretend that I'm normal, and my other life, where I'm a multiple personality working to integrate. I don't know how to blend the two worlds into one, so I keep showing up and doing the best I can.

*****

I have the day off, and Mom is coming over to work with me.

Placing her coat on the chair, Mom settles down in the rocking chair across from me. "What's cooking?" she asks.

"Heart wants me to start with the regional vice president who came to work the other day. His name is Carl ..."

Interrupting me mid-sentence, Norma asks, "When Carl comes to see you, do you go to a story in your mind or do you stay in the moment and look at this man for who he is? What I'm inviting you to do is to pay attention to your thoughts so you can respond in a way that helps you."

Tears silently slip down my cheeks.

"What are you so upset about, Serena?"

"You don't understand, Mom."

"Then tell me."

It's difficult putting my feelings into words. "So much is going on all at once; I'm managing the money, answering the client's questions, and he's standing behind me taking notes ... and he's holding a clipboard!"

"Yes," Norma says, "and ask that child ... what does it mean when he stands behind you with a clipboard? Serena, please listen to the answer. This will help you. I don't need the answer, you do."

With a cry and a rush of emotions, I hear, "I'm not safe, I'm not safe!"

"This is how you can help yourself, Serena. You're the only one who can hear these children. I'm not at work with you. When your emotions become intense, go to the bathroom and run water over your wrists while breathing deeply. Ask yourself questions to better understand what is upsetting you.

"Now ... I want you to listen as I talk to this child." Pausing a moment, Mom's voice fills with compassion as she says, "This has happened before, hasn't it? They hold clipboards whenever they do experiments on you, don't they?"

"Yes!" she screams.

"Tell me about it."

"They always write things down," she wails! "They tell me I'm doing it wrong, but I don't know what they want me to do!"

"I understand why you would be angry," Norma gently states in a soothing voice.

Turning her attention to me, she states, "Serena, can you understand why you would be upset at work?"

Without pausing, Norma turns her attention back to the child. "Have you ever seen what they write?"

Shaking her head, no, the child is silent.

"Can you see the angel that is standing next to you, sweetie?"

"Yes."

"You can go with her. She will never let them hurt you again. Would you like that?"

The child doesn't answer, but the anxiety I was feeling completely vanishes as the child falls into the angel's arms. As I continue breathing, Mom invites all the other children who are afraid to come home to the angel.

"Let's take a moment to breathe together, shall we?" Smiling at me, Mom closes her eyes and leads me in breath.

"I really needed that. Thanks, Mom."

"Of course. You can always let me know when you would like to breathe with me. That's how you can help yourself. Now, ask Heart what else she would like us to talk about."

"She says we need to talk about money.

"So, what is money, Serena?"

"What? You're asking me what money is?"

"Notice, Serena, you went to fight instead of staying with me." Stating this, Mom sits back and waits.

I'm fighting again, dammit! Rubbing my forehead, I close my eyes and take a breath. It seems that's all I ever do. Asking myself what money is, I hear an explosion of answers. Taking them one by one, I relay the answers to Mom. Money is bad, money is powerful, money is corrupt, money makes you bad …"

"Are those Heart's answers, Serena?"

"No ... it's the answers I heard from the others."

"Good. It's important that you're aware of your mind's answers. Now, ask Heart what money is?"

"She says that money is a tool like a hammer or a fork. What does she mean by that?"

"Ask her what she means, Serena."

"Money is a tool like a fork. A fork picks up food and brings it to your mouth. It's an instrument. Money is an instrument that humans use to allow themselves to have freedom."

As I repeat the words out loud, I sense their truth, which has nothing to do with my mind. "So money gives me things, and that's good?"

"Notice," says Norma, "when you go to the idea of good, you're in judgment, which is your mind. We are discussing money from the awareness of higher consciousness. Money is neither good nor bad. Money is paper and metals, nothing else. Can you sense what I'm saying?"

"But everyone says that money corrupts ..."

"When did we start choosing to follow what everybody else says? Do you want to be a prisoner to your old beliefs, or do you want to discover a new way of living? I love money. It's a doorway to freedom for me. It allows me to do what I want, when I want. Do you have that freedom, Serena?"

"No, I don't."

"Would you like to have the freedom to do what you want?"

"Yes, I would."

"Then notice how quickly your mind says no. I want you to play with the idea of money. When you are counting it, notice: does it have power? Can it do anything to you? Or is it just paper with numbers on it? You get to decide, Serena. This is your life."

"When I'm in the vault, I count thousands and thousands of dollars, and it's weird."

"Why is it weird?" Mom patiently asks.

"Because it's so much money, and it's just lying there. There can be a hundred thousand dollars just lying there on the counter."

"I know. It doesn't do anything until you decide how you want to use it. Ask Heart if there's anything she can lend to this conversation."

"She's laughing, Mom."

"I know. Heart has a wonderful sense of humor; ask her why she is laughing."

"She's laughing because she's delighted with how this job is going to help me learn and grow. She wants me to play with my ideas about money and notice whether money has power in and of itself. She says we can talk about it again, but this will help me to discover the truth."

"And that's what we're all about, isn't it, sweetie?"

Chapter 24: FIGHTING NEVER WORKS

I have a presentation on interest-bearing accounts to give at work today. I'm so afraid—I can barely breathe. Looking down at my notecards, I try to focus.

"Serena," Jeanette asks, "are you ready?"

Standing in front of my seated co-workers, they wait for me to begin. My face is numb, my voice quavers with anxiety, and my pulse is pounding so loudly in my ears that I wonder if they can hear it too. Taking my seat while still speaking, I try to gain control over the panic. Discreetly placing my hand on my belly, I focus as best I can, but it doesn't abate. Quietly excusing myself, I make my way to the breakroom to call Mom.

"Mom!" I frantically whisper, "I just gave my speech, but I was so afraid, I could barely breathe!"

"But you gave the speech?"

"Yes …"

"And you were aware of your fear, but you kept breathing?"

"Yes?"

"You gave yourself a gift with this experience, Serena. Even though you were afraid, you kept going. You didn't retreat into fear. You can either see this experience through judgment or from compassion. Which do you choose?"

Taking a more conscious breath, I respond, "I will see it from compassion."

"Good," Mom replies. "You chose to help yourself, and that's what matters."

"But I was so afraid when I spoke."

"That's not the issue, Serena. Do you get that?"

"You're right, Mom, I focused with my breath, because I wanted to."

"Yes, the power of your choice is what matters. Now, choose to come deeper into your body. Listen to the sound of my voice, and let that help you."

After breathing together for a couple of minutes, I'm feeling better. "Thanks, Mom, for being there."

"I'm glad you called. When do you get off work?"

"The bus picks me up right at 5 p.m., so I should be home no later than 5:30."

"Good. Then I will come over so we can work a bit. Would you like that?"

"Absolutely, Mom!"

*****

Arriving home a little before 5:30, Mom is waiting in her car in the driveway.

"Why don't we have a cup of tea before we start?" Mom suggests.

"That sounds good." Going into the kitchen, I prepare the pot to boil.

Settling down on the couch a few minutes later, we set our hot mugs on the carpet so we can talk.

"Why can't I be normal like everyone else? I got so afraid when I gave my speech this morning. It felt like I might pass out! What's wrong with me?" I angrily demand.

"Did you hear what you said? I've asked you to listen to the words you say about yourself." Norma responds with a sigh. "You say such cruel things without thinking. Where is your compassion for yourself, Serena?"

Instead of feeling compassion, I'm angry at myself. I know Mom is here to help me, and the last thing I want to do is to fight with her. Turning inward, I breathe, settling deeper into my body, and finally, after minutes of dedicated breathing, my anger diminishes enough for me to speak. "Heart wants me to repeat exactly what she is telling me. She says I have a plan for how I should be, and when I don't live up to that plan, I hate myself for it."

"And what is that plan, Serena?"

"That I should be normal like everyone else!" As I utter the words, I'm instantly angry all over again. "I should be better by now!"

"Can you hear the anger you have toward yourself?"

"Yes! I'm angry! I should—"

"Do you hear yourself repeating what your mind says you should be? Does Heart tell you that you should be better or different?"

"No, but—"

"Yes, I know, you need to fight. What if you didn't have anything to fight about? Be still a moment and sense: if you had nothing to fight?" Emphatically raising her voice, she asks, "What would you do?"

"It would be wonderful!" I angrily retort.

"I will not stay here and fight with you. I'm serious; I will leave if you want to fight." Remaining silent for a minute before continuing, she says, "Don't you feel the push that screams for you to be normal? Doesn't that tell you something?"

"Yes?"

"Will you sink deeper into your core and ask your mind what 'normal' means?"

Without a moment's hesitation, I know the answer. "Normal is like everyone else. I watch the people at work, and they don't struggle as I do. They don't seem to be in turmoil like I am!"

"And how do you know that, Serena? Do you know what's going on in their lives? You make judgments based on what you see. Sense a moment, and tell me: what is normal?"

I repeat: "Normal is like everyone else."

"And if you don't know how everyone else is, how can you be normal? Don't you sense a bigger push here? Do you feel the desperation that says you have to be normal? Go behind that and sense: what is it you really want?" Leaning back in her chair, Mom waits, knowing that it's up to me whether I will go any further with this.

Inhaling, I close my eyes and feel what the desperation is really about. "It's the training. I can feel that I must be like everyone else! I hear the words, repeated over and over again in my mind, that if I stand out or am different in any way, I'll be hurt!"

"Yes, and who is telling you this?"

"Jack and the men from the government are leaning into Jennifer's face, yelling at her. They are threatening her that she had better not attract attention to herself, or she will pay for it!" As I say the words, anxiety pulses throughout my body.

"Serena, you say the words, but take a moment and feel how real this threat was. Will you breathe and integrate it? You're the only one who can do that. You ignore when you are pushed from within. Those children know this was no idle threat. Will you take the time to be there for them and then integrate the belief?"

"You say I ignore the push, but most of the time I don't even feel it."

"You ignore it, because you're so good at it, Serena. You've pretended your entire life that if you didn't like something, then it wasn't there. This will not go away. You have to pay attention to how you feel." Raising her voice, she adds, "all of the time! That is what being conscious is all about, and when you feel emotionally pushed, know that it's memory that you need to pay attention to."

"I didn't know it would be this hard, Mom. I thought that I would just be normal somehow."

"This is a part of growing up. Your entire life has been spent as a child. When you accept what is, without fighting, we will have made a giant step forward." Smiling at me, she continues, "I'm not judging you, Serena, but as long as you want to fight more than you want to live, you will stay stuck. You are the only one who can do this. I can cheer you on from the sidelines, but it is ultimately up to you. Now, ask Heart what else she would like us to look at."

"She wants me to talk about the speech I made today. She says I was being unreasonable with what I expected from myself."

"Do you know what Heart is talking about?"

Ignoring her question, I angrily retort, "It's not that big a deal to talk for five minutes in front of a few people."

"Serena, do you realize where this fear comes from? When Jennifer was forced to stand naked in front of the people in the cult, she was tortured and humiliated. Do you think being in front of a group of people is such a trivial experience? I'm not asking you to live in the past, but when you have that big of a reaction, some child within you is screaming to be heard." Leaning toward me, she adds, "After all these years, you still choose fear over anything that Heart or I tell you. That is insulting to me."

"That isn't true!"

"I will not stay here and fight with you." Standing, she leans in, close to my face, and says, "You are the only one who can stop this game. Until you grow tired of it, there's nothing I can do. Be with that truth. I have to go now."

"But, Mom—"

"There is nothing left to say. I love you, Serena, but until you decide to love yourself, we can't go any further with your integration."

I'm dumbfounded as I watch her close the door behind her.

"She loves you so much that she's willing to be honest with you, even if you don't like it," Heart says. "She can't make you integrate your self-hatred. That is up to you. Feel what I'm telling you, Serena. You chose to believe the mind's stories instead of asking me. Feel and be with this truth, for it cannot change until you face it without judgment."

It would help me if I got into the tub. As I undress, I obsess over whether I should call Mom. I want to fix it with her. Knowing that is not the answer, I take a breath and shout, "Please, Heart, help me! I can't do this integration for Mom, but the truth is, I want Mom's love more than anything else. When she says she can't do it for me, I know that's true!" Crying with frustration, I stop myself and take a breath, because crying is such a waste of time. Getting into the tub, I lower myself into the hot water and implore, "Heart, fill me with the desire to do this integration work just for me! I can't make myself feel this, but you can."

"You cannot love yourself from your mind, Serena. Breathe with me and discover."

Willing to do anything to change how I'm feeling, I breathe, and slowly my mind quiets. I feel Heart's presence with me.

"Why is this so hard, Heart?"

"Please, listen without judgment. You love to fight. It's not right or wrong; it's just the truth. Let yourself feel how much your love affair with fighting is hurting you."

Closing my eyes, I lean back against the bath pillow and breathe.

"Okay, Heart, I'm willing to feel it. What do I do?"

"Breathe and let yourself feel the energy of fight. Don't be afraid. I won't let it get so big that it hurts you."

Letting go, I allow the energy of fight to grow within me. I feel impenetrable, and I like how that feels. I hear the words, "No one can hurt me now." The statement is absolute, and the resulting emotions make me feel safe. As I continue breathing, I watch the body being repeatedly raped, while switch after switch occurs. As each new child awakens, their awareness of the previous rape is gone.

I become aware of another presence, the child who whispered, "No one can hurt me." She watches from a distance, believing that it is someone else who is being raped. She believes she escaped. *Wow ... this is how my multiplicity worked!* Taking a breath, I let myself feel the truth that there was only one body that endured it all.

"Please, Heart, I know I can't do this without you. Help me feel that fighting never worked!" Breathing slowly, I become aware that a shift is happening inside of me. The pretend feeling drops away, and I feel—really feel—that no matter what story Jennifer told herself, the nightmare happened only to her.

"Can you let these aspects of memory come home to me, Serena?"

"Oh, yes, Heart!" My breath, with my intent, brings each of these memories home to my Heart. "What else would you like me to see?"

"Will you feel how much you love this energy, Serena? No judgment. It's important that you be honest with yourself. The habit to fight is just that, a habit. It helped you to stay alive, but you no longer need it. Feel that you are safe! You are no longer in the cult or being trained by the government, but you act as if you are, by being on guard and ready to fight at a moment's notice. You are still on guard after all these years. You don't need to live that way anymore." Heart's voice gentles as she adds, "You are free. Will you let yourself feel that?"

Breathing quietly, I feel the awareness that I'm free blossom within me.

"Don't pretend, Serena. Your love of fight is not over yet, but you have made an important step in your integration today."

Feeling grateful for what I've accomplished, I realize the push to call Mom has completely vanished, and in its place, I am at peace.

Chapter 25: WHAT IS SOUL ?

"What's cooking?" Mom asks, upon answering the phone.

"I couldn't sleep very well, because the wind's howling reminded me of someone screaming."

"So what did you do?"

"I asked Heart for help."

"When you say you asked Heart for help, what does that mean?"

"It means that I asked Heart for guidance."

"I'm glad you chose to help yourself last night, but would you play with me a moment? Who do you sense Heart really is?"

"She's my Soul."

"And do you feel your Soul in your body?"

"Yes ... I feel my Soul in my belly and chest."

"Now, take a breath and stay open. So where are you in your body?" Mom asks, as she quietly chuckles.

Responding in kind, I laugh because I know that we're discussing another distorted belief that I have. "I'm aware that my Soul is in my belly and chest, and that I am here too ... but I don't know which part of my body I am in."

"You're still insisting you are separate, which is multiple thinking. Would you be willing to see Heart as you really believe she looks?"

Closing my eyes, I look inside and see her smiling at me. "Her face glows with a radiance that is not of this world, and her eyes, ... they invite me to come home to her whenever I look into them. And when I hear her voice, I am comforted, plus her warmth fills me from the inside out whenever I am close to her!" Pausing, I sigh happily.

Laughing with merriment, Mom replies, "When you are willing to be honest, we both win. So, keep sensing: is Heart ... really Soul? Don't answer yet; instead, let yourself feel the truth. I will wait."

Breathing slowly, I recognize that Heart is my constant companion, and since she is all-knowing, that feels safe to me. I don't know if I'm ready to give up what I think Heart is for something less tangible. "The truth is, I like how I feel with Heart, and I know it's multiple thinking, but the idea of Soul doesn't connect for me in the same way."

"That's because you've created a psychic package around the word 'Heart.' I'm not here to push you, Serena. If you want to keep things the way they are, then that's okay with me."

Keeping Heart in the old way is another way of staying stuck, and Mom's guidance has only led me to freedom. "I want the truth, keep going, please."

"Do you remember how much you believed that Robbie was real?"

"Oh ... yes." Sighing happily, I recall his smile and sweet, freckled face. I know he wasn't real, but the vivid imagery still remains.

"Good. So let yourself feel what you experience when you open to Heart."

Closing my eyes, I breathe deeply and intuitively open to her. Immediately, a comforting warmth fills me. The thought that it might disappear if I let go of Heart scares me. "I like this feeling, Mom."

"I understand, Serena. It's wonderful that you have allowed yourself to feel this much love, but would you be willing to go for the truth?"

"Okay."

"Then hold up your hand, and look at it. Is it there? Do you have to concentrate to keep it attached to your wrist?"

Laughing, because this isn't the first time I've been asked this question, I retort, "Of course I don't!"

"Good ... now let yourself feel that Soul is here, just like your hand. You don't have to concentrate to have Soul here, because she is always with you. She was with you from the beginning, and she is here with you now, just like your hand."

I ponder what she said, but it really doesn't have meaning for me. "Would you tell me what Soul really is? Maybe that will help."

"Of course, but will you sense what I'm saying, instead of listening with your mind?"

"Yes." Taking a breath, I drop deeper into my belly.

"Soul is the actual aliveness of every human being. Let yourself feel that first. The aliveness we have worked so hard to bring into your body through your breath is your Soul. How does that feel, Serena?"

"I like that. It feels real."

"When I breathe with my Soul, I'm staying with the awareness that all is well. This choice feeds my body with energy, filling me with a sense of well-being and gratitude.

"Every organ of the body has a specific function. For example, the liver filters the blood, removing impurities from the body. The brain controls our speech, the movement of our arms and legs, and the function of our organs. Your brain is a physical organ in your body, Serena. For most people, the brain is a wonderful tool. It stores data and is trained to perform specific functions, such as speaking and writing.

"When we turn on the computer, the electricity is the spark of energy that allows it to do its function." Raising her voice, Mom stresses, "The computer is not alive of itself. Do you really get that, Serena?"

"Yes, I do."

"Stop me if you're not following me, alright?"

Nodding, I am silent. *What has this got to do with Soul?*

"Mind is where our thoughts and emotions, beliefs and imagination, are stored. But your mind is different from other people's minds because it was programmed from the very beginning of your life. Every single day, you were tortured with one intent: to program your mind with a specific belief system so that the government and the cult could completely control you. This rigid belief system demanded your absolute obedience, or you would be hurt, many times, by your own hand.

Do you remember how you used to burn yourself whenever you ironed your clothes or used the oven? For the longest time, you believed it was an accident, but eventually you realized it was a child programmed to perform a specific job. These children had one purpose: to keep the secrets at all costs. They burned you because you were telling me the secrets. Only through integrating the children who were programmed to burn you were you able to stop hurting yourself. That is why I have repeatedly stressed that you cannot afford to get angry. You are not like other people! You were trained to express anger excessively, with the intent to hurt yourself or someone else. Does this make sense so far, Serena?"

"Yes, like never before!"

"Good, because when we work with truth, we set you free."

"But what has this got to do with my understanding of what Soul is?" I impatiently ask.

"Please, Serena, stay with me. It all ties together. You have always believed that the voices in your mind were alive because you were trained that way. You have lived completely from your trained mind, so you knew no other way. It's only been through us working with each one of these beliefs that you have discovered the truth, and that is what we are doing now."

"I never realized how connected it all was," I remark.

Chucking, Norma replies, "That's why we are having this discussion. Now, drop deeper into your core and sense: the awareness that lies beyond the programming of your mind ... is your Soul. Stop a moment and let yourself feel what I just said." Speaking slowly, Mom repeats the statement again. "Soul is the awareness outside of your mind, Serena."

Breathing quietly, I feel it. "It's a knowing, isn't it?"

"Yes. This knowing is our own inner wisdom, our spark that can guide us every moment of every day. Do you sense what I'm saying?"

"Yes, I really do." The awareness I am feeling requires no explanation. "Please, keep going, Mom."

"When a baby is born, the mind creates anxiety as a result of new experiences. It can be as simple as the baby seeing a new face or hearing a loud sound, which triggers the release of the hormone adrenaline into its bloodstream. Hoping to calm the crying baby, the parent puts a pacifier in its mouth, and as the baby sucks, endorphins are released, setting in motion a game that all humans play until they awaken.

"Your body and mind have been addicted to this game for decades. When your body's adrenaline levels drop, your mind automatically kicks in, creating a fearful story that floods your bloodstream with adrenaline, giving you a false sense of energy. But since you don't like the emotions that come from that fearful story, you seek relief by doing a myriad of things to get an endorphin rush. As these two hormones fluctuate back and forth in your bloodstream, this yoyo effect drains your body of energy, hurting you in the process. It is an exhausting game to play, but if you choose to be done with it, you can by staying aware.

"That is why I have repeatedly stressed that you cannot afford to get overly angry, because you are not like other people! You were trained to express anger excessively, and that hurts you. Understanding how this game works, combined with examining your beliefs about Heart and Soul, will help you make new choices. How are you feeling about what I have shared so far?"

"I get it, Mom, it's not a random concept that I have to think about. I have lived this way for most of my life, and I am tired of it! "

"And having clarity supports you in making new choices. Being a Soul having a physical experience simply means that you and everyone else you meet are Souls having a human experience. It's that simple. But when you insist on holding onto a child's understanding of what it means to be human, you stay stuck.

"Most humans want the Soul to be something special. They want it to be this wondrous thing that is separate from the daily living we humans do, but that is not the truth. Your Soul is the living essence of you, and my Soul is the living essence of me. Every single person on this planet is the living essence of their Soul. As long as you want your Soul to remain separate, you will continue to come from your mind.

"When you accept the truth, you get to experience life with ease and grace. Gone is the need to prove your worth; you no longer struggle to survive. Instead, you live from higher consciousness, knowing that you are intuitively guided in every step of your life. And when you falter or don't know what to do, you're not surprised. You take a breath, surrender to the greatness of who you are, trusting your next moment will be perfect for your unfoldment. This way of being gives you the freedom to be authentically yourself at all times. And I can tell you from experience, there is no better way to live!

"So, take a moment and sense, what do you believe a Soul is?"

Immediately, I feel a sense of awe. Relaying this to Mom, I state, "Soul is wonderful, all-knowing, never makes mistakes … you know, better than being human."

"Yes," Mom says, "and what is human?"

I hesitate before answering. I'm aware of the hatefulness of my mind's answer, but I am not interested in that. Faltering, I slowly state. "A human is someone who lives in a body." I try to sense what more there might be, but I'm blank. "I really don't know how to describe what a human being is."

"Isn't it fun to find out you really don't know? It leaves room for discovery!"

Taking a breath, I try to ground myself. "You've shared a lot, Mom."

"I know, because it's all connected. Do you get that?"

"Yes, and I'm ready to let go of my idea of what Heart is, and discover the truth about my Soul."

"I'm glad, because your ideas of what Godmother and Heart are is for a child who needs to hide, but you are not a child anymore."

Despite feeling anxious, a sense of strength emboldens my decision to let go of my childish thinking.

"Play with the idea that every human you meet is actually a Soul in physical form," Mom suggests.

"And wanting my Soul to be someone I can run to is keeping me stuck, isn't it?"

"Yes. Breathe that part home to your Soul, Serena. Be gentle with yourself. When you go to work today, and you're interacting with people, let yourself feel the truth of who they really are. Don't go to your mind. Instead, feel and notice. This will allow you to discover what you aren't aware of yet."

"I feel better knowing I have time to be with this," I reply.

"That's great. We can talk about it another time. Have a good day, Serena."

"Bye, Mom."

Chapter 26: ASPECTS

"I'm driving!" It's the first time in over ten years that I have driven a car, and it feels wonderful! Driving around the abandoned parking lot, I giggle joyfully.

"Breathe, Serena. It won't help if you get too excited. Stay focused, and shift the gear. Do you hear the engine revving? It's telling you that it's time to shift."

Nodding, I shift the gear effortlessly.

"You're doing great." Trading seats, Mom drives the short distance back to my house. "Now, I want you to see how it feels driving down your street, with cars passing you by."

I inhale anxiously; the street is narrower than the parking lot, and there are children walking on the right side of the road.

"What's going on, Serena? Are you listening to your mind? Do you think that you would be driving if Soul and I didn't think you were ready?"

I'm surprised that she knows what I'm thinking.

Parking the car in front of my house, Mom turns off the engine. Turning toward me, she asks, "Can you allow yourself to have freedom, Serena? Your Soul and I trust you, but if you're listening to your mind, then you had better not ignore what it's saying."

"That I'll get into an accident and hurt someone."

"And do you believe that?"

"I don't know … but it makes me afraid, Mom."

"Notice: you're trusting your mind more than your Soul."

Discouraged, I sigh loudly.

"If you want to be a victim, then we're done for today, Serena. Do you want to drive or give up?"

"I want to drive!"

"Then choose. Driving will give you freedom. Do you want that?"

"Yes!" I resolutely declare.

"Are you going to let your cruel mind choose for you? This is what having freedom is all about: you choosing for you! Can you feel what I'm saying?"

Without reply, I nod and open the door to trade seats with Mom. Turning on the engine, I pull out onto the road. Coming to the end of my street, I make a U-turn and go back the other way. "After driving up and down the road a few times, I ask, "I'm feeling better; can we go onto a busier street now?"

"Not yet, Serena, that will not serve you. Instead, I want you to get used to being behind the wheel. Drive down the road again and pay attention to what your mind is saying."

Driving up and down the street, I listen to my thoughts. My mind is quieter, and I'm feeling less anxious. "I'm doing great, aren't I?"

"And how does that feel?"

"It feels really good."

"That's what freedom is all about, Serena. You get to do what you want, when you want to do it."

*****

Coming into the house twenty minutes later, we take seats across from each other. "Soul wants you to explain what an aspect is, Mom."

"Do you remember how you believed Robbie was real?"

"Yes, and I know he was a personality, but to me, he still seems real somehow. I can still see his face, and I remember how his voice sounded ..."

"Of course you do, Serena, because he was an integral part of you. So let's slow this down so you can have clarity. What do you believe a personality is?"

What is a personality? I really hadn't given it much thought before now. "I really don't know. I know the personalities in my system weren't real people, but to be honest, they seemed real to me."

"That's what kept you alive. If you hadn't believed they were real, your multiplicity would never have worked. Ask your Soul what a personality is."

"When Jennifer was a child," Soul explains, "her life was a nightmare that she could not escape, so I created personalities from our energy pool to step in and do specific jobs to keep her alive and sane. A personality is nothing more than conscious energy, created to keep all of you alive."

"With Soul, *anything* is possible, Serena," interjects Mom. "Our Soul is the energy of God, and with God, anything is possible! When you believe the lies of your mind that tell you you can't, you stay limited, because you're creating from fear. But when you create from your Soul's brilliance, you have a different outcome. Are you following us so far?"

"Yes."

"Now ... Jennifer learned to *never* let anyone know the truth of what she felt or thought. She learned very early on to pretend. This was a part of the training from both the government and the cult. By the time she was five years old, all of the authentic child had been put to sleep by your Soul."

"But how does this relate to aspects?"

"I'm getting there. Please, hear this next part from compassion. What if every one of your personalities were just an aspect of memory and nothing more? How would that feel for you?"

"What?" I retort. "How can that be? Are you saying that every personality I knew was only a memory and nothing more?"

"Yes. Can you be brave enough to face this truth from compassion?"

"But ... then am I an aspect?" I hesitantly ask. "I was born into the system, too."

"Ask your Soul that question, and listen carefully, please."

Feeling anxious, I take a breath and close my eyes to hear my Soul's answer. "You are not an aspect, Serena, because you are the conscious chooser in the body. At first, you lived amidst the chaos of the other personalities, unaware of who you really were. Your job was to learn how to stop switching into other personalities. As you chose your breath over fear and discovered the truth of what your life had really been about, you began to know stability for the first time. That stability was the beginning of the authentic you being created."

"Wow … this is amazing, Mom! This work has been so slow at times that I wondered if I would ever integrate, but now, I realize how my Soul literally weaved me into one person a breath at a time; no wonder it has taken so long!"

"Yes, Serena. Each personality had its own job, and your job was to birth authentic human consciousness into the body so that the whole of you could live. Soul, Jennifer, and all the other personalities are parts of the energetic *whole* of you. But as long as you were disconnected from the physical body, you stayed disempowered. That's why we had to connect you to your body. As long as you obeyed the training of your mind, you couldn't make choices to help yourself. That's why this has taken so long. As we integrated each aspect of memory along with its pain into the core of you, you grew stronger, Serena."

"I really get it! So when a person gets afraid and fearfully inhales, they create an energetic package of memory that needs to be integrated. That inhalation holds the memory outside themselves until they breathe it home to their Soul. We are always creating, aren't we?"

Whether it's from fear or love, unconsciously or consciously, we are the ones who do the creating," Mom states emphatically. "I've told my students that it's similar to putting a memory into a container, sealing it tight, and putting it into a space within ourselves until we're able to work with it. That's what integration is … being with the truth of an experience, owning it without resistance, and then breathing it home into the greatness of who we are. You and your Soul are one Being, and this piece of separated energy can now come home into wholeness."

Grasping the enormity of what we have accomplished, I exclaim, "My mind could never have orchestrated this!"

"I am glad you realize the limitation of your mind, because it is not where you will find peace. You have believed your mind for a very long time. Becoming conscious of your thoughts requires your presence in each moment. It isn't a magical fix that will finally quiet your mind. You must notice where your thoughts are coming from; are they judgmental, filled with anger, are you feeling pushed, or anxious? These are dead giveaways that it is your mind, because the energy of fear uses these tactics to control you. Judging is also a tactic the mind uses. Each time you catch yourself reacting to a thought from your mind, and you take a breath without reacting to it, you break its hold on you, Serena. This stops the cycle of feeding it your energy. The more you do this, the more you will experience freedom.

"When you have a thought that is from your Soul or a true feeling from you personally, the experience is filled with peace, warmth, and kindness toward yourself. Your Soul is always there, guiding you, filling you with her energy of compassion, strength, and … oh, so many different, sweet moments, if you stay open to her. It becomes a relationship that is personal and highly cherished." Sighing deeply, Mom's entire body radiates with pure joy.

"I have always believed the fearful thoughts of my mind, but I'm tired of living that way," I firmly declare.

"I'm glad, because it isn't until you tire of the game of fear that you will stop playing it. Fear is never grander than the truth of who you are, Serena. When you breathe and allow yourself to feel the energy of your Soul, you know there is nothing that can seduce you from the truth of who you really are. Now, play with me. Say these words out loud, and feel how they resonate within you …. 'I Am that I Am.'"

Repeating the words out loud, I feel strength, peace, and a knowingness hold me in stillness. There are no thoughts, just solid feeling. I feel I am God; that we are all God; there is nothing to discuss, nothing to prove, just quiet awareness filling me. "I feel the truth of it, without needing to explain anything."

"Yes, Serena … hear this: aspects are never the voice of God. They are only the game of fear, and forgetting who you are. Your Soul created each aspect to help Jennifer cope with the brutality of her life, but you, as the adult, can make new choices. Compassion is an experience your mind will never understand. When you operate from a deeper realm, a fuller life will open for you.

"Learning to differentiate our mind's voice from our Soul voice creates this opening. Our mind's voice says you should, you must, you did it wrong; but our Soul's voice tells us how brilliant we are, how loved we are, how exquisite we are. Our Soul honors and encourages us; she never judges us. She holds us with pure love, no matter what we do or what we experience."

As Mom continues speaking, my Soul whispers, "Yes. Yes."

"This compassion is unending, every moment of every day, every moment of every night. It's within every human, Serena, and it's waiting for you to open to it. The more you consistently stay in stillness, the more you will begin to sense the radiant vibration that actually moves out through your body, going out before you. When we activate our inner core from this realm, the radiance that flows out from us is this exquisite self-acceptance, called compassion. Do you want this compassion, Serena?"

"Oh, yes, I really do!"

"Good, because you are the only one who can give it to you. I want you to take out your notebook and draw a line down the middle of the page. On the right side of the page, write what your mind is saying, and on the left side write what your Soul is saying."

Retrieving my notebook, I draw a line down the middle of a page.

"Alright. Listen to what your mind is saying about this conversation."

Writing quickly because the words are coming fast, I relay, "My mind is angry at you for telling me this, and it's yelling that it's a bunch of lies!"

"Notice how threatened your mind is. That is an aspect of memory, trained to keep you stuck. Now, listen to your Soul and write her words."

Unlike my mind, Soul's words are calm and unhurried. "I'm proud of you for letting us guide you even when it makes you feel uncomfortable. Your mind tells you things to shut you down and repress the fear, but it ends up intensifying it. As you learn to discern your fearful thoughts and let them go without a fight, you will experience an ease in your life you have not known before. Keep letting me lead you, dear one."

I like the words of my Soul; they feel kind and encouraging.

"Can you feel the difference between the two? Who do you want to listen to?"

"I like the words of my Soul."

"Good. Then, will you practice this method so you can begin to discern the difference between the two? After you have practiced this for a time, you will become familiar with your Soul's energy more easily, and it will be the only one you respond to."

"This is wonderful! I won't be manipulated as easily as I have been. I'll be able to choose differently because I'll feel the contrast between the two thoughts ... and that will really help me!"

"It can, if you let it," Mom calmly states. Now, I don't mean to change subjects, but I have been meaning to ask you if you know what post-traumatic stress disorder is?"

"Yes, I was diagnosed with PTSD when I was in the hospital. Dr. Barnes told me that's why I got triggered so easily. Even when I knew someone was coming, I would hysterically scream when they entered the room. I thought it was crazy that I reacted that way, but Dr. Barnes said that was the PTSD triggering me. He told me that was the reason I switched so much into different personalities because I was triggered by the most trivial things."

"Yes, post-traumatic stress disorder is what happens when people have extended periods of trauma. They're in a cycle of memory, stuck in a loop, where the slightest provocation causes them to be triggered. The work we've done has allowed you to truly integrate the PTSD, which is why Soul and I could trust you to begin driving today." Raising her voice, she sincerely asks, "Do you realize what a miracle you are?"

"You know, I actually feel it, Mom. It isn't something I need to think about, I feel it, and that awareness moves throughout my entire body, filling me with joy and accomplishment!"

"These are remarkable, miraculous changes, Serena! When we came to Colorado, that was the first time you ever felt safe. I had used the word 'safe' before, but for you, it was a theory, an unknown idea, connected to nothing. Authentic 'safe' began slowly as you lay on the couch watching television. We distracted your mind with a captivating story on the television so that your body began to relax, trusting the sensation of the fabric's softness against your skin, and feeling the gentle, rhythmic beating of your heart. This experience brought your body a level of comfort it had never known before. You noticed that you were safe as you did things around the house; safe became an actual experience, grounded in physical reality, and compassion was the key element.

"That's why you can feel the truth without having to think about it. You are connected like never before, and celebrate that!

"I am grateful for how far I have come," I reply.

"The fact that you are following this conversation as you are shows both of us how much you have changed."

"I know ... I'm not struggling to understand what you're saying. I was the one who made the choices that got me here—no one else did that! No matter how many times I fell down, I always got back up again!"

"Yes," Mom replies. "You are the one who created it from your passion to integrate. That's why today is a red-letter day! You chose to drive; no one else did that but you, Serena."

Chapter 27: A NEW BEGINNING

I'm going to the debut of Timothy's documentary film, which is showing in Albuquerque, New Mexico, this weekend. I haven't seen him for seventeen years. I've seen Stephen and Aaron a couple of times, but we haven't been together as a family since I took them to North Carolina in 1998. I had hoped we would get together this time, but Aaron has to work.

Standing on my front lawn, I look up into the night sky, seeing a multitude of shimmering stars twinkling above me. Lifting my arms to the heavens, I joyfully sing, "I'm alive!" Driving down the mountain to the airport, I'm wrapped in a cocoon of peaceful joy.

Waiting to board the plane, I close my eyes and breathe. I'm amazed that despite all the people hurrying by me, I'm at peace.

The flight is short, and within an hour, I'm hugging Stephen.

"Where's Tim?"

"He's in a press conference. He said he would meet us later. I'm sorry, I know how much you wanted to see him."

"That's okay ... Tim's in a press conference, wow, that's cool!"

"You're going to love his film, Mom. I saw a rough cut, and I was impressed!"

"I can't wait to see it!"

"Let's get your suitcase and go to the hotel. Are you tired? Do you need to take a nap?"

"No, I feel great." Standing in front of the baggage area, we watch as my suitcase comes down the shoot.

"Why did you pack such a huge suitcase for only three days?" he asks, chuckling.

"I wanted to make sure I had everything I might need."

Pulling the suitcase onto the floor, Stephen unzips a flap on the top of the suitcase and pulls out a handle.

"I didn't know that was there!" Pointing to the strap attached to the side of the suitcase, I admit, "Instead, I used that to pull the suitcase behind me. I had to walk quite a distance, and the suitcase banged me in my calf the entire way!"

"Oh, Mom, I can tell you don't travel much."

"No, I don't. This is the first trip I've taken since I took you guys to North Carolina, so this is a big deal for me. I'm so happy I get to share it with you and Tim."

*****

My room is on the first floor. Opening the window to let in some fresh air, I start unpacking.

"Have you had lunch yet?" Stephen asks.

"No, do you want to go out and get something to eat?"

"I've already eaten, Mom, but I can go to the grocery store and get you a few things. Would you like that?"

"Yes, and while you're gone, I'll lie down for a few minutes."

"I'll be back before you know it," Stephen cheerfully remarks, closing the door behind him.

Lying down on the king-sized bed, tears of gratitude slip out from beneath my eyelids. "Thank you, Soul, for allowing me this time with my sons."

"You are greatly loved, Serena. Enjoy this time, because you're the one who gave it to you."

I dial Mom with the cell phone she lent me. "I'm here!"

"Good! And how was your flight?"

"It was good. I was afraid when the plane began to taxi down the runway, but I took a breath, connected to my Soul, and everything was fine after that.

"Ask your Soul if there's anything we should be aware of."

"She says I'm doing great!"

"I hope you know that you are the one who gave you this gift by doing the work you did to integrate."

"I know that. I'm proud of what I have accomplished, which is something new for me."

"I'm glad, sweetie."

"Oh ... there's Stephen. He went to the store to get me some groceries. Can we talk later?"

"Of course."

Stephen comes in and puts the groceries away. He's leaving, but he'll be back in a couple of hours.

Lying down so I will be fresh for this evening, the hours pass in sleep.

Answering the phone, I hear Tim's voice. "Wait for us in the lobby. We'll be there in five minutes. I'm excited to see you, Mom."

Hanging up the phone, I give the mirror one last glance. Grabbing my purse, I take deep, slow breaths to calm the huge, happy emotions I'm having.

Rushing toward Tim, I grab him in a bear hug. Leaning back, I look into his face, laughing with sheer joy.

"Hi, Mom," he says, while grinning sheepishly.

"Oh, Timothy …" I can barely speak without crying.

"Thanks for coming. I didn't know if you would," he quietly remarks.

"I'm so grateful I could come." I want to tell him I wouldn't miss it for the world, but that would be a lie. Everything has come second to my integration, even my sons. I missed their college graduations, Aaron's and Stephen's weddings, and numerous other things that mark the passing of time. My heart ached, but I had to put my healing first. It required a level of commitment beyond anything I could have ever dreamt at the time.

Looking at my son, standing 5'9" tall, with blue eyes and blond hair, I realize I missed seeing him grow into a man.

"We're going to our hotel to get dressed," Tim says. "Then we'll go to the theatre to make sure the sound system is working right."

"I don't care where we go. The fact that we're together is all that matters."

"Oh ... don't be surprised by how messy our room is. There are five of us crammed into it!"

"Tim, you should see *her* room!" Stephen exclaims. "It's bigger than ours, and she has a fridge, TV, and bar area, plus her windows open! We should have stayed there, plus it's less expensive!"

"We couldn't," Timothy flatly states. "The film festival's committee wanted all the submissions to stay in one place. There's a lot of publicity going on, and they wanted to be able to reach us quickly if they needed to."

"Oh, okay," Stephen mumbles. "I was only thinking of the money we could have saved."

Eyeing their room, I quietly laugh. With two beds and three cots, plus electronics, clothes, shoes, trash, and beer bottles strewn everywhere, messy is an understatement. Clearing a pile of clothes off a chair, I take a seat and wait for them to get dressed.

"I'm ready," Stephen says, "but Tim needs more time." Pulling his guitar out of the case, he asks. "Would you like me to play something?"

"Play a John Denver song."

Stephen plays "Rocky Mountain High." Our voices aren't the greatest, but I don't care. It feels good singing together. When my sons were growing up, I would play John Denver music for hours. It inspired me.

"Play something else!"

"Do you like the song, "Hallelujah"? I've been practicing it for a while now," Stephen proudly admits.

"I love that song!"

As Stephen plays, gratitude fills me to bursting. I can barely contain my joy. Taking deep breaths, I rub the side of the chair, reminding myself, this is the here and now. I can't allow my joy to engulf me, or I won't stay grounded.

"I'm ready. Let's go!" Tim calls.

Putting his guitar back into the case, Stephen stands and gives me a hug. "I'm so glad you came, Mom. I've missed you."

"Oh, Stephen." Returning his hug, I hold back my tears. "I can't tell you how happy I am to be here with you and Tim."

*****

I've been to the movies hundreds of times, but I've never sat in a dark theater, ready to watch a movie my own son made. *I hope everyone loves it. I hope I love it. What if I don't like it?* Realizing I'm in my mind, I take a breath and drop deeper into my body.

Through home movies, Tim introduces the audience to the two main characters, portraying them as sweet young boys. When one of the boys wiggles and squirms in his kindergarten recital, I'm reminded of when my sons were little, and I wistfully sigh with longing.

As the audience laughs, Tim leans in and whispers, "It's wonderful. They're laughing in all the right places. I didn't know it would feel this good."

Taking his hand, I whisper, "It's a wonderful movie. You should be proud of yourself, because I am."

As the story unfolds, the boys' sexual orientation and the bullying they endure become the focus of the film. One boy responds by standing up for himself, speaking publicly, and not allowing the cruelty to defeat him, while the other child internalizes the abuse and withdraws further into himself. I feel love for both boys and admire the outspoken child for his bravery. But in truth, I identify with the one who believed what his tormentors were saying about him. In the end, the boy who internalized the bullying takes his own life, while the boy who spoke out against the intolerance grows in maturity and strength.

As applause fills the auditorium, I look over at Tim. He is smiling and nodding.

"I told you they would love it!" Stephen exudes.

"It was wonderful," I happily exclaim.

"Thanks, Mom," he says, squeezing my hand. "I need to answer questions from the reporters and audience members. You stay here."

*****

Sitting on the patio of an Italian restaurant a couple of hours later, I watch my sons, the crew members, and the families of the two boys interact. As the evening continues, their laughter grows louder. Sandwiched in between Stephen and Tim, I am quiet. The wind is blowing, and I'm cold.

"Here, Mom, take my jacket," Stephen offers.

"No, take mine. It will fit better," Timothy kindly offers.

Pulling it around my shoulders, he pats my back before sitting back down.

"Are you tired?" Stephen asks. "Do you want to go back to the hotel?"

"Yes, after we have dinner, I will be ready to go."

*****

Back at the hotel, I slip into the warm bathtub filled with bubbles. I'm amazed at how today went. I didn't struggle to stay present. I wasn't afraid, even though I was with strangers. And, even more remarkably, as I met each person involved with the film, I spoke easily. I didn't think cruel thoughts about myself. Even though people knew I was Tim's mother, I didn't shrink in shame when being introduced to them. I was proud to be by his side. The guilt and condemnation I had carried for so long were gone, and in their place was a feeling of happiness.

*****

The moment Mom answers the phone, I happily declare, "Last night was wonderful, Mom!"

"Oh, Serena, I'm so happy for you. Tell me all about it."

"I felt comfortable with myself the entire time, can you believe it? I met lots of people, including Robert Redford's wife and a Grammy-nominated musician, but I didn't switch or become afraid. I had fun, plus the movie was amazing!"

"I know you're happy, Serena, but don't get too happy," Mom stresses. "Remember, let yourself enjoy this moment of joy without pumping too much happiness. You can't afford to create big emotions."

Breathing slowly, I lie back against the pillows. "Will you breathe with me then?"

"Of course."

The minutes pass in quiet breath, Mom leading and me listening.

"Ask your Soul if there's anything she wants us to look at before we get off the phone."

"Let yourself feel the precious gift you created," my Soul says. "Mom and I guided you, but it was your unending commitment to your integration that made this trip possible. I say created, because you kept showing up. You did that," she stresses. "No one else did."

"Do you get what your Soul is saying?"

"I think I do."

"Don't think it ... let yourself feel what she said. You are the one who created this opportunity to see your sons this weekend. We could only do our part, but you met us at every turn. Take that in, eat it like a sweet cookie, so it fills your entire body with the awareness that no one else gave this to you, but you. That is how you take ownership of your life. Now, there's a reason your Soul is asking you to notice this; can you sense what that is?"

"Because I'm the one who made the choice, no matter how hard it got."

"Yes, but sense: when Soul says you created it ... you were the one making the choice to integrate. That was you, Serena, creating from your passion. Let yourself feel that. This is a new beginning: because you are experiencing firsthand what it feels like to live without fear, and most importantly, you're discovering you like this new way of being.

"Yes, this is a new beginning for me; living life without fear controlling me!"

"Yes, life can be easy, Serena. That's what I mean when I say that I live my life with ease and grace. It means my Soul goes out before me, to make the corrected places straight. I don't have to think about it; it flows naturally from within me. Now ... I have to go, but we'll chat later, sweetie."

"Okay, Mom!"

"I'm loving you and sending you a huge hug!"

Hanging up the phone, I reflect on what my Soul said, realizing I like feeling empowered. I don't have to be a victim anymore! What a relief.

*****

"What are we doing today?"

"We want to get tattoos to commemorate the occasion," Tim replies. Watching to see if I will react, he adds, "Do you have a problem with us getting tattoos?"

"No, why should I?"

"Well, I thought you might."

"It's your body—you get to do what you want with it." Surprised by my response, I happily smile.

"Great. This will be fun!" Tim declares.

"I'm getting one, too!" Stephen exclaims. "I've always wanted one, and this is the perfect occasion."

As we drive to the tattoo shop, I hear an odd, rattling sound. "Do you hear that? I think it's coming from your car, Tim."

"Oh, don't worry, Mom. I was fine coming out here, and I'll be fine going back."

"What do you mean, you were 'fine'?" I dubiously ask.

"The tires are bald," Stephen interjects.

"And you're driving on them?" I say, aghast.

"I don't have the money to replace them," Tim casually replies.

"But you drove for over two thousand miles on bald tires?"

"Yeah." Tim chuckles. "It was scary a couple of times. You should have—"

"Stop!" I shout. "I don't want to hear it!"

Closing my eyes, I ask my Soul if it would be for my highest good to buy new tires for Tim's car. I don't want to rescue him, but over the years I've missed so many events in his life that this would be a gift for both of us. It doesn't erase the pain I still have about the past, nor does it change anything that's happened. In order to truly love myself, I know I'll have to let go of the heartache and the what-ifs, but I'm not there yet. My Soul knows this; consequently, her answer of yes comes from the depths of her compassion for me.

"Tim, after you have gotten your tattoos, I want to buy new tires for your car. Stephen, would you find a tire store nearby and ask how much it will cost?

I need to stay within the three-hundred-dollar range. Find out if that is possible, please."

"Wow … thanks, Mom. You don't have to do that, you know," Tim replies.

"I know, but I want to. Plus, knowing that you're driving home on new tires will make me feel much better."

*****

I've never been inside a tattoo parlor; the music is literally blasting my eardrums, and I can't hear what anyone is saying. Every room is at capacity, and five people are ahead of us in line.

"Ma'am, would you like to get a tattoo?" the male receptionist shouts.

"Me? Oh, no," I laughingly shout back.

"Come on, Mom, it would be fun," Stephen jokingly declares. "You could get a tiny one that doesn't show."

For a split second, I consider it, but my Soul is adamant, I'm not to get one. I don't care, because it hurts to get one anyway. "It's okay, I'll have fun watching both of you get tattoos."

*****

The new tires make a huge difference in how the car is handling, and that sound has completely disappeared. I'm relieved to know Timothy and Stephen will be safe driving home on new tires.

*****

Checking my watch for the umpteenth time, I wonder where Stephen and Timothy are. They told me they would be here by 9 a.m. Since this is our last day together, I don't want to waste a minute of it. Dialing Tim's number, I listen to it ring.

"Hello?" Timothy groggily answers.

"Did I wake you?"

"Yes. What time is it?"

"It's 9:30, when were you planning on picking me up?" I ask.

"Stephen's still asleep, and I'm tired. Would it be okay if we didn't come until later, maybe around 10:30?"

"Of course. Do you still want to go out for breakfast?"

"Yes, but after we sleep a bit more," he replies.

I have to leave for the airport in a few hours, and it seems as though time is just slipping away. Settling back against the pillows, I close my eyes and breathe, purposely letting go of the plan my mind has.

"I know you don't want to leave," my Soul whispers, "but this is just the beginning. You will have more of these sweet experiences in the future."

Taking my Soul's promise to heart, I feel the truth of her words resonate within me. This isn't an ending; instead, it's a new beginning.

*****

"Where do you want to go for brunch?" Tim asks.

"Let's go to Sloan's," Stephen suggests.

Stopping in front of the restaurant, we notice people standing outside, waiting to be seated. Stephen goes in and comes back to the car a few minutes later. "There's a twenty-minute wait. Is that okay?"

"That's fine," Tim says. "Let me park the car while you add our name to the list."

When at last we're seated, and the server has taken our orders, Tim turns to face me. "I've been angry with you, Mom."

"I know you've been angry. Can you tell me why?"

"When you sent us to live in the placement home, I hated it!" Trying to control his emotions, he inhales quickly. "You didn't even try to find my father!" Tears pool in his eyes, but he doesn't give in to his feelings.

Breathing deeply, I wait to see if there's anything else he wants to add.

Voice filled with anguish, he adds, "Stephen and Aaron didn't have it as bad as I did."

"Would you like to know the truth?" I gently ask.

"Yes."

"When I went into the hospital for their twenty-eight-day program, I expected to learn how to cope with my multiplicity in that amount of time, but instead, I completely fell apart. I was told that if I didn't willingly give you to foster care, the state would come in and legally take you from me. Then I would never get you back. That terrified me, Tim!" Stopping, I take a breath. I want to be honest with him, without giving him excuses for what I did.

Dropping deeper into my core, I ask Soul to speak through me. "I remember giving my phone book to someone in charge so they could try to locate your father. They came back and told me they had done an extensive search but couldn't find him, and I trusted them. At the time, you were living with your aunt, who found the placement home. It came with wonderful credentials, and the foster care worker said this was how the three of you could stay together."

I stop sharing and wait for Tim to respond. Emotions flit across his face. I know this isn't easy for him, so I remain quiet. I'm grateful he was honest with me; it took courage for him to share this.

"I guess I understand," he sadly comments, "but it doesn't make what happened any less painful."

Nodding in understanding, I continue sharing. "After I moved to Colorado and didn't talk to the three of you, I did it because there were only inner children present. In the past, it had been hurtful and confusing for the three of you when my child parts tried to talk to you, and I didn't want to do that to you again. I had no contact with outside people for six and a half years. If someone came to the door, I hid out of sight until they left. It wasn't safe for me to go outside for any reason. The commitment it took for me to integrate was bigger than anything I could have imagined. I know it was hard on you, and I wish that things had been different, but they weren't. Only through self- love have I been able integrate and accept my past without judgment."

Taking a sip of my chai latte, I breathe. This was a lot for both of us. Knowing I can't fix it, I wait. After several minutes of silence, I ask Tim an incidental question, but his response is swift; he's still mulling over what I've shared.

After a long silence, he asks, "Did you know Stephen was my first friend?" The statement seems casual, but I sense that he's sharing something special for him.

"I didn't know that. What about Aaron?"

Shaking his head no, he states, "Aaron never let me in. He was always in his own world, but Stephen and I have always had a special friendship."

"I was always in the middle," Stephen adds, "because I was close to both of them."

Looking at these two young men, whom I love deeply, I share, "I wish I had known how to raise the three of you, but I didn't. I discovered that I lived by a script of how I thought things should be, and the three of you did things that were way outside my limited understanding. I was confused and afraid all the time, which meant I wasn't emotionally available for any of you."

Again, there is silence. I know this is a lot to take in this morning. Breathing, I allow them to digest what I said.

"I got an A in anatomy class, Mom," Stephen kindly says, changing the subject.

"That's great! Did you like the class?"

"I really did. It's interesting to learn how the body works. I have to take chemistry next semester, and I don't think I'm going to like it much."

As the conversation shifts to something lighter, we finish our breakfast while they share what they have been doing over the past few years.

*****

Our time together is coming to an end. Timothy is leaving first.

Standing at the boarding gate, Tim wraps his arms around me. "I was afraid this weekend might turn out to be awful. I didn't know if I would even like you, but you're so different from the person I remember. I really love you, Mom."

"Oh, Timothy, thank you for inviting me to come. Your movie was wonderful! Plus, I like the man you have become. This trip has meant so much to me." Holding him close, I try not to cry. Stroking his cheek, I look into his eyes and smile. The energy of love that passes between us is more important than any words spoken. Holding him a moment longer, I add, "I love you, son. Will you be good to you?"

"I'll try, Mom."

Taking leave of Tim, Stephen, and I walk to his boarding gate. When we arrive, I hug him tightly.

"This has been a wonderful weekend, Mom. I sure love you."

"I love you, too, Stephen. I hope you know how proud I am of you. I'm not saying this because I'm your mother. I've watched you with Tim and Aaron; you are genuinely kind to both of them. Over the years, even when you hadn't heard from me, you kept writing. I don't know if you realize how important those letters were for me. They were a lifeline to the three of you, which helped me through some very difficult times. I hope that someday you believe what a wonderful person you are."

Awkwardly shrugging his shoulders, Stephen smiles and gives me a final hug.

When I arrive home later that evening, I get a call from Tim, telling me his film won first place in the documentary category at the film festival. I couldn't be prouder.

Chapter 28: I'M DONE WITH DARK ENERGY

Feeling discouraged, I call Mom before going to work. "I don't know what's happened, but the peace I felt on my trip seems to have disappeared."

"Did you sense with your Soul what's going on?" Realizing that I hadn't, I turn inward for clarity.

"I wrapped you in a blanket of love," Soul responds. "I quieted the aspects that we haven't integrated yet, so that you would know what true peace felt like. Did you like it?"

Surprised by her revelation, I sadly exclaim, "What? You mean that wasn't the real me?"

"Are you going to fight or go for the truth, Serena?" Taking a breath, I answer, "I want the truth, Mom."

"Good. Then get out of your mind so you can hear your Soul."

"I wrapped you in a thick blanket of love. It allowed you to feel what it's like to live in peace. I gave you a gift: a weekend with your sons, free of inner conflict. A weekend of peace so that no matter what happened on the outside, you remained unruffled. Did you like it?" my Soul asks again.

"I loved it! But I thought I felt that way because of all the work we had done."

"As long as you want your lie more than you want the truth, you will stay stuck," Mom calmly states. "The truth is, we still have work to do. Do not overlook the fact that you're the one who allowed yourself to stay in that space of peace. You chose to love and take care of yourself the entire weekend. If you had not chosen to do that, Soul's blanket of love would have been ineffectual."

Surprised by her statement, I state, "You're right, Mom. I'm the one who allowed it!"

"No, Serena," Mom firmly states, "You chose it."

"I want peace; it was liberating to go about my day without struggle. I didn't try to figure out how to be—I just was. "Tell me how I can have that, Soul."

"We have done a level of integration that has brought home many of the aspects created to survive," my Soul responds. "The next phase of your integration is working with the original child. The truth is, you were never more than one person. Would you agree with that statement?"

Speaking aloud what my Soul is saying, I stop to marvel at how obvious that is. "Yes, I feel it! It isn't an idea from my mind, but a knowing that I feel all the way down to my toes!"

"It took us years to get to this place," Mom remarks. "We have worked with the original child intermittently throughout the years, but for our purposes, do you really get what that means?"

"I think it means the person who wasn't split yet. Is that right?"

"Yes. We started our work with the trained child, because that's what presented itself first. But your parents started with the original child, and through their training, pieces of consciousness split off to help Jennifer survive. As the years went on, that original consciousness was completely covered over by those pretending to be someone else. Those parts that were fragmented from the original child now have a chance to integrate."

"I love how my Soul always knows what the next step is!"

"Yes, she has led us perfectly up to now," Mom replies, chuckling.

"Unfortunately, I need to leave for work now, but can we pick this up tomorrow?"

*****

It's early, and I still have an hour before I have to leave for work. Picking up the phone, I call Mom.

"I'm sensing that there is still something we need to look at outside of working with the original child, and admitting that aloud makes me anxious."

"I'm glad you're willing to be honest with yourself. Ask your Soul where she wants to go with this."

"Rage is intentionally blocking you," my Soul states. "Your rage was created at an early age from the experiences of the original child. That's why you sense there is a connection between the two."

My anxiety is growing. Taking a breath, I drop deeper into my core and close my eyes. I allow my awareness to open, and as I do, I feel the rage pulsating on the right side of my body.

"It intentionally blocks me," I slowly murmur. "I can feel it … this rage wants to destroy me! No, it wants me dead! You mean after all this time, the rage still wants me dead?" I incredulously ask.

"That's its job, Serena. Rage is an energy meant to destroy. Please, stop a moment, and sense why you keep pretending the rage isn't here? Don't answer me quickly. Really, be honest with yourself."

Placing the phone in my other hand, I wipe the tears off my face. Dropping deeper into my belly, I continue breathing, while opening to the truth. "I don't want the rage to be here. I would rather pretend that I'm doing great." I'm surprised by my own admittance. Shakily inhaling, I choose that the rage must come home to my Soul immediately!

"It's important you realize the full scope of what this rage does to you. There's a constant dumping of toxins into your body from this energy. We have used different words for it over the years, but they all mean the same thing. Whether we call it fight, anger, fear, anxiety, or hysteria—they're all the same energy. When you create any of these emotions, you are feeding your energy to the rage, and your rage is trained to destroy.

"Remember, we aren't talking about anyone else's experience but yours, because unlike other people, they trained you by using torture to control you. It started with Jennifer when she was a baby. Her anger at her parents, the cult members, and the government officials grew the older she got. But Soul's brilliance kept Jennifer's anger separate, keeping her sane. But as time went on, that anger grew into a massive, destructive rage.

"You experienced fear to the extreme, and you used it to the extreme. Just as your multiplicity was an extreme case, so is your rage. From your stomach issues, to the pain you have suffered for most of your life, to overeating, being tired, insomnia, and your financial issues, they are all a result of one thing: your self-hatred." Raising her voice, Mom states. "Your self-hatred is an aspect that sees you as a separate person, and it wants you dead. As long as you push that truth away, you hurt yourself!"

"Then hear me," I urgently declare. "I'm speaking from the very depths of my being! I choose to be done with my rage!" Inhaling deeply, I implore, "Do you hear me, my Soul?" Speaking passionately, I avow, "I am choosing to be done with all dark energy!"

As Mom leads me in breath, we call upon Jesus, Kuan Yin, and all the other light beings who have been involved in our work to be present. Passion fills me as my entire body resonates with the knowledge that in this lifetime, I am done! Resolute determination fills me as I breathe. Despite our being on the phone, our connection to this choice bridges the distance between us, holding us in a cocoon of yes that flows outward.

I had hoped the rage could be completely integrated in that instant, but I discovered that was not to be. Instead, my choice to be done with rage was the invitation my Soul had been waiting for. She knew of things I had yet to discover. Only through her compassionate love was I able to face the dark, hidden parts of me.

*****

Listening as the phone rings for the third time, I'm relieved when Mom finally answers. "Do you have time to talk before I go to work? It's important that I tell you about a memory I had this morning."

"Of course, Serena."

"I'm around two-and-a-half years old, and Jack is smiling, moving back and forth in front of me. He stops and stands on my right side, telling me I can't see him, and I agree wholeheartedly. But Mom, that was a lie, because I clearly saw him! I was already lying to myself when I was only two. I created a psychic wall, pulling the shades down over my eyes, so I could block him from my view to please him!"

"Yes, Serena, I get it, but I'm glad you're finally getting it."

"I told myself I couldn't see him! That was me!"

"Yes ...?"

"Even at that young age, I was manipulating and lying to myself."

"I understand, Serena. Would you be willing to see the truth? You can't afford any judgment about this; otherwise, you won't be able to help yourself. This is the nightmare you lived every single day of your life," she stresses, "and today, he's smiling at you. Feel it. Don't listen to what I'm saying; instead, feel it! If you play along, maybe he won't hurt you. You love him, you want to please him, and on top of that, he's smiling at you! Can you feel the desperation you felt back then? Just one kind touch, just one kind word ... you would do *anything* for it. Since you're only two, you aren't split very much, so a large part of the authentic child remains. This allows you, Serena, to feel this memory more deeply because the dissociation is not that dense."

"I feel how intense it was; my entire body screamed with how much I needed Jack."

"This is the beginning of 'the right hand knows not what the left hand does.' These are two different aspects playing a game, Serena. The one who knows the truth, which is the authentic child, and the one who pretends she can't see Jack, which is the trained aspect. This game started even before you were two years old and continued until you were so divided that you believed your own lies.

"As he stepped from your right side to your left side, he would say, 'Now you see me!' Then he would laugh and smile. You were desperate for his kindness, so you played the game. It seemed innocent at the time, but nothing that man did was innocent. Every single thing was calculated to create an unconscious person controlled by others. So you pretended you didn't see him, but you did! What we're going for is the bigger picture. Feel how much you wanted Jack's love. No judgment, Serena! If you hold onto any judgment, you will stay stuck."

Feeling upset that I was that desperate for Jack's love, I take a breath and drop deeper into my core out of judgment. I'm willing to do whatever it takes to integrate my rage.

"I want to ask your Soul something, Serena. Please, don't get in the way."

"Okay …" Taking a breath, I let go as much as possible.

"I have felt for some time that there is a reason Serena has not yet integrated," Norma states. "I sense it has to do with psychically holding onto Jack. I need absolute honesty if we are to be done with her rage. It needs to be out in the open, no matter how unpleasant it is!"

"There are aspects of Serena still tied to Jack," my Soul calmly responds.

"What does that mean? I want the complete truth. If we are to accomplish this integration, I need it now," Mom passionately insists.

"The rage is holding onto Jack, feeding its energy to him even as we speak. I couldn't tell you this until she was done playing this game."

After moments of silence, Mom admits, "I can't help but be upset by this. After all these years of giving my energy to this work, and Serena, only to find out that it's been going to Jack, is astounding!"

"I understand, and I'm not minimizing your feelings, but I couldn't tell you because it was too dangerous. Trying to let you in on the secret meant the rage might have picked up on it. Since we were dealing with Serena's dissociation, I knew that if she went unconscious, the rage could kill the body much more easily.

"Inviting Serena to feel meant she would feel the emotional impact of her rage. It was a delicate balancing act between fueling her passion to live while confronting the truth about her past. It's only been in the last three years that we could move toward this final goal to integrate her rage completely."

"I hear you, but I need to deal with this because I'm stunned. I'm going to get off the phone now to take care of myself."

"I know how overwhelming this feels, Norma. I'm sorry I couldn't tell you this before."

"I understand."

Serena, for me to accept the fact that there are aspects of you still feeding Jack your energy and mine is stunning. Can you face this truth, without running?"

Feeling extremely upset, I implore, "Don't go, Mom, I will face it, I promise, but it's important that these parts that are still holding onto Jack be severed now, before you get off the phone! Do you hear me?"

"Yes, Serena. I'm not rejecting you. Over the years, I've had to face some difficult truths. This is just one more. Ask your Soul if we breathe now to sever all ties with Jack, will it be accomplished today?"

Immediately, I feel the answer resonate throughout me. "Yes, this is the time. My Soul is saying that it can be done now because my choice is clear!"

"So before we breathe, take a moment and feel the truth. You, Serena, have been feeding Jack your energy and mine. I have given you my energy all these years, holding you in a sweet cocoon of love with your Soul, so you could stay alive and integrate. I never imagined you could be connected to Jack in any way, but that was my fault. I wanted to believe you wanted to integrate as much as I wanted it for you, but that was not the truth."

It's not easy to hear her put it that way. Choosing to own what I have done, I breathe deeply. I will not run from this reality, no matter how uncomfortable it makes me. I know Mom loves me, but do I love myself enough to own what I did without judgment? I have played the game of being multiple parts my entire life, pretending it was someone else who was making the choices, but I'm the new consciousness in this body, and I am choosing to take full ownership of all that has happened. It's not easy facing the truth, but I am.

"With every breath, I receive my Soul's strength into me and sever all ties with Jack now!" I resolutely declare."

"Breathe, and choose to live, Serena. Know that all psychic ties with Jack must be severed now because that is what you desire!" Raising her voice, Norma declares, "Every aspect, every piece of dark energy holding onto Jack, must now go into the light of Soul. They no longer have permission to stay!"

"Yes!" I passionately announce. "Jesus, you have said that where two or three are gathered together in your name, you are there with them. Be with us now, strengthen my choice, that all dark energy that has been holding onto Jack must be integrated now!"

"Breathe, Serena!" Mom invites.

Our combined breaths are the only thing that matters. I have identified with being a victim my entire life, so it's been easy for me to pretend the rage wasn't mine, but I won't do that anymore! I love myself more than ever before, and this old way of living must stop today!

"Every time you make a decision, Mom states, "go to Soul first. This will force the remaining rage to come out of hiding. Plus, it will empower you, Serena."

"But, Mom, that means I was the one hating you; I was the one who would hit you with my energy when we were working; I was the one who said hateful things to you! It was no one else but me," I sadly admit.

"Yes, and as long as you pretended it wasn't you, it had permission to stay here and continue acting out."

"This isn't easy for me to face."

"No, it isn't. I'm the first to admit that. This journey has been very difficult at times, but your Soul warned us years ago that it would be harder than anything we could imagine, and she was right. Now, before we hang up, it would be helpful for you if you had more clarity about your rage."

"Yes, but I thought you needed to get off the phone to take care of yourself," I anxiously remark.

"I do, but this is equally important. I will take care of myself shortly. We can't afford to leave this part of the discussion for later, because your rage will use it to judge you. So … drop deeper into you so you can hear me without judgment.

"Jack exemplified the perfect tyrant. He seemed never to be hurt. Instead, he was the authority, demanding that his orders be followed to the letter. No matter what he did, he seemed impervious to attack or pain. As a young, impressionable child, you watched your parents. Which one do you think you wanted to be like?"

"That's obvious. I wanted to be like Jack!"

"You answer so quickly, but you brush aside the implication of what that really means," Mom says.

Feeling anxious, I inhale slowly.

"Describe to me what that young child liked about Jack, and listen carefully to what you say, Serena."

"I liked that he was powerful, that he could go anywhere and do anything, and no one seemed to get in his way!" As I speak, an exhilarating strength fills my entire body. "No one could hurt him!" I defiantly declare.

"Yes, Serena. Do you notice how you feel right now? That is the energy of your rage."

"I feel all-powerful!"

"Yes, that was the energetic package that your Soul created in those early years to help Jennifer. If she had not felt rage pulse throughout her body, she would have easily given into the despair of death. Can you sense what I'm saying?"

"I'm surprised," I reply, "because it sounds like you're saying the rage was good."

"You're listening from your mind, Serena. Drop deeper into the stillness so you can hear me. The rage kept passion alive in your body. If Jennifer had only experienced pain and the despair of abandonment, she would have given up. Your Soul knew that if the body became overly filled with the energy of death, Jennifer would have let go and died. Rage fed the body energy and kept it warm, thus Jennifer stayed alive. Now describe Lois's experience, and again, let yourself feel what you're describing."

"Lois was constantly afraid, and even though she obeyed Jack, she still got hurt!" As I say the last few words, the contempt I feel for her is massive. I want to bash her for being so spineless. Surprised at my reaction, I relay this to Mom.

"Even now, you feel the energy of what was lived some sixty years ago. Your choice to follow in Jack's footsteps was huge. Can you recognize this without judgment?"

"Yes, because I can feel that choice radiate throughout my body even now!"

"That's the rage that's still inside you, Serena. You watched Lois be stabbed, raped, bullied, and intimidated on a daily basis. You chose to be like your father. You adored him, and in the beginning, your choice was made from a child's perspective: be weak like Lois or be strong like Jack. But as you grew older, your love affair with the rage intensified.

"Now you have the choice to live your life differently, and what you used to do unconsciously, you can no longer afford to do. You must stay conscious of what you are feeling ... all the time! There can be no excuses for going unconscious, Serena.

"Now, I have to go, but remember that I love you very much. This doesn't change anything between us. I need to take some time for myself, but that is part of being a conscious human being. Before you make any decision, ask Soul first. This will bring your rage out of hiding."

"Okay … Mom."

Hanging up the phone, I take a breath. I can't afford to feel sorry for myself. Breathing deeply, I ask my Soul to help me own the truth that this rage is an aspect of me.

"Play with me, Serena," my Soul directs. "Go behind the rage to the pain that has been feeding it."

I intuitively move behind the wall of rage and feel indescribable emotional pain.

"Breathe. Allow compassion to fill you, Serena. It's only through compassion and loving this part of you that this rage can fully integrate. Stay deep in your core, and allow the energy to move. I am here," assures my Soul.

Breathing with the energy of yes, I feel my body relax as compassion fills me. Holding still, I allow the energy of rage to move home to my Soul. Internal screams shatter the stillness within me, but I don't run. I feel solid, determined as I make a new choice, owning a level of truth and love for myself that I have never felt before. As my compassion continues to grow, the rage melts, integrating into my Soul.

"Don't be fooled, Serena," my Soul advises. "There is more rage hiding in the shadows. Stay conscious because you love yourself, and together we will integrate it."

*****

The ability to energetically move beyond the confines of the physical body is something everyone knows how to do. Our Soul energy is larger than the human body we live in; it surrounds us, flows through us, and comes from us.

When I was three days old and lying on the cold, dank grass, I desperately needed to connect to the warmth of another human being because my body was cold and filled with pain. I went out energetically and sought warmth, and the first body I found was Jack's. His body's heat helped me stay alive that night. As I grew older, my need for Jack and his warmth only intensified, and with that, my obsession with winning his love and approval increased. When I chose to be done with my rage, I had to face the truth of what I had done and what I was still doing. Only through compassion was I able to integrate all the aspects that were still connected to Jack.

*****

I've been working for months on integrating the rage. I feel physically ill today; the rage is taunting me with its lies. As I sit across from Mom, my mind whirls with cruel thoughts.

You'll never win!

Look at her.

Do you see how tired she is?

You're doing that to her!"

You're killing her.

Why don't you give up and die!

Breathing deeply, I quietly beg my Soul for help.

"Ask your Soul if she is ready to bring up the authentic child for integration," Mom suggests. "But before you do that, make sure all the rage you are feeling is integrated."

Taking a breath, I let go more deeply into my Soul, choosing light and love no matter what. After a while, my Soul tells me it's safe: she will bring the authentic child to the forefront.

I feel a shift in my body as the child's energy joins mine. We are seeing things simultaneously, but our experiences are separate. As she looks around the room and sees the dogs sleeping on the floor, she attempts to speak. The mouth opens, but no words are spoken.

"Serena, stroke your face. Help her to feel safe."

Stroking my face helps Jennifer feel comforted. A sigh escapes my lips. Pointing to herself, the child says, "Not afraid." Her words are stilted and slow. She repeats the words again, while I continue to stroke our face. Then, ever so slowly, the separateness between us melts, and I become one with her. Her awareness is mine.

"Feels good, alive ..." Warmth fills me as awareness dawns.

Mom smiles and whispers, "Yes."

My awareness is new ... it's beyond a concept. I'm feeling a level of consciousness I've never felt before. It's opening a place within my physicality where death energy has always lived.

Feeling joy, I touch my face again. I am pure child consciousness without trauma. As I breathe, joy floods my body, allowing me to relax more fully into my Soul energy. "Me, me," I repeat, as I touch my chest. I get that this body is mine! Words are no longer needed to bridge the gap between thinking and knowing: I feel it. Repeating the word "me" over and over. I touch my face, my arms, my legs, and my hands. I am filled with sheer bliss. Looking at Mom, I see her radiantly smiling back at me. There's nothing but this moment.

As Soul, and I, and the original child integrate, we become one. "I feel I am more than just Serena." My words are no longer stilted. Instead, I feel a flow of awareness that is mine.

"You are, just as I am more than Norma."

Completely understood, outside of mind's understanding, I continue to receive the love that is filling me. "Did you know that Serena was never fully in the body?"

"Yes, I did," Mom states quietly. She knows change is still occurring.

"You don't know this," I continue, "but the push to give up had gotten so big. The lies kept running in Serena's head. I know I'm speaking in the third person, but the human part of me seems to have integrated into this new me that is sitting here now. The rage kept telling her to leave. It said you will never get what Norma is offering you. You have done everything, and look where you're at. You will always be a person of fear. But Serena kept silent, refusing to speak those lies."

"Yes, and her courage to stay present and not to give into the rage has forced it out of hiding," Norma states. "Serena always lived from her mind first, but as this part of the original child brings her essence of pure, untainted love into the body, it allows for a whole new beginning for you."

"I know ... and it feels wonderful."

Then stay with it, and keep breathing," Norma kindly directs.

"Oh, I will," I promise.

*****

When I met Norma in 1996, I lived in a state of absolute unconsciousness, where separateness ruled. My life was an artificial presentation, meant for one purpose only: to keep what I had lived a secret from everyone, including me. The revolving door of aspects flowed seamlessly to support this way of living. Each aspect of personality was segregated, defined by its identity, traits, and job. When I wrote in my book that my left hand knew not what my right hand did, that was not an exaggeration.

Undoing that degree of separateness by bringing authentic Soul consciousness into my body was a significant part of the work Norma and I did. Intentionally coming into my body to feel, to stay without running when things got difficult, was a necessary ingredient in becoming whole. If it were not for higher consciousness supporting us in this endeavor, we would have failed. We entered into this work in innocence, unaware that it would take over two decades to finally achieve our goal.

Towards the end, when I was integrating my rage, I had to sit in its presence, in non-resistance. It screamed for my attention, cursing me with its vicious lies and flooding my body with uncomfortable emotions. I knew that if I reacted, I would feed it my energy, making it stronger. It was difficult staying rooted in my core, breathing the compassionate breath, but as days turned into months and I chose compassion over rage, the pain connected to my rage finally integrated.

I realized that the rage that I had judged as bad had actually kept me alive. Its energy provided me with purpose and determination. Its energetic pulse kept my body warm, while simultaneously walling off huge pockets of pain that could have overwhelmed me, pushing me into insanity or death. I knew that without it, I would have died. My gratitude for its presence in my life dissolved the last of my judgment, ultimately freeing me from my past. By choosing stillness, I allowed compassion to expand, opening me to the true essence of my nature.

If it were not for Norma's unwavering compassion and honesty, combined with my own commitment, I would not have been able to walk into my new life, whole and free, knowing unequivocally that I was a soul having a human experience.

*****

I hope this book has inspired you to discover your authentic essence. If you invite your Soul into your life, your Soul will joyously honor that invitation. Talk and share freely with it and be open to its guidance, and when the going gets tough, don't give up! Remember: your Soul is *always* filling you, surrounding you, walking with you, or you wouldn't be alive. I know you can create a magical, working relationship with your Essence, because I did, one breath at a time.

EPILOGUE

When I began the arduous and extremely slow journey into the light in 1996, I was unaware of the grander plan my Soul had for me. I discovered my Soul contract in bits and pieces over the course of twenty years. I was born into one of the evilest environments on our planet for the purpose of experiencing all that the darkness had to offer so I could choose between it or the energy of love, and through that process, awaken from the game of fear so I could be done with it entirely.

The passion I had to fully embody my Soul required that I synchronize with a higher frequency. I couldn't achieve this because my body still held the residue of trauma in its tissues, which caused it to vibrate at a lower frequency. Beginning in October 2024 and continuing until Christmas Day 2025, a complete transmutation of my physical body was accomplished, during which even my DNA was restructured to align with a higher frequency, enabling me to become the embodiment of my Divine Essence in human form.

The chronic abuse I endured resulted in chemical toxicity, causing a long-term dysregulation of my body's natural stress-response systems and neurotransmitter balance. This ultimately led to systemic wear and tear, creating increased vulnerability for my body. This was not exposure to an external toxin; rather, my body's own stress chemicals became toxic due to overactivation. I had pain in my joints, and in my toes and hands. I had an infection in my mouth that would not heal. My eyesight was worsening, and I had the beginnings of cataracts. I had difficulty with my muscles; they often cramped and were sometimes stiff. My knees and lower back ached, and my spine often burned with pain. Plus, my weight always fluctuated.

When my Soul invited me to begin this process of transmutation, it was essential that I was alone, without outside stimulation. As the months went on, it grew increasingly difficult. November and December of 2025 were the hardest. I resisted the urge to surrender to the abject terror and hopelessness I felt. At times, all I wanted to do was die. My mind had shattered into multiple parts to contain the truth of my past, but my body had experienced every moment of extreme, horrific abuse for decades. It never got to escape through dissociation. The intense emotional terror and powerlessness I was gripped by during this last phase of my healing seemed never-ending. At times, its intensity overwhelmed me to the point that I was unable to distinguish between the release of memory and the present moment. In these instances, I would insist that my Soul fortify me with her strength and resolve. Thankfully, she always did. Sometimes it took the entire day for the terror to begin to wane. Her fortification was evidenced by my ability to stay focused while breathing. Mercifully, my trust in her never wavered.

This process enabled me to grasp more deeply how the dissociative energy had served me. That young, defenseless child that I was would not have survived without it. My body had to grow into adulthood before the task of integration and healing could begin. Every step in my healing process required a new level of strength, maturity, and presence on my part. I entered this final step of healing in innocence, trusting that my Soul's promise of complete transmutation of my body would be fulfilled.

The passion I have to share my message, "With Spirit, Anything is Possible," resonates in the very fibers of my being because I followed my Soul's daily guidance, creating with her the miracles that literally transformed my life.

I hope that my memoir inspires you to discover the true Essence that dwells within you. It is important, though, that when I invite you to open the door to your Soul and invite it into your life, that I don't oversimplify what that really means. This choice depends on your belief system, how it aligns with your Soul's intent, and how willing you are to fully surrender to your Soul's guidance. I know from experience that this alignment takes time. Allow your journey to unfold from a place of compassion and self-love, because it is not an instantaneous fix.

I promise you that this relationship will fill you with a love beyond your imagination. You will have a partnership with a brilliant, compassionate Being who loves you limitlessly, who can provide you with the answers you seek, walk with you into every moment of your day, and embolden you with foresight, intuition, ideas, and strength. Isn't that a fabulous promise to make?

Please remember that once you open the door, your journey will unfold with perfect timing from Divine Intelligence, a breath at a time.

*****

www.ingramcontent.com/pod-product-compliance
Lightning Source LLC
Chambersburg PA
CBHW051857160426
43209CB00006B/1333